Grasping the Nettle

A story of courage, joy and victory

by

Joyce Donovan

Copyright © 2007 by Joyce Donovan

GRASPING THE NETTLE
by Joyce Donovan

Printed in the United States of America

ISBN-13: 978-1-60034-870-9
ISBN-10: 1-60034-870-X
Library of Congress Control Number 2006937498
UK Copyright 264030

All rights reserved solely by the author. The author guarantees all contents are original and do not infringe upon the legal rights of any other person or work. No part of this book may be reproduced in any form without the permission of the author. The views expressed in this book are not necessarily those of the publisher.

Unless otherwise indicated Bible quotations are taken from
1. New International Version Copyright © 1984 by Oxford University Press
2. Revised Standard Version Copyright © 1973 by Collins

www.xulonpress.com

TABLE OF CONTENTS

Dedication		vii
Acknowledgements		ix
Foreword		xi
Preface		xiii
Commendations		xv
Family Tree		xix
Chapter 1	Beginnings	21
Chapter 2	Growing up	45
Chapter 3	Ted	65
Chapter 4	War	81
Chapter 5	The Christmas Raids	103
Chapter 6	Liverpool, Ireland, Sweden	123
Chapter 7	Dublin Again	149
Chapter 8	Canada	163
Chapter 9	Boston	189
Chapter 10	Holland	205
Chapter 11	Back to Boston	225
Chapter 12	The Tape Library	247
Chapter 13	The Valley of the Shadow	267
Chapter 14	England Again	293
Chapter 15	The Jesus Fellowship	305
Chapter 16	The Living Spirit	319
Chapter 17	Community	343
Chapter 18	Cancer	361
Chapter 19	The Last Lap	379
Epilogue		393

Dedication

Encouraged by friends, Joyce was inspired to write down her memories for her children and grandchildren. So with that in mind this book is dedicated to the children who survived her, Anthony and Liz, and to her grandchildren of whom she was very proud: Stephen, Alan and Jonathan. It was Joyce's desire that these recollections would tell of God's power and love and that all who heard them would be drawn nearer the truth.

Acknowledgements

It is with deep gratitude in my heart that I say thank you to all those who helped to get *"Grasping the Nettle"* into the shops. Their patience, love and understanding helped enormously all along the way. My thanks to Tracy Owen who laboriously typed Joyce's complete original material; being computer-graphically literate, she (together with Olivia Scott) put all the graphics into the correct format as well as helped with the final proofreading. Thanks also to Pat Avstreih for putting all the material into chronological order and a big thank you goes to Selina Charleton who bravely got us off the ground with the first 'go' at editing the manuscript. I am without words in how to thank Teresa de Bertodano for all her insight, enthusiasm and editing expertise, who brought the manuscript into its finished state, without whom this book would not have been published.

I must mention the dedication and hard work of my younger daughter, Liz.

FOREWORD

Joyce Donovan tells her story with simplicity, humility and candour. There was always a refreshing realism about her approach to life. Joyce managed to combine very high aspirations for her spiritual life with a very sober assessment of herself and those around her. She spoke straightforwardly about her desire to live a holy life, but that was quite endurable because her vision of holiness was sane, human and attainable.

I knew Joyce in the last twenty-five years or so of her life, and it was a pleasure to read her account of those many years I had missed. On page after page I found myself thinking "this really is the Joyce I knew; no pretence, no re-inventing herself for the historical record."

Jesus said that He came "not to be served, but to serve" (Mt. 20:28) and that very well describes the way Joyce and Ted lived their lives in the several decades that I knew them – I found them to be unpretentious with a genuine spirit of service. As a houseguest, I regularly witnessed their devoted prayerfulness and was moved by their very evident, sensitive attentiveness to the circumstances of so many people.

Repeatedly in widely scattered parts of the world, many times in the last years of Joyce's life, Ted and Joyce would quietly sit with someone, listening to his or her concerns and praying with them. In spite of age and Joyce's grave illness, they devoted themselves to long hours praying for and with people, and when necessary travelling long distances to do so. Many people speak very gratefully of the care and love shown to them by this couple. The last years of Joyce's life were difficult, as she struggled with a prolonged and ultimately fatal illness. Through it all she continued to serve and she bore the increasing pain and weakness with real serenity.

My enduring memory is of the youthful zeal which remained with Joyce to the end.

Bruce Yocum, Servants of the Word, Ann Arbor, MI

PREFACE

This book is delightfully written. The early chapters are a fascinating period-piece of history, which need to be treasured as a record for the future. It is both warm and winning, and reveals a character blessed of a profound trust in God from an early age; her faith being remarkably relevant.

Joyce was a frequent attender at the regular renewal meetings we organised at St. Andrew's Chorleywood, in days gone by. But now when the past seems less defined, her face still abides in the mind as brightly radiating an unforgettable light. Her story is rare in its purity; her prayers were remarkable in their efficacy and her conversation rich with its encouragement.

She may never be remembered as a stained-glass window saint, but she will never be forgotten as a real-life one by those who knew her. I am so happy to commend *'Grasping the Nettle'*. It is a book which will refresh hearts and re-focus lives.

Bishop David Pytches, Chorelywood, Herts. UK

COMMENDATION

In *Grasping the Nettle*, Joyce Donovan shares her unchanging faith in God in the context of constant change within the Church and the world. Joyce was never doctrinaire in her views or critical of the lives and opinions of others. As her children left home, the things of God assumed ever more importance in Joyce's life. Her detailed account of the way in which she and Ted became involved with the spirituality and gifts of the Charismatic movement indicates their willingness to change in their relationship to God and to other believers.

As she grew older, Joyce increased in Christian wisdom, the wisdom that comes only as a result of increasing submission to the guidance of the Holy Spirit. Besides suffering the loss of people she loved, Joyce had also to cope with mental affliction due to stress, spiritual affliction in the form of desolation of spirit, and physical affliction due to a leaking heart valve. She eventually had to contend with cancer and leukaemia. These sufferings served to test, purify and strengthen Joyce's faith. I feel confident that readers of this book will find an engaging description of a life lived to the full.

Fr Pat Collins cm, Dublin, Ireland

COMMENDATION

Readers of *'Grasping the Nettle'* will discover a personality as lively as the story she has to tell. There is never a dull moment, never the impression of a boat becalmed.

Joyce Donovan responded wholeheartedly to the Lord at an early age. Her commitment to God was the source of her life; the center of her life, and enabled her to be committed to her family and to God's people. She lived for the glory of God and for the good of the brothers and sisters; for all those who needed the mercy of God.

I came along late in Joyce's life, when she and her husband Ted were pillars of the Antioch Community in West London, where they were an unfailing source of service and hospitality. Over the years I have heard many stories of Joyce. *Grasping the Nettle* is a revelation of the breadth of Christian experience incarnated in her and of the international background of her life with Ted and family. I came to appreciate that the steady and adaptable dedication of Joyce and Ted was not a recent acquisition. It was rooted in their following the Lord over long years and through countless challenges.

The Book of Hebrews speaks about the "great cloud of witnesses" who went before us and who "surround us". Joyce is within that cloud and *'Grasping the Nettle'* is her witness to the Lord Jesus, "the pioneer and perfecter of our faith". May it reach out to many readers.

Steve Clark, Ann Arbor, MI

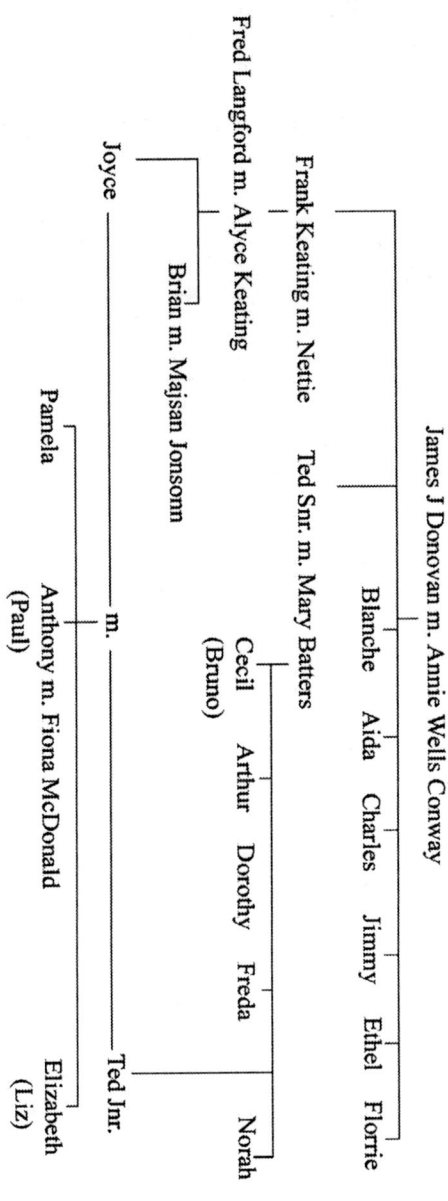

1

BEGINNINGS 1921-1928

"I have known a great many troubles but most of them never happened".

Mark Twain

The story is told of a farmer in China who had just one horse with which he ploughed his fields. One day the horse ran away. The neighbours came to console the old man. 'What bad luck' they said. The farmer replied: 'Bad luck, good luck - who knows?' Sometime later the horse came back bringing a whole herd of wild ponies in its train. The neighbours came to congratulate the farmer on his good fortune. He responded: 'Good luck, bad luck - who knows?' When the farmer's only son tried to tame one of the wild horses, he fell off and broke his leg. The neighbours came round to commiserate: 'Bad luck, good luck' said the old man. 'Who knows?' A few days later war was declared. The military arrived and rounded up all the able-bodied young men. The only one left in the village was the young man with the broken leg. Good luck, bad luck - who knows!

This story means a great deal to me. Apparent disasters in my life have sometimes proved to be very well-disguised blessings. I thank God for *not* answering some of the requests with which I have bombarded him! His plan for my life has been infinitely better than anything I could have imagined or planned for myself.

I was born in Dublin on October 18 1921 in the midst of armed conflict between the Irish and the English. My father was an officer in the British Army who had been sent to Ireland to head up troops from England known as the "Black and Tans": a name infamous to this day in Ireland. During the First World War, father had worked closely with the future Prime Minister Clement Attlee. Daddy spoke of Lord Attlee with affection and said that he had done his best while he was in the army but had been a square peg in a round hole. While fighting in that terrible war, my father's lungs had been badly affected by gas which left him with a legacy of emphysema. As a young girl I can remember

My father

having to rush for his white pills when he was literally gasping for breath. I also remember being brought to see Daddy reviewing troops in Dublin on his white horse. I must have been about two and a half.

My mother, Alyce Keating, was Irish. She became one of the very early film stars – amazing for someone of her nationality and background. The film industry began very early in Ireland and mother worked for the Irish director Fred O'Donovan [no relation!] In 1977, Trinity College Dublin held an exhibition of some of the first Irish movies. It was with amazement that I saw pictures of my mother with other people she had mentioned when I was young.

My mother

Alyce met Fred Langford, my father, at Dublin's Milltown Golf Club. My mother's family had been founder members and my father was a first class player. The relationship flourished but neither family was pleased at the prospect of Alyce Keating marrying Fred Langford because of the difference in religion. Alyce was Roman Catholic while Fred's family was staunchly protestant which really meant that they were anti-Catholic. Both families appeared to base their 'religion' on bigotry and prejudice and none of them seem to have had any real relationship with God. At the time of the marriage Alyce was seventeen and Fred was twenty-five.

The Langfords already had experience of a 'mixed marriage' - as Catholic/Protestant alliances were then described. One of my father's aunts had apparently fallen in love with a Roman Catholic and eloped with him by knotting her bed sheets together and climbing out of the window! When her flight was discovered her picture had been turned to the wall and her name inked out of the family bible! By the time my mother came on the scene the Langfords were slightly less intolerant, but the marriage was certainly not welcomed although it proved to be exceedingly happy. My parents were not only lovers but great friends and I remember much shared laughter and a lot of private jokes. When they had been apart for even a few hours they would rush into one another's arms as if they had been separated for weeks! Despite their great love for one another, my parents were certainly not perfect – who is? My father would occasionally get drunk which was unpleasant. He never became violent but his speech would be blurred and he was inclined to become sentimental. After these episodes he would always ask my forgiveness and I know he did the same for my mother.

Father eventually decided to leave the army and we moved to England which was his home. I was quite small at the time and my memories of the actual move are dim. I know that when we arrived in

England times were hard and my parents were brave and courageous in their acceptance of the switch from the comparative affluence of army life to near poverty. I was not particularly aware that we had become 'poor' because I had the greatest gift a child can receive – the unconditional love of my parents and an awareness of their love for one another. This was my rock!

The only position my father had been able to secure was that of a purser with the Harrison shipping line which sailed out of Liverpool – so Liverpool became our home. Father's job took him away frequently but what excitement when he was home from the sea! He called me his 'little Lulu-belle' and one of my treats was what he called a 'bicycle ride' when he placed each of my feet in one of his hands. He would make the motion of a bicycle and let me pretend I was going to school! Each night he was home we would have this playtime together and Daddy really entered into it. He would say: 'Careful, now we go slowly round this corner' or: 'A little faster here as we are going downhill and are nearly at school'. He must have been about twenty-nine.

When we returned to England some uncles and aunts entered my life – my father's brothers and their wives and his sister, Aunt Mabel who had been persuaded to turn down offers of marriage so that she could look after her parents in their old age. Uncle William was an accountant and later on he taught me bookkeeping which came in useful. I found Uncle William somewhat cold and remote and later I learnt that he had disapproved particularly strongly of my mother and her Catholic relations. This probably explained his coldness.

Uncle Ernie was an uncle after a little girl's heart! He was in the army, had some horses and taught me a little riding. For some reason the family considered that Uncle Ernie was not very respectable and they found him unreliable - which probably added to his attraction as far as I was concerned. Sometimes Uncle Ernie would turn up 'out of the blue' and take me out for the day or suggest that I come to stay overnight with him and his wife.

There was one uncle I heard about but never met – Uncle Stanley who lived in America. Uncle Stanley had committed some undisclosed misdeed which had warranted a thrashing from his father. Stanley did not take kindly to the thrashing and ran away to Salt Lake City where he married into a staunch Mormon family and never came home again. He did not convert to Mormonism and continued to drink and smoke which did not find favour with the Mormons. Perhaps he did something else as well because he was apparently barred from attending the wedding of his own daughter! Uncle Stanley sounded fascinating!

My Liverpool home

Our house in Liverpool was close to Wilberforce Square, named after William Wilberforce, the most prominent and successful of the anti-slave-trade campaigners. Liverpool, like Bristol was one of the main ports to which these unfortunate human beings, were brought; whole families were often separated and small children removed from their mothers. My father took me down to the Goree on the quayside to see the place where the ships had disgorged the slaves during the eighteenth century. The rings to which they had apparently been attached were still there. Years later, reading Harriet Beecher Stowe's *Uncle Tom's Cabin*, I was able to imagine the buying and selling, the horror, the heartache and the tragedy. Down on the quayside there was also a synagogue that was always unlocked. Sometimes I would steal in there with great trepidation and wander around by myself.

Monday was wash day and I always remember Mondays as fine and sunny – but it must have rained sometimes. On Mondays, the whole house was up before six to heat the water in the copper clothes boiler. On wash day I was just an onlooker, as I suppose I would have been more trouble than I was worth if I had tried to 'help'! Washing was an all day job, with the sheets, tablecloths, napkins, aprons; never mind the shirts and normal clothing. It was done by hand, with the help of a 'dolly' (a sort of three legged stool on a stick which you swished around in the large hot water vats), and a rubbing board, which was made of wood and steel. One rubbed the extra dirty clothes on this board until they were clean. This was a world without washing machines and driers. There was no soap powder, no water softener (unless it was washing soda) and no gloves. No wonder that the women who came in to help had 'washerwoman hands', which meant that their hands were red, hardened and cracked. Some women did nothing but go around and help with the washing. They either did it on the premises or took it home and did it there. The clothes were pegged out on huge lines, and the overflow placed on large bushes.

We all needed 'clothes-horses' in our kitchens on which the clothes were aired. These were enormous racks with six or eight rails which were suspended from the kitchen ceiling because of the constant heat rising from the coal fire and the oven. Clothes horses were raised and lowered with a rope and pulley. Early on in my own marriage we had one of these contraptions, but I doubt if many youngsters today would know what I was talking about.

When I was five, something happened that changed my whole world. Another baby arrived - a boy, Brian Frederick. My mother was overjoyed as she, like many Irish mothers, felt special pride in a son and in the family name being carried on. I felt extreme rejection and have a vivid memory of people coming to see the new baby. I rushed to the door but my mother pushed me out of the way, saying: 'Go and sit quietly on that chair', pointing to a corner. I felt really squashed. To make matters worse, my

Brian and me

mother proudly lifted up my brother to show him off. She told the visitors: 'He is *such* a good baby, not at all like Joyce when she was born'. There rose in me an anger and resentment of which I had to repent years later. Worse was to come! That night and for many a succeeding night, I would nip out of bed when my brother was asleep in the cot in my room, I pulled his thumb out of his mouth and pinched him till he cried. Brian Frederick was not going to gain points for good baby behaviour if I could help it!

For the first time, I felt starved of affection and experienced a sense of rejection, which was to last for many years. At least I knew that I had a father who really loved me, for whom I was 'Lulu-belle', his favourite. How much the love of my father has helped me to appreciate the love of God - despite the fact that Daddy himself had no faith, no interest whatsoever in the Almighty as far as I could see. His indifference, and in fact his subtle opposition to my mother going to church weakened her own commitment to attending Sunday Mass.

School

When I was about 5½ I started school. My mother, as an 'on and off' practicing Catholic took me to visit one of the best convents in Liverpool where we saw the Reverend Mother. My mother asked if the nuns would take me as a pupil and she had to do a really brave thing which she must have found humbling. She had to explain to Reverend Mother that she was in no position to pay anything whatsoever - but would try to pay something in the bright future which she hoped was in store for her husband and family. Reverend Mother agreed to take me for free!

My mother bought material and sewed as much of my school uniform as possible in order to save money. She did her best, but my uniform was never quite the right colour, and never just the same pattern as the uniforms of the other girls. They were rather unkind about it.

My first day at school was awful. My mother left me at the door and I knew no one. My teacher was not a nun, but a lady with a 1920's fringe wearing a red dress. I must have started in the middle of the school year because there were only a couple of other new girls. One unfortunate girl who started the same day as me must have been even more nervous than I was because she wet her pants. This was disgrace *par excellence*. The unfortunate girl had to sit miserably with the telltale pool of water round her feet. The mistress was not kind, and I had a horror that I might do the same thing! This was one of the many useless worries I should never have entertained. I think now of the words of Mark Twain: "I have known a great many troubles but most of them never happened".

All the 'old' girls had small attaché cases for books. This was a great hurdle for me because we 'new' girls were each told to bring some money the following day for an attaché case. The thought of having to ask my parents for money appalled me, as I knew it had been a struggle to rig me out for school. Little did I know that this was the first of many requests to bring money: for Reverend Mother's Feast Day, black babies, for outings, presents for teachers, posters, picnics – the requests were legion and caused me much anguish. I would have cheerfully washed floors for a few pennies rather than bother my parents.

Each day I was given one penny for my fare. I had to choose whether to walk to school and ride back in the tram or the other way about. Most of the time I chose to take the tram to school and walk back because something in me dreaded being late for school. For most of the time I went to school I was the first child to arrive. I felt a great sense of injustice when report cards were sent home and one of the items under 'behaviour' was punctuality. The nuns gave me only 'satisfactory' for punctuality when others got 'excellent' and I knew that they were sometimes late! I had never seen an alphabet before going to school, and I can remember the letters on the classroom wall. There were animals with names that started with particular letters. I began to get the hang of reading and will never forget the day I realised I could read all by myself. It was in the middle of a small party of six or eight school friends which I was giving at home. We were playing hide and seek, and the cupboard in which I was hiding had some books and a little chink of light. The other children were long in finding me and I opened a book. I could read it!!! Christopher Columbus could not have been more excited when he discovered the New World. I thought the guests would never go so that I could get down to the important business of reading on my own.

The nuns were not a packet of fun, but they certainly saw that one learnt about the Catholic faith and they taught me a spirituality that has stood me in good stead throughout my life. They made a point of reminding us to remember God every time the clock chimed or the bell rang for a change of lesson. This was an invaluable starter for perceiving the presence of God at all times. We were taught many beautiful, powerful, instructive hymns which I had no difficulty in learning by heart. Now, in this latter part of my life these hymns are included in the repertoire when my husband and I go to Mass together.

The nuns also set great store by 'novenas' which consisted of special prayers or devotions to be recited on nine consecutive days for a particular intention. I firmly believed that things 'happened' when you prayed – and I still believe that. We also had 'indulgenced' prayers which we were taught could remit all or part of the punishment due for our sins, even after the sins had been forgiven by God. This concept of 'indulgences' I certainly would not share with any of the ecumenical communities with which I have been so happily involved in my latter years.

My feelings about school remain very mixed. There were some subjects in which I never got more than ten marks out of a hundred and this left me feeling dim, unhappy and very frustrated. When it came to subjects I was rather good at, I had a very annoying habit which I suppose I developed in order to assert and affirm myself. When questions were asked in class, a girl was expected to put up her hand and wait to be called on to give the answer. I could never wait and invariably shouted out the answer.

Again and again I was reprimanded but I did not stop. Every time I 'called out' in class I would be handed *The Penny Catechism*, as it was known in those days, and told to leave the room. I would go outside and sit at the top of the stairs for hours, days, maybe months! Far from being a punishment, this was a real bonus because I learnt so much about God while sitting in exile!. The second question in *The Penny Catechism* particularly delighted my heart: 'Why did God make you'. The answer was: 'To know him, love him, and serve him in this world and to be happy with him forever in the next.' Bare bones, perhaps, but God put flesh on the bones over the years. He placed in me a desire to know him that will only be fulfilled when I shall see him face to face, and shall know him as I am known' [I Cor.13:12.I Jn 3:2] I learnt all sorts of things from *The Penny Catechism*, as I had ample time to read *all* the questions and answers over and over again. Being sent out of the classroom never bothered me - and I don't suppose I was missed!

Grandma Nettie

At various times my mother's mother, Grandma Nettie would visit from Dublin. Even I could see that Grandma Nettie was upset by the lower standards in our household. She and my mother were always at loggerheads by the end of the visit.

One wonderful outcome of Grandma Nettie's visits was an invitation for me to go and stay in Dublin. Every summer from the time I was five, Grandma Nettie paid for me to travel across to

Grandma Nettie

Ireland and stay with her for the entire summer. Each year I would be taken down to a ship of the B&I line and placed in charge of the stewardess. I always had a single cabin of my own which was a tremendous thrill - especially when the stewardess brought me a cup of tea with a biscuit in the morning. I would always be awake before dawn and it was a recurring delight to see the land coming into view. There was the excitement of watching the buildings getting larger and larger and, as the years passed, recognizing and naming them. I have always loved the sea, and I suppose this early introduction had something to do with it.

After I had travelled across by myself for a couple of years, my mother and Brian came with me. This time the stewardess said to my mother: 'Please let me know if there is anything you need, and if the children are seasick, please ring the bell and I will come'. My mother replied: 'My children wouldn't dare be seasick - I would push them through the port-hole'. I had never heard of being 'seasick' and my mother's words burned into my mind. Later in life I had a few ghastly crossings of different seas and although I have sometimes felt like death I have hardly ever been seasick. Perhaps in my subconscious I always remembered the threat of being 'pushed through the port hole'!

Grandma Nettie had not a clue about how to cope with a small child in her house in Dublin. I began to visualize the sort of childhood my mother would have had as Grandma Nettie's daughter. It would have been: 'Speak when you are spoken to", "Come when you are called" and "Shut the door quietly". Grandma Nettie was also 'in bondage' to punctuality. It was a sort of sin for her to be late which I found tiresome at the time but has proved to be good training!

Nettie was always over-anxious about what I might blab to others about my life in England and extremely rigid about what was 'done' and 'not done'. It was 'not done' to run around too much for fear of getting hot and the bow falling out of one's hair and romping was for the times when Nettie was not around. It was awfully boring to be monitored so strictly. Later on, when I had met my Irish cousins, we romped to our hearts' content and these included wonderful games of hide and seek in an enormous garden and energetic games of tennis. I have happy memories of going down to the sea with the cousins and coming back covered with sand and looking like a ragamuffin.

Every day Grandma Nettie read the newspaper from cover to cover but I never saw her read a magazine or a book - although there were plenty in the house. I inherited my love of reading from my mother who would almost rather read than eat. The only books in Grandma Nettie's house that gained my attention were Butler's *Lives of the Saints* in the original edition. These volumes seemed to leave a great deal to be desired. Butler presented a most jaundiced view of the saints. I gained the impression that there were certain people who were called by the Lord to live very generous lives, and the closer they came to the Lord the more they suffered. In a nutshell, it was as if God was saying: 'Come closer to me and I will clobber you with suffering!'

Nettie was not 'religious' and not, therefore, a typical Irish Catholic woman of her generation. I never saw her say the rosary, go to benediction, or make novenas. This was perhaps because her background was so different from that of her contemporaries. She had been educated in England at a progressive school near Manchester. I can never remember Nettie 'hearing' my prayers, or talking about Jesus. She would go faithfully to Mass every Sunday, and twice a month she would receive Holy Communion. This had to be preceded by 'going to confession'. After her confession there were special prayers which she read aloud and then there had to be silence. It was as if Nettie felt that she might sin if she chatted and then she would feel unable to receive Holy Communion the following morning.

In the afternoon when there was no-one else in Church Grandma Nettie and I sometimes walked around the side-altars. I enjoyed this but was completely baffled by her remarks about the saint in whose honour the first altar was erected. It was someone called 'St. Thérèse of Liseux', a French contemplative who had lived at the end of the nineteenth century and died in her Carmelite convent at the age of twenty-four. Nettie would snort as she passed Thérèse's altar and say: 'We won't stop here, *she* never answers any prayers!'

I remember Nettie taking me to visit a retired bishop who lived in a convent. I had never met a bishop before and was fascinated with his ring which was very ornate. He let me play with it. After tea, a nun came and asked if she could take me to the convent chapel. I was allowed to go with her and when we reached the chapel, the nun lit a candle and we both knelt down. I have no idea whether or not I prayed because I was nervous about the whole situation. As we were walking out of the chapel the nun turned to me and said sweetly: 'Do you know what I prayed for?' I dutifully said: 'No Sister'. Her reply floored me: 'I prayed that you might become a nun'. I can still feel the horror. I thought Grandma Nettie and I would never get home. When I was able to get to my room I closed the door, rushed to kneel down at the foot of my bed and said: 'Dearest Lord, please don't listen to that nun!'

At one point Nettie and I had a real personality clash. On that occasion – and many others - I was rescued by my grandmother's best friend, Kay Cantwell, Auntie Kay, as I called her. Auntie Kay had also rescued my mother when she and Grandma Nettie had clashed. If things were ghastly with Nettie and we had reached a point of not speaking, I would sneak out to a neighbour whom I was allowed to visit. She allowed me to phone Auntie Kay secretly and Kay would breeze round in her car and say: 'Just passing, Nettie. I thought I would take Joyce out for the day tomorrow'. It was through the kindness of Auntie Kay that I was to meet my future husband. I had heard whispers that Grandma Nettie had a brother somewhere in Dublin. But there was a lot that was for grown-up ears only – and I wasn't too interested in Grandma Nettie's brother! My husband Ted was the son of that brother!

When I was about seven I 'fell in love' with my cousin Gavin who was nine and lived in Dublin. I thought Gavin was Prince Charming, and the fantasies I wove in my mind would have filled many a Barbara Cartland novel. Gavin was handsome, assured, and full of fun - and he even considered talking to me! I remember him making me a partner in a 'trick' - doubtless because there was no one else interested in helping him! The 'trick' was an illusion that one could make a large 'old' penny go through the bottom of a glass of water, through the table on which it was standing and onto a hankie underneath. We had this trick off 'pat'. Everyone probably knew how it was done, but Gavin and I were always applauded and we lapped it up! One day Gavin 'egged me on' to put my head through the bars of the day nursery in his house. I loved him and would have done anything to please him. I pushed my head through the bars and it got stuck – Gavin and his brother tried to get me out but my ears kept getting in the way and the boys panicked which did not help much! Rather blue in the face, I eventually managed to get my head back through the bars without their help. Afterwards a little bit of the glitter seemed to have disappeared from Gavin!

First Communion

Back home in Liverpool I prepared to make my First Confession and First Holy Communion at the age of seven. In those days people were tartars about children learning things 'by heart'. The nuns went over word-by-word what we were to say on the day of our First Confession. In those days it was the custom to have a 'dry run' the day before. This meant that each child went into the coal black confessional (without the option we have today of seeing the priest face to face). Each little girl was expected to say "Pray Father, give me your blessing, this is my First Confession". When the priest made some response such as: "Bless you, my child", you were supposed to tell your sins.

For the 'dry run' there was a very stern Reverend Mother behind the grille. I didn't say the exact words, and instead said: "Pray Father, give me your blessing*s*" - instead of 'blessing'!! In icy tones Reverend Mother said to me: "And pray, how many blessings would you like?" She always had icy tones, but I did not recognise that this time they were frozen icy. I was really surprised, and thought to myself: 'I never knew you got more than one blessing - how wonderful - I shall be coming back all my life to confess my sins if I can have more than one blessing!' In all innocence, and thinking that one should not be greedy, I said "May I have three please?" The response was dramatic and unexpected. Reverend Mother thought I was being cheeky, and ordered me out of the confessional. In front of all the other girls, she marched out of her side of the confessional 'box' and gave me a dressing down – but it was like water off a duck's back. Despite Reverend Mother's anger, I had received a great light from the Lord during that 'dry run' confession. Suddenly and in the depths of my being I knew that I would really be meeting Jesus himself the following day when I made my 'real' First Confession. I knew Reverend Mother wouldn't understand, but it didn't matter one bit.

The next day, my First Confession was the start of an ever-deepening relationship with Jesus Christ that I know will come to fulfilment in eternity. I have read of many occasions when people have had a special meeting with Jesus at the time of their First Communion. For me, the 'meeting' took place during my First Confession. Jesus became totally real to me and I fell in love with Him. He also gave me a special language, the 'gift of tongues' which enabled me to praise God in a language which I did not understand. I imagined that this gift was unique to me in the whole wide world. Sometimes I would speak it out loud when I was alone on the beach and there were moments in the future when I was to fear that this 'secret language' might be a sign of madness. It was not until the early 1970's when visiting the community in which my youngest daughter lives that I realized how many people possessed this gift which had first been recorded at Pentecost{Acts 2:1-4}

I made my First Holy Communion in a shack-like Church which was bitterly cold. I had a white dress with a headband, which I am sure my mother had made lovingly. The ensemble was not improved by the warm black stockings which I had had put on in the morning and was only allowed to remove when we reached the church vestibule.

In the afternoon of the First Communion day, a small party was held at the convent. Parents were invited, but mine did not attend. This was sadness for me but I now realize that Daddy would have been away at sea, and my mother would have had to stay at home to mind Brian who was only two. My principle memory of the party is of embarrassment. My overcoat was very worn so my mother gave me an ornate white wool cloak with beautiful embroidery that she had worn when she was my age. It was 'different' and I felt dreadful. When I was waiting at the tram stop a lady asked me if I was the May Queen – goodness knows why since the date was December 8th – the feast of the Immaculate Conception. Years later my husband Ted and I compared notes and discovered that we had both made our First Holy Communion on the same day, December 8th 1928.

At the time of my First Confession and First Holy Communion, Jesus also gave me a love of Scripture and I sought out and devoured books on the saints and became fired up with their love for Jesus.

With tremendous trepidation I also asked my parents if I could go to daily Mass and, amazingly was given permission: "unless you get too tired!" If I had been dead on my feet I would never have admitted it! This ability to get to daily Mass was a grace that is beyond my telling. I did not have an alarm clock, and yet I woke every morning, summer and winter, and walked the twenty minutes to the Church of St Philip Neri. There was a side-chapel in the church devoted to St. Philip and I discovered a little about his life. I was thrilled to find that St Philip had been full of fun – contrary to what I might have supposed from reading Grandma Nettie's copies of Butler's *Lives of the Saints!* For a number of years this little girl of seven was the only parishioner attending the early morning Mass. I wonder what the parish priest made of me.

Before I crept out of the house to Mass on weekday mornings, I would heat the huge kettle to boiling point and pour it carefully into the large sink in the corner to kill off dozens of horrible cockroaches! It was a fact of life that old houses were homes for cockroaches too – not to mention bedbugs – but we did our best to get rid of the ones we could see! On one occasion my mother bought a piece of second-hand furniture which must have been infested with bedbugs because we were eaten alive for weeks. They literally clung to us and sucked our blood. They were revolting! We had special powder which helped to deal with cockroaches and we knew that many people were putting up with similar conditions so we were philosophical about them and also about the bedbugs! At times I have to chuckle at the hygiene mania of today. During my childhood the killing of cockroaches was as routine as eating breakfast!

There was a curate who used to come and visit my mother from time to time. I suspect that he was trying to encourage her to become a fully practicing Catholic. She had definitely drifted away and I can remember coming to her bedside one particular Sunday morning and trying to cajole her into coming with me to church. My father got cross with me and told me that Mummy was too tired. I now realise that it is vital to have support in ones faith and I realise that God gave me special grace to enable me to persevere completely on my own. My mother certainly made sure that Brian and I went to Sunday Mass and there were occasions when she would accompany us – but as she slipped away from regular church going, Brian slipped with her.

The final crunch came when we were going on a picnic one Sunday and had to be up early as the journey was a long one. No way would *I* not go to Mass, and my father and mother knew this. In the end, my mother came to church with me and brought Brian with her – he was very reluctant. We came out of the church at the Last Gospel, which was the final part of the Mass before the liturgical reforms of Vatican II in the 1960's. Many other people would slip out of church at that time but on this occasion the parish priest was in the vestibule and said to my mother in a loud voice: "I think it is a scandal that you take two young children away from Mass before it is ended'. That was the last straw. My mother rounded on him and dressed him down in no uncertain terms about the so-called 'scandal'. She went on to tell him about certain things 'going on' in the parish to which he was a party. I cannot remember the details but I remember only too well that I wanted to crawl beneath the floor. My mother never again darkened the door of that church and seldom attended any other!

2

GROWING UP
1929-1937

"We don't know what [God] wants us to be; the finished work will be unveiled in God when we come to die; but we know quite surely what He wants us to do."

Ferdinand Valentine,
'Whatsoever He Shall Say'

Just before the start of the Christmas holidays of 1929 I began to feel awful - terribly hot and with a dreadful sore throat. When I arrived home from school my father was in the house and obviously very concerned; he took me in his arms and held a cold wet flannel to my forehead. Daddy must have been very alarmed indeed because he and my mother did something dramatic - they sent for a doctor! In those days before the National Health Service doctors were expensive and you did not call one out unless there was an emergency. The doctor arrived and diagnosed the dreaded diphtheria, which was a killer – in

1929 there were no antibiotics, no penicillin. If you managed to survive at all you were very likely to be left with some disability. I was rushed to the isolation hospital in an ambulance, and the school was notified and closed for several days in case any of the other children had contracted the disease.

I spent three months in that isolation hospital and the experience was very unhappy and traumatic. Christmas came and went and then Easter. Part of the treatment involved lying flat – no pillows allowed. We were not permitted to sit up or even to raise our heads and at mealtimes the nurses would spoon feed us. One of the things we dreaded most was constipation because a ghastly sludge would be administered which tasted of licorice. To this day I cannot abide the taste of licorice.

The greatest suffering was the isolation. Parents were not allowed to visit their children and reading was not permitted because it was considered to be bad for our eyes. The nurses were unable to help us much apart from the daily necessities. They were obviously bored and probably underpaid. As a result they seemed to turn in on themselves and I recall a great deal of unkindness. One nurse told me that my parents had abandoned me, and were never coming back - I suppose she thought it was a joke. That isolation hospital gave me a fear of hospitals that was not healed for years. The unfortunate nurses, and the whole situation left me feeling trapped - and I was totally convinced that my parents had abandoned me.

My mother and father in fact visited the hospital faithfully and were once allowed to glimpse me through the door of the ward – but I never knew about that until I returned home. Mummy apparently sent in edible goodies to bolster my health. I don't know what happened to them because they never reached me! One thing that I did receive from her was skeins of coloured wool which I was allowed to work while lying on my back. This was a great relief to a small girl of eight for whom the hours were long – there is so little one can do while lying flat.

I could still pray which was a lifeline – though at times a very slender one. I was obviously unable to get to Mass on Sundays – let alone weekdays - and the well-meaning nuns had instilled into me the importance of attending Sunday Mass. They had not got around to explaining that the obligation was lifted in the case of illness. I was under the impression that missing Sunday Mass under any circumstances was a very serious sin which hurt God and that caused me considerable suffering. A kindly Anglican minister came to visit us from time to time but I wonder why there was never a Catholic priest?

After three months I was allowed out of bed to go home. But I was unable to walk after all that time on my back. It seemed ages before I could use my legs again – let alone run about. I remember having to sit down for long periods and my mother began to teach me embroidery which I loved. In due course I was able to go back to school and life continued as normal.

Evergloss

In 1933 or thereabouts my father seized a business opportunity which really paid off. I do not know where the money came from but perhaps he came into an inheritance. Whatever the source of funds, it enabled Daddy to buy a polish manufacturing firm and eventually take over as director. The firm had the unimaginative name of 'Evergloss' but the polish was super. These were the days when elbow grease went into cleaning furniture and good polish was essential for every household. Evergloss was made from pure beeswax and had a lovely lavender smell.

The factory was on Dock Road down in Liverpool's Wapping. For a while Daddy used to work from home and when I was twelve he made a bargain with me. If I could teach myself to type and work for him in the evenings after school I could have fifteen shillings a week- [75p in today's money]. This 'bargain' was really an order and I was well aware that if Daddy's new venture was to succeed it was going to be a case of 'all hands on deck'. I obediently learnt to 'peck and hunt' type with two fingers. I never had a lesson and, to this day, know nothing about touch typing. 'Peck and hunt' has served me well, however, and many people have benefited from my unprofessional efforts.

In typing for my father there could be no mistakes and spelling had to be perfect so I made good use of my dictionary! Most nights of the week there would be lots to type and Daddy would dictate letters. I developed my own form of shorthand and became very familiar with the ways in which he expressed himself. In time I could almost read his mind and was often able to write routine letters for him to check and sign. But it was often after eleven at night before we were finished. I was aware that I would be getting up in the morning to walk to church before going to school - and I needed my sleep. Plus there was the warning: 'If you are ever tired, I will stop you going to Mass'. Into the bargain, my father loved company. As often as not, when the letters were completed, he would drive down to the General Post Office to catch the last post at midnight and he liked me to come along for the ride. The Lord was always faithful in waking me up in the morning. Even without an alarm clock I was up in time to get up and boil the water, kill the cockroaches and walk to Mass. But the late nights created an anxiety about getting enough sleep, which is still with me.

After we bought the polish firm, the family was able to move from Wilberforce Road to a big house on Merton Road in Bootle - these were years of the economic depression and property prices must have been low. Our new house stood in its own grounds with iron railings around it. These were removed during the Second World War when all such ornamental railings were melted down as part of the war effort. The house had three storeys and a decent sized garden at the back. There was a huge drawing room, a fair sized dining room, and a large kitchen with pantries and other rooms off it; upstairs were four bedrooms and then a further five bedrooms up another flight. One of the five was so large that it could be used as a ping-pong room. Another was devoted to Brian's electric trains so that he could leave them out all the time instead of having to tidy the trains away at teatime.

The house could certainly be described as a handsome dwelling – but it was a cold one. All large houses were cold as ice in winter. There was always a huge fire in the drawing room and the kitchen was warm – but you froze in the dining room When anyone went out of the room one always called out: 'Close the door' or, more pointedly: 'Were you born in a barn?'

One had to be *very* ill for a fire to be lit in your bedroom In the winter I went to bed in a long woollen nightie with layers of jumpers and cardigans, and mounds of blankets on top of me. A hot-water bottle was a treasured possession – mine was made of stone and felt like a log of wood. It never seemed to keep the heat for very long.

A wonderful woman from Ireland called Jo came to be our housekeeper. Jo had her own living quarters on the ground floor. She was fat and kindly and probably in her forties. I loved Jo dearly and there was a sense of kinship because she was a practising Catholic.

When my mother married at the age of seventeen, she claimed that she had never been in a kitchen in her life and couldn't boil an egg. She had done her best, but she just wasn't interested in cooking. Fortunately, she was wise enough to decree that no daughter of hers would grow up ignorant of cooking. I was put under Jo's expert tutelage and was eventually able to cook the Sunday dinner every week, and the desserts on weekdays. I enjoyed cooking and was 'promoted' to preparing a buffet supper on my own nearly every Saturday evening when my parents used to go out to 'the dogs'. Greyhound racing was a very popular form of entertainment, and a lot of people backed 'the dogs'. I went along a couple of times when I was older, but greyhound racing bored me silly. It is strange that, with all the Irish blood in me, I do not have an ounce of gambling spirit. I have known so many Irish people who really loved a 'bet', but I am not one of them.

Discoveries and difficulties

As I entered my teens there were many changes in my life. For starters, I no longer had to do office work with Daddy in the evenings. That was now done in the company office at Wapping. My father still worked at home in his study - these days he would have been called a workaholic. My mother was now employed in the business and she and Daddy certainly worked like trojans. In those days it was considered odd for mother to work outside the home but Mummy had great personality and must have found the outside interest rewarding as well as being of considerable help to my father.

Although the Depression of the 1920's and 1930's was lingering on, the firm was doing well and we were certainly better off financially. Mummy and Daddy each had a new car every year – and the cars had a lovely smell of leather. Mummy always had a Ford and Daddy a Humber. In 1934 when I was thirteen, Daddy took delivery of a beautiful green Humber and proudly drove off. He came home late with his hat on the back of his head and it was clear that something had happened because the shiny new car had had its front all pushed in! Daddy was very honest about the cause! He had been driving along behind a tram and spotted a pretty girl who was waiting to get off at the next stop. My father was always a bit of a flirt and was only about forty at the time. He raised his hat to the young lady which diverted his attention from the road. The tram stopped abruptly and into the back of it went the green Humber! Daddy came off worst because the tram was big and heavy. As a final indignity, the young girl laughed at her admirer's misfortune!

At about this time, I had a very difficult experience with my father. On Ash Wednesday it had long been the custom to go to church and get a blob of ashes pressed on one's forehead, as a starter for Lent. The priest said: 'Remember man that thou are dust, and unto dust thou shall return'. This particular year I think the priest must have given me at least five portions of ash - and it was extremely obvious. In previous years the ashes had usually worn off by the time I got home and there would have been little more than a smudge which went unnoticed. This time the ashes looked like a huge bruise. Daddy asked what it was. I tried to explain but he was horrified, and said 'No daughter of mine is going out of this house like that - go and wash it off'.

I wept, but my father would not budge. I was still under the impression that one should not touch the ash but allow it to fall off. The nuns had clearly overdone the significance of such things! I went to my mother but she backed my father. This, I felt, was treachery as she had been accustomed in the past to coming to church to receive her own ashes. Then I went to Jo. She backed me up, but pointed out that she could not say anything to my parents as she was only an employee. In the end I had to go and wash it all off.

Sometimes Daddy would mock me for going to Confession, and would quiz me about what I had confessed. I found this excruciating. I told him some of the things I said, and he would say: 'Why don't you come to me instead of going to Confession? Anyway, you do the same sins over and over again, so what good does it do you?' At times I felt that we were eye-ball to eye-ball in conflict. My father was sufficiently astute to realise that I had a real relationship with Jesus and he must have felt that he therefore had a rival for my affections.

In my early teens I developed a devotion to two saints who were to become my friends. One was St. Anthony of Padua who had lived in the thirteenth century and was a friend and collaborator of St Francis of Assisi. The other was St Thérèse of Lisieux of whom Grandma Nettie thought so poorly. I suspect that I started being interested in St. Anthony because I was a pragmatist and knew he had a reputation of finding lost things. He certainly found a lot of things for me. I was fascinated by Anthony's life of poverty and suspected that he spoke louder to the Lord on my behalf if his beloved poor were tended. I am afraid that I used to 'bribe' him with promises about the money I would give to the poor if he did this or that for me. I do wonder how on earth this must come across to my brethren in other churches!

St Anthony's evangelistic zeal also sparked off a response in me although I was a little dubious about some of the stories attached to him. It was hard to believe that Anthony had actually preached to the fishes. Years later when I was married and living in Boston I was amazed to see a splendid mosaic depicting this event on the wall of a church dedicated to St Anthony.

St Thérèse of Lisieux also had an influence on my teenage life. Perhaps I was impressed by her insistence on asking the Pope for permission to enter her convent at the age of fifteen when the local bishop was delaying matters. I had a battered copy of Therese's autobiography but found it a bit sugary although I came to understand her better when I was married and my husband explained her spirituality. Years later, I read her autobiography in the translation by Ronald Knox and found it excellent. I was told that Knox had been reluctant to translate the autobiography but eventually succumbed to pressure. At the end of his life he wrote to a friend : 'I have a [suspicion] that [St Thérèse] was asked in heaven who she'd like best as her translator, and replied: 'Ronald Knox – he'll mind my style terribly, and the great thing is always to do something you don't like!"

I sought out and devoured books on all sorts of saints and became fired up with their zeal and with their love for Jesus. One story in particular helped me greatly. It was attributed to St Catherine of Siena but I have never been able to find confirmation of this. Catherine apparently suffered from a particular aberration. She believed that one had to keep on doing good works in order to 'earn' heaven. She had a supply of beans and every time she did a 'good work', into the jar went a bean!. She counted the beans every night and gave herself ratings. One night she had a vision or a dream about Jesus in which he emptied out her precious bean jar! "Lord, why are you doing that?' said Catherine in amazement: "It is all for YOU", Jesus replied "My daughter, learn this. You can do nothing *for* me, you can only receive".

At about this time I acquired my own Bible. At school we each had our own copy of the New Testament and complete bibles were certainly available – although the Old Testament was barely touched upon in religious education classes. Now I started to read the gospel of St John with fresh understanding and found it tremendously exciting. At the time of my First Confession and First Holy Communion, I had begun to know and love Scripture but it was as if the words were now leaping off the page. Nothing delighted me more than to get to bed as early as possible and read and learn by heart long passages from St. John. In retrospect I would have expected a girl of thirteen to prefer the Acts of the Apostles as a great adventure story – but for me it was always St John.

I was certainly an 'odd' little girl, but not so odd that I did not read ordinary books as well as spiritual ones. I can remember my father calling for me and muttering under his breath: "I'll bet she's curled up in a corner somewhere reading a book". My mother was especially helpful about books because she knew a librarian [whom I never met] who took an interest in me and sent along about three books a week. I read classics like *Anne of Green Gables* and the subsequent books that grew out of this little story set on Prince Edward Island off the eastern coast of Canada. I really entered into these stories and lived them vicariously. I remember going to the bathroom, and weeping privately when Anne's adopted father, Matthew died. I wove a romance about the hero Gilbert and my Irish cousin Gavin Halpin who I still felt to be my own Prince Charming.

I can remember laughing uncontrollably at Richmal Crompton's *William* books and having to ram a hanky in my mouth! Even today I chuckle inside at some of the silly escapades of William and his friends. I think of Violet Elizabeth, daughter of Mrs Bott - the little girl who used to get her own way with William and his unwilling 'Outlaws' by saying with a lisp "I'll thcream and thcream and thcream till I make mysthelf thsick". I have met quite a number of ladies who manipulated and manoeuvred like Violet Elizabeth. I have also met one 'Mrs Bott' who was a lady of the manor, and thought that everyone should tip their hats to her.

As far as my deepest beliefs were concerned, I kept them to myself because I still had nobody with whom to talk about them. But at long last somebody was about to come into my life with whom I could share the things that were most important. A retreat was to be held at the school - three days of talks and prayer to be led by a Dominican priest, Ferdinand Valentine. The name meant nothing to me and I had no idea that Father Ferdinand was a famous preacher and retreat leader. In his long white habit and hob nailed boots he seemed hugely tall but in no way intimidating. He had a wonderful sense of humour and there was a lot of laughter during the retreat which made it clear that it was fun to know God. We had never come across a priest like this! He didn't just 'preach', he 'shared' with us. One of the girls was called Eva Ramos, and any time she said anything, or answered a question, Father Ferdinand would say: 'All right, come on Adoramus' which made us laugh.

The main talk each day was always on prayer, and Father Ferdinand's words touched my heart. I was in the habit of talking to Jesus every day in a familiar way but often wondered if I was praying 'properly'. Father Ferdinand had spent most of his life teaching people to pray and to move into deeper relationship with the Lord – as far as I was concerned he was a gift from heaven! I had a gut feeling that God had sent this priest to open a door for me and I was determined to walk through it and get as much help as possible. Father Valentine's method of prayer was apparently classical - but it was certainly new to me He used the acronym ACTS – the four letters stood for 'Adoration', 'Contrition', 'Thanksgiving' and 'Supplication' and it offered a way to use the time one had set aside for prayer. When I have found it difficult to pray I have frequently gone back to ACTS.

At the end of the retreat Father Ferdinand gave us each a copy of a little leaflet he had written on ACTS. On the back of it I found his address and did something which seemed to me very daring. I wrote and asked if I could send him a letter from time to time, asking for help in my spiritual life. He wrote back to say that he would be very happy to answer my letters and help me. This was the start of a correspondence which extended over more than twenty-five years! I would share my difficulties with Father Ferdinand and he would write back most helpfully and suggest books which I might find useful. Years later, he published *Whatsoever He Shall Say* which was presented in the form of letters between a young girl seeking advice and her spiritual director. I am sure that the book drew, anonymously, on many of the letters he received. But each of the questions posed by the 'young girl' in the book – Theophila - had certainly been raised by me at one time or another.

New Horizons

These were years when Hitler was coming to power and war clouds were gathering over Europe. We were the most unpolitically minded family imaginable and in the mid-nineteen thirties I had never heard of Hitler. The Burning of the Reichstag in 1933 and the 'Night of the Long Knives' in 1934 only came to my knowledge years later.

In the 1930's, the cinema was very much part of our lives, and the family would go to the films once a week. In my mid-teens I was also allowed to go to the cinema on Wednesdays. I went with my best friend from school, Julie Jeffers, and another girl. There were no violent pictures, no fear of anything upsetting - just sheer entertainment although everything was still in black and white. We would cry a little, laugh ourselves silly, and have a really good time. The Westerns were the films I liked least, but even the Westerns often included a love story – with a happy ending and the right side winning! Sometimes there was a musical with, say, Jessie Matthews, Cicely Courtnedge, or Sonny Hale and we would come home humming all the tunes!

1935 was the Silver Jubilee year of King George V and Queen Mary. The Jubilee was celebrated in every town and village in the land with bunting, streamers and decorations. There were prizes for the best decorated streets and we had a holiday from school on the day the King and Queen visited Liverpool. I can remember getting hot and sticky while waiting for what seemed like hours to see them pass majestically in an open car, which did all of five miles per hour! Queen Mary did not smile much but she was every inch a queen. I don't think she changed her style in the whole of the reign but maintained her high toque hats, the chokers of pearls, and the tight-waisted dresses. In summer she held a tiny parasol.

I had seen the King before his visit to Liverpool - which sounds grand. When I was a little girl I remember holding my father's hand on a country road near Chester where Granny and Grandpa Langford lived. A large car came towards us. Daddy must have spotted the Royal Standard. He lifted me up and told me it was the King. I was very impressed because the King raised his hat to the two of us.

In January 1936 the King died and his eldest son was proclaimed as King Edward VIII. One day the milkman told my mother about a lady called Mrs

Simpson and her liaison with the King. My mother did not believe him, and berated the man for taking someone's character away! The milkman was so incensed at my mother's disbelief that he gave an American newspaper to our maid to give to my mother. There were lurid headlines 'Broadway Babe leads Britain's King' and a cartoon of a smart lady leading a little puppy dog with the face of the King. We were to learn that the story was all too true. In December 1936 King Edward VIII abdicated to marry Mrs Simpson and his brother became King George VI.

In 1937 I remember going up to the top of the Royal Liver Building to see the aircraft carrier HMS Ark Royal being launched from the great shipyard Cammell Laird, on the other side of the Mersey. The first submarine to be built on Merseyside by Cammell Laird, Thetis, was also a source of great excitement until tragedy struck. On June 1st 1939 the Thetis made her first dive with many distinguished visitors on board. Unknown to crew and passengers, a torpedo tube had remained open to the water. As she dived, the sea flooded in but, due to poor communications, the plight of the Thetis was not discovered until the morning of June 2nd. Eighteen feet of her stern were sticking out of the water and men in small boats were able to knock on her side and hear frantic knocking in return. As one did ones shopping, people would be asking one another: 'What is the latest about the Thetis?' I am sure many people must have been praying. Four men were saved out of the 95 on board and on the morning of June 3rd

the Admiralty announced that there was no hope of further survivors.

When I was nearly sixteen, Daddy decided that I should acquire a few of the accomplishments which he considered useful for a young lady. These were ballroom dancing, Ju-jitsu and fencing! What a strange assortment. I suppose my father felt that dancing would give me a certain gracefulness, and be useful in the life of the day. But why ju-jitsu? Perhaps he suspected that we were entering an era of violence and I would have to defend myself. I didn't get far with ju-jitsu and I never even began the fencing.

For ballroom dancing I went to a dancing school every Saturday evening which was not far from home. I found it a dreadful business. I knew no one and felt terrified because I was very shy and completely lacking in self-confidence. I would be delivered to the door about 8pm and had to be home (again collected!) by 10.30pm.

The class took place in a huge room with a beautiful floor. The boys sat on one side, the girls on the other. I suspect that we were all equally nervous but the others seemed better able to conceal the fact. The instructors were a very handsome couple, Mr and Mrs. Marshall. There was some sort of mystery about them and I discovered subsequently that one of them had been divorced, which was quite a scandal in those days. The Marshalls demonstrated different steps in old-fashioned ballroom dancing, and then got the pupils to practice. A few advanced students were available to help newcomers.

There was a break when we had had a cup of tea, followed by the awful moment when boys were invited to ask a girl to dance. I had never had any camaraderie with boys and found it sheer agony to sit waiting to be asked. Some of the boys were even more gauche than me and I found myself praying that 'so-and-so' would not ask me to dance but 'such and such' would! I loathed the humiliation of waiting to be 'picked'. If nobody chose you there was the ignominy of dancing with one of the female advanced students. It was even worse to find oneself dancing with the expert Mr Marshall.

I made friends with a girl called Pat and we could make small talk together while the boys were plucking up the courage to ask someone to dance. One day Pat did something that really shook me. She took out a cigarette, made a display of lighting it and then became engrossed in smoking her cigarette until someone asked her to dance. At that point she gracefully stubbed it out and off she went with her partner. My mother and father smoked heavily and I now saw a way of getting around the awful business of being a wallflower. I could take up smoking and give the impression that my cigarette was tremendously important to me. If someone asked me to dance I could convey surprise and gracefully stub out my cigarette as Pat had done.

I didn't quite know how to approach my father on the subject of smoking and had a feeling that it might be sticky. Choosing what I thought to be the right moment, I said casually, with my heart beating fast: 'Pat has started smoking'. Daddy was sitting at his desk and there was a long silence before he said: 'Has she darling?' I became bolder: 'May I smoke too?' Another long silence. Daddy said, without looking up: 'Of course you can darling, just as long as you pay for your own cigarettes'. Well, that finished it! I was getting five shillings a week [25p today] Out of that I had to buy my stockings and I was luxuriating in pure silk stockings made by Bear Brand, which seemed to cost the earth and snag when you looked at them. To pay a shilling [5p in today's money] for twenty cigarettes seemed the stupidest thing imaginable.

3

TED
1937-1939

At the age of sixteen, I was quite sure that I was going to be an old maid. How was I ever going to meet anyone I could possibly want to marry in a backwater like Liverpool? About a year earlier I had started what turned into a perpetual novena to St. Anthony, asking him to find me a husband and promising that if he did so I would call our eldest son 'Anthony'. Perhaps I was beginning to have doubts about Saint Anthony, because I now started bombarding Our Lady with similar requests. I do not think that my faith was especially high and I had no idea that St Paul had told us that God: 'will do infinitely more than we ever dare to ask or imagine" [Ephesians 3:20] I suspect, though, that deep inside me there was hope – and hope is a powerful virtue.

I was still making my annual visit to Grandma Nettie and still had a crush on cousin Gavin. He was now eighteen and had passed his driving test the previous summer. Gavin had arrived back at the house exultant and I had been the first person to whom he showed his new driving license. I was probably the only person around and he had to show that license to somebody! But this 'loving gesture' encouraged me to weave all sorts of useless fantasies around Gavin.

In Nettie's house I continued to hear snatches of conversation about 'Edward' who I suspected of being a distant relative. Occasionally Nettie would also mention 'Ted' and 'Mollie' – but if I enquired further she shut up like a clam. This particular summer, dear Auntie Kay Cantwell took me swimming at Blackrock Baths. When I came out of the water she suddenly said: 'When you are dressed, I will introduce you to your uncle Edward Donovan'. My uncle! I had an uncle in Dublin! In fact he was my great-uncle, as he was Grandma Nettie's eldest brother. Auntie Kay took me across to be introduced to a gentleman in plus-fours who shook my hand and asked politely after my health. 'Very well thank you' I replied - just as politely. Great-uncle Edward then introduced me to three of his children – one of whom was Teddy or Ted. Little did I imagine that I was meeting my future husband!

My newly discovered uncle asked if I would like to go bathing with them the following day. He did not wait for an answer but announced that he would pick me up from Grandma Nettie's at eleven o'clock sharp. I was dumbfounded and when I got home and told Nettie, she was as near speechless as was possible for her. I discovered later that great-uncle Edward and Grandma Nettie had not spoken for twenty years because they had quarrelled over a family will. Her immediate reaction to me was: "You can't go of course" followed by: "What time did Edward say? Who else did you meet?" and "Let me look through your clothes!"

With all the fuss about my clothes, I was ready at least an hour before Uncle Edward was due to pick me up. Nettie posted herself at the drawing room window where she could see but not be seen. Uncle Edward's large car drew up and Nettie came into the hall to open the front door for me and herself moved back into the shadows to watch me walk down the long flight of granite steps to the iron gate. Uncle Edward ushered me into the back seat where I found myself sitting beside a middle aged lady in hat and gloves. We were never introduced and Uncle Edward addressed never a word to this lady throughout the day. Nettie told me later that she must have been his wife Mollie. With my experience of the warm relationship between my own parents I was astounded that husband and wife could spend the day together without chatting. The back seat was spacious and my other companions were Uncle Edward's daughter Freda – and his son Ted.

I was far too shy to open my mouth, so conversation was anything but sparkling although the young people were certainly friendly and it was arranged that Uncle Edward would pick me up every morning at 11.00 so that we could go bathing regularly. When I was dropped home, Nettie did not open the door to me until the car had driven off. Then the inquest began. Who had been there? What did we do? Where did we go?

Horsefly

I was astonished that in a place the size of Dublin Grandma Nettie and Uncle Edward had managed to avoid speaking to one another for twenty years! They had been founder members of the Milltown Golf Club where my parents had been introduced and club rules had facilitated the estrangement. Ladies were allowed to play only at the least popular times and *never* allowed to enter the 'Gentleman's Lounge'!

Inadvertently I managed to heal the rift with the help of a horsefly! One afternoon I felt a sharp prick on my arm and looked down to see the large yellow brute. I brushed it away and thought no more of the matter. Two days later I began to feel ill and noticed a round red mark and realised that the glands beneath my arm were swelling. On the third afternoon I was having tea with friends in Dublin's famous Grafton Street and began to feel hot all over. By the time I reached home I had a high temperature, my arm was throbbing and the lump had swollen alarmingly. Nettie was in a real panic and totally unaccustomed to dealing with anything medical. I suspect that in the back of her mind was the thought of her own baby son who had died of convulsions.

She put her pride in her pocket and telephoned Uncle Edward. He responded magnificently and arrived on the doorstep with his own doctor. By this time I was ensconced royally in Nettie's own bed – but too ill to appreciate the honour. The doctor examined me and announced that he would be back with a surgeon and a nurse. Two hours later they arrived and I was given an anaesthetic so that the huge lump beneath my arm could be lanced and also a smaller one on my wrist. How strange all this must sound to my children and grandchildren, but in the 1930's it was common practice to operate at home.

I was not yet out of the wood because there was apparently a danger of blood poisoning. The doctor and nurse continued to call every day and – wonder of wonders – Grandma Nettie and Uncle Edward became fast friends. All thanks to a hungry horsefly – good luck, bad luck, who knows?

During my convalescence, the Donovans made daily calls and really took me under their wing. Sometimes Teddy came on his own and although he was tall, dark and handsome I did not have the slightest romantic notion about him – Ted and I know nothing about love at first sight!

At the end of my holiday there were polite goodbyes and Teddy told me that he would write but I never really expected him to do so. Letters from Ted did however arrive occasionally and then with increasing frequency. It was nice to know that I had not been forgotten.

Career

Back on the home front in Liverpool, I was giving thought to my future – still praying my head off for a husband! At school there was talk of preparing for 'School Certificate' which was the entry into higher education. I was good at games and gym but although I also loved to read there was no doubt that my academic record was far from brilliant. One day I met the new headmistress in the corridor – not the

Reverend Mother who had admitted me. I asked her when I could sit 'School Cert' and her response went to my heart: 'Never!' she said coldly: 'It would be a waste of paper!'

At least I had my games expertise – perhaps I could be a gymnastics teacher like our pretty games mistress. I had a bit of a crush on her and got hold of a college prospectus. To my horror, I learnt that trainee games teachers could not be accepted below the age of twenty-one! I was heartbroken – twenty-one was aeons away – right over the horizon. I told my father that I really wanted to train as a games teacher but I would have to wait because they would not accept me until I was twenty-one'. 'Rubbish' said Daddy. 'You'll be married before you are twenty one!' I ran upstairs and wept copiously.

My mother realised that something would have to be done to take my mind off my troubles. She came up with the bright idea of getting me trained to operate a comptometer - a machine which looked rather like a typewriter but was used for adding up figures and saved a lot of time in offices. I duly enrolled on the course and although I did not particularly enjoy it, I must have done quite well because I was subsequently offered a job teaching other girls to use comptometers.

While I was still training, my mother and I went off on a shopping spree one day. Mummy loved pretty things and on this occasion she spotted a beautiful blue Russia leather handbag with thick golden frame. It was lined in the softest pale cream calfskin and she fell in love with it on sight. I determined to buy that bag for her birthday.

I was going to have to save up and was very much afraid that the bag might be sold in the meantime! I had one shilling [twelve pennies] a day set aside for lunch [5p in today's money] and spotted a Salvation Army pantry offering 'cheap food'. I cased the joint and discovered that two pennies would buy me half a meat pie, a thick slice of bread and margarine and an apple - plus a small cup of tea to wash it all down. This would leave ten pence each day towards the bag – marvellous. I hid my hoard of money in the wardrobe. One day I nearly met my Waterloo! I spotted my father just as I was coming out of the Pantry - fortunately he was looking the other way because he would certainly have stopped me getting my lunch courtesy of the Salvation Army!

It took months to collect the vast sum needed but the great day eventually dawned when I had every last penny. I went to the shop and thank goodness the bag was still there - even more beautiful than I remembered it. The assistant wrapped the bag in layers of pristine tissue paper and enclosed it in a very posh box – in those days purchases nearly always came in boxes. The next hurdle was to get the box home without being detected. I decided that if either car was outside the house I would hide the precious parcel in the front garden and retrieve it later.

Fortunately everybody was out and I could smuggle my treasure up to my bedroom undetected. Every night before I went to bed I opened the box and unwrapped the beautiful bag. I could hardly wait for November 30th – Mummy's thirty-fifth birthday. At last the day dawned and I proudly handed over my gift. Mummy always loved beautiful things and her delight in the present made it all worthwhile. Fortunately she never asked where on earth I had got the money – she probably imagined that my father had financed me.

In due course I was asked to join the staff of the comptometer school and on the day I was due to receive my first wage packet the director's wife called me into the office. She asked if I had ever earned any money before: 'No' I said. I had, of course, received fifteen shillings a week for helping Daddy with his typing but had always thought of that as pocket money. The director's wife handed over my wage packet, telling me that it was a pleasure to do so and that I would never forget this day. She was right. It was 1937 and I had joined the workers of the world.

After some months teaching at the school and receiving the welcome wage packet, my father decided that he needed me as a sort of personal secretary in the polish business. My comptometer training was clearly to be tossed to the wind but I didn't care. I never wanted to see another comptometer.

At about this time I witnessed a little drama that remains clear in my mind, and was an interesting lesson in human nature. I was walking past a canal where a crowd of women were making a commotion. Being curious, I stopped to see what was going on. At the centre of the group was a woman crying her heart out. "My poor Ivy", she sobbed: "My poor darling Ivy!" At that moment a police launch drew into the side of the canal. On the deck was a policeman holding the dripping body of a child. Could this be 'Ivy'? The little girl appeared to be about five years old, her golden ringlets were sodden and she looked like a bag of wet washing draped across the arms of the policeman. The poor mother's voice rose to a scream and many of the other women screamed with her. The policeman climbed out of the launch and handed the dripping bundle to the distraught mother. At that moment the 'body' gave a loud cough and shook itself. "Ivy", yelled her mother, "I will murder you when I get you home!" This has turned into a family saying when Ted and I have been particularly concerned about one of the children – only to find that all was well after all!

Occasional letters arrived from Ted and in one of them he told me that he was coming to England to visit his old school, Ampleforth in Yorkshire, where all the Donovan boys had been educated. One of the brothers, Cecil, had entered the Benedictine community at Ampleforth and Ted was coming over to see him – or so I thought. I was allowed to ask Ted to stay with us and he confided to me that he felt God was calling him to become a monk at Ampleforth. He was going up to Yorkshire to talk to the Abbot. I thought that it would be nice for Ted to join his brother in the community and felt not the slightest twinge of disappointment.

Much later Ted told me that he had been not a little chagrined at my lack of concern over his great decision. He was definitely miffed and I imagine would have preferred me to wipe away a little tear

– or stifle a sob! At least I told him that I would pray for him – a promise to which God has certainly given me the grace to be faithful. Apparently that visit to England was the beginning of his desire to make me his wife.

Ted duly travelled up to Ampleforth to see Abbot Herbert Byrne –'Sweaty Herb' as he had been affectionately known during his years as a parish priest in Liverpool when he was always in a hurry. The meeting was not really satisfactory to Ted because the Abbot told him to complete his engineering degree at Trinity College Dublin and then reapply to the monastery.

He obediently returned home and as far as our correspondence was concerned, the postal scene changed completely. Letters became more frequent and we ended up in daily correspondence. How much one can learn about someone from his letters. I discovered that Ted had the very highest ideals, wanted to serve God and was fervent in prayer. He was a man filled with hope - I have never met anyone so consistently hopeful.

This relationship with Ted was a very good friendship but marriage did not enter my head. I was still making my Tuesday evening novena to St Anthony and it did not occur to me that my prayers might have been answered. Other members of my family were, however, looking at matters in a different light. Every day I tried to waylay the postman bearing my letter from Dublin. If I missed him Daddy would take the letter and either hide it – rather obviously – or else prop it up against the marmalade and invite me to read it out to the assembled company. I was never in fact made to divulge the contents but I was teased a lot and sometimes resorted to reading Ted's letters in the bathroom.

Dublin and the Donovans

In September 1938, Prime Minister Neville Chamberlain returned from Munich with his signed 'peace agreement' with Hitler. But storm clouds were looming - although the general reaction seemed to be: 'they can't afford to have a war'. It had, after all, been only twenty years since the 'war to end all wars'! In our house, no one ever talked of war, so there was no apprehension in my heart. I was much more interested in the fact that I was turning seventeen and the world was my oyster.

In the summer of 1938 I was invited to stay with Ted and his family and luckily Grandma Nettie did not mind me staying with her brother instead of herself. I had never received such an exciting invitation and was scared silly. My parents bought me a lovely black coat in honour of the occasion and I had a white ermine muff with hat to match – the little black ermine 'tails' peeping round the side of my head! Very chic! Daddy made the most of the occasion and told me that I could *fly* to Ireland. I had never met anyone who had so much as stepped into an aeroplane so this was excitement indeed.

The morning I was due to leave I walked down our red carpeted stairs in my black coat and ermine accessories. Daddy was standing at the bottom. "Stop!" he said dramatically. "Don't move! You look like Anna Stein!" That made me feel a million dollars. Anna Stein was my father's favourite actress and the only resemblance between us was the fact that we both had blonde hair. Anna was tiny and I was 'pleasingly plump' but the fact that Daddy could think that I resembled her in any way at all made me aware of how much he loved me.

In 1938 Liverpool's Speke airport was little more than a couple of sheds. The tiny plane carried eight passengers plus pilot and stewardess. It was filthy dirty and looked as if it might fall out of the sky. We were not instructed in safety procedure but were issued with brown paper bags! I could not imagine why we needed such things but it soon became obvious when the passengers started being sick. I managed not to be sick – perhaps remembering my mother's words about pushing Brian and me through the porthole if we dared to do such a thing!

When I arrived at Ted's home I was struck immediately by the fear in the house. For some reason all the children seemed afraid of their father. Uncle Edward was now a widower because Aunt Mollie had died of a stroke two months previously. I wondered if this might be the reason for the atmosphere in the house. There was no light chatter when Uncle Edward was around; no jokes or banter. There was also a curfew which I found very alien – we always had to be back home by the time he decreed.

The house stood in an acre of garden with full time staff to run it. I shared a huge bedroom on the top floor with two of Ted's sisters, Freda and Dorothy. Freda would have been about twenty-two and Dorothy a couple of years older. Dorothy was exceedingly courageous because she was permanently lame and had to get about with a walking stick. This did nothing to diminish her constant cheerfulness – but I soon realised that she did not get on at all well with her father.

Freda was forever arranging parties to go to balls and to the Saturday night dances at the Gresham Hotel. These were great fun – except when Ted asked me to dance. I liked Ted very much – but he couldn't dance to save his life and always seemed to have two left feet.

After a dance we usually got home late, bringing a group of friends along with us. I wondered what Uncle Edward would say about that but I soon discovered that Freda had found a way of dealing with Uncle Edward and his 'curfew'. We would all creep into the drawing room, quiet as mice, and Freda would go up to her father's bedroom and knock on the door. "What time is it?" Uncle Edward would enquire. Freda would tell him whatever time had been previously agreed and he always believed her.

This would be the cue for us all to tiptoe upstairs – avoiding the creaking stair on the way to the top floor. We would change out of our dancing finery into more manageable clothes and creep down again to prepare a clandestine meal. We would base ourselves in the back drawing room which had a priceless Aubusson carpet and tiptoe down to the maids' quarters to raid the larder for eggs, bacon, bread and a frying pan. Back in the drawing room, we switched on the electric fire, turned it onto its side with the frying pan on top and set to work on 'breakfast'. When I think of the risks we took I cannot doubt the existence of guardian angels! One day I picked up a bowl of 'fat' in the kitchen and brought it upstairs – only to discover that it was not fat but soup. That night we had fried eggs and bacon boiled in soup! One morning we finished our meal and decided to go out to see the sunrise. We pushed the cars down the drive before starting them and managed to get back home again before the maids were out of bed.

There were evenings when Uncle Edward went out to his club and we had the house to ourselves. Cecil Donovan was home on holiday from Ampleforth and he regaled us with ghost stories. One evening he reached the most frightening moment when there was a rattle at the drawing room window. We were scared out of our wits and somebody eventually summoned up the courage to open the curtains – it was brother Arthur wanting to get in and knocking on the glass with his walking stick!

At the end of the garden was a large coach-house with a loft in which Ted and I made an interesting discovery. The loft was packed with copies of the 'Illustrated London News' dating from around 1860 – collectors' items even in 1938! They made fascinating reading but some of the advertisements would not have conformed to the Trade Descriptions Act. There were 'secret potions' to put in ones' husband's tea to stop him drinking or smoking – and 'bosom cream' which enlarged the bosom and was delivered in a plain wrapper! We spent hours with those old magazines and I had a sneaky feeling that Ted might be going to propose to me. The idea scared me silly and I avoided going near him whenever I thought that he might be plucking up his courage. Later he told me that I had been very provoking.

I returned to Liverpool and to my job as my father's secretary at the Evergloss factory. Before I left Dublin I had been invited to return the following summer so I realised that I must have passed muster with Uncle Edward. In the summer of 1938 I took off for Dublin again. During the first dance I spotted Ted approaching – and my heart sank at the memory of his awful efforts at ballroom dancing the previous summer. I could not refuse to dance with him and gritted my teeth in the hope that he would not walk on my feet too many times. Ted swept me into his arms and what was my delight to discover that his dancing had improved beyond recognition. During the intervening year Ted had not only gone to classes but had won a silver medal. He could do 'fishtail turns', 'running right hand' turns and I who had been so snooty was now hard pressed to keep up with him.

On my last evening Ted invited me to come out to a film – just the two of us. Freda and Dorothy had bought a car and graciously loaned it for the occasion. The film was 'Bachelor Mother' and made us laugh. On the way back afterwards Ted asked me to marry him. He was twenty and I was eighteen. Things seemed to be getting out of hand. Despite my constant novena, the idea of marriage was in fact leaving me feeling rather panicky – a bit like an unfledged chicken. I said firmly 'I will think about it and let you know, but I think that it will take me years to make up my mind.' We crept into the house and I tiptoed up to my bedroom where Dorothy and Freda were shamming sleep – they usually talked into the small hours! I didn't get much sleep that night and the following day Ted took me to the airport. We said goodbye staidly – at that stage never having exchanged a kiss. Ted's final words were: 'I will wait!'

4

WAR
1939-1940

"…if we know that He hears us – whatever we ask –
we know that we have what we asked of Him."
1 John 5:15

The flight to Liverpool provided me with breathing space. I certainly wanted to marry somebody who was walking with God. Ted was obviously doing that and he went to Mass every morning like me. There was quite a lot in his favour. I seemed to be coming around to the idea of marriage!

When we landed, my mother was there to meet me at the airport and, on the way home, I blurted out the news and added 'I have told Ted it will take me ages to make up my mind. You won't tell Daddy about this, will you'? Mummy did not seem surprised. In hindsight I realise that she and my father must have long since discussed the possibility of marriage between me and Ted. She told me that she was not at all sure about it because we were first cousins once removed with Grandma Nettie and Uncle Edward being brother and sister! It had never occurred to me that that could be a problem.

When we got back, my father was not home. At last I heard him at the front door and rushed into the hall to give him my usual bear hug. I knocked his hat off flinging my arms around his neck – and blurted out the news. So much for asking my mother not to tell him! So much for self-control and taking years to make up my mind about an engagement! All of a sudden I was engaged to be married!

My father's response was shattering. 'You are far, far too young, and I need you as my secretary'. I was crushed. Not only was I not going to be able to get married for years but I soon realised that Daddy was going to make the most of the situation and get some fun out of it: "I had to ask Grandma Nettie for your mother's hand in marriage and this young man of yours will have to come to me. Tell Ted to come over and ask my permission and I will think about it!" That night Ted phoned to see if I had arrived home safely. I told him that I could give him my answer. It was "Yes! I then told him about Daddy's ultimatum and that he would have to come to Liverpool. "No problem!" said Ted.

My father had first met the Donovans in Dublin while he was wooing my mother. Daddy was playing in an exhibition golf match at Milltown Golf Club and met Uncle Edward who invited him to his home, Thorndale, for a meal. My father was asked if he would like to see the new baby. He dutifully said yes and the youngest Donovan was carried in by his nurse. Daddy told me that he little thought that he was looking at his future son-in-law!

It was now late summer and war clouds were gathering. On August 25th Britain had signed a mutual assistance treaty with Poland, warning Hitler that invasion would warrant British intervention. On September 1st Germany invaded Poland and the following day Prime Minister Neville Chamberlain presented Germany with an ultimatum: withdraw from Poland by 11.00am on September 3rd or face war with Britain. On September 3rd the Prime Minister was due to make a radio broadcast at a few minutes after 11.00. When the time came I was alone in the drawing room. I remember only the words: "This country is at war with Germany". My heart sank.

Later that day, Ted telephoned and told me that he intended to volunteer for the Irish army. He and a good friend went along to enlist together. The friend was accepted but Ted was turned down on the grounds of his sight which had been damaged by a golf ball during his school days. He had to remain in Dublin and complete his degree.

As far as my own little world was concerned, Ted was going to come to Liverpool to ask for my hand. He made arrangements to come over a few weeks later so as not to clash with his exams. One evening I turned on the radio to hear shattering news that stopped me in my tracks. There was to be no travel between England and Southern Ireland until further notice and the ban was expected to last until the conclusion of hostilities. Never in my wildest imaginings had I dreamed that Irish neutrality would lead to such a rift. That evening Ted phoned to tell me that the news was only too true. In addition, he told me that the thousands of young Irish men and women who had volunteered to serve in the British armed forces would be in danger of arrest if they wore their uniforms in neutral Ireland.

My father was clearly disappointed that Ted could not appear in person. He asked, instead, that Ted write him a formal letter and claimed that he had no idea what his answer would be. He continued to insist that I was far too young and that he needed me as his secretary. It was a game and he was loving it. He really was maddening.

Ted duly wrote to my father, asking to marry me and asking whether our engagement could be announced on his 21st birthday, June 29th 1940. I think I still have that letter hidden away somewhere. Daddy showed it to me – completely deadpan – and told me that he would have to give the matter some thought. He would write to Ted and he would let me know his decision. Infuriating!

A few days later I spotted a white envelope addressed to Ted propped up on the mantelpiece. I said nothing and pretended to ignore it. Nobody referred to the letter and Daddy eventually asked me if I would like to see what he had written to Ted! I seized the envelope and tore it open – only to find that there was nothing at all inside. Daddy was still enjoying himself! "Do you think" he enquired: "that I could possibly put on paper what I have to talk to that young man about?" I have booked a telephone call to Dublin!"

Almost immediately the phone rang. Daddy walked slowly into his study, leaving the door ajar. I sat on the stairs outside. For ages and ages my dear father talked pleasantries. At long last I heard him say: "I got your letter, Ted! My dear boy, you don't know what you are planning to take on. She can be a virago and you can't get a civil word out of her before eleven o'clock in the morning. Believe me; she will spend every penny you ever earn! Yes, of course you can marry her. I have kept her for eighteen years. Now you can take responsibility – but you will have to wait a year!' I had heard enough – I rushed into the study and flung my arms round Daddy's neck. Suddenly a year did not seem too long after all – the war would probably be over by then anyway.

My father agreed to our getting officially engaged on Ted's twenty-first birthday and exciting plans were afoot for a big party in the grounds of Thorndale. I assured myself and everybody else that the ban on travel between England and Ireland was only temporary. I must have been convincing because my mother started speculating about what she might wear for the party. January 1940 dawned and the ban on travel was still in place. By the spring, the so-called 'phoney-war' was coming to an end and England was moving onto a serious war footing – but the ban showed no sign of being lifted. Meanwhile we continued to live in cloud-cuckoo-land – believing the propaganda that the war would be over in months.

The Visa

I was determined to get across to Ireland in June by hook or by crook. When I was reading my Bible one day, the words seem to leap off the page. "...if we know that he hears us in regard to whatever we ask, we know that what we have asked him for is ours."[1 Jn 5:15]. I knew that I had to exercise my faith in this matter of getting official permission to travel to Dublin.

I took my passport down to the consular section of the Liverpool passport office, handed it over to an official and requested a visa for Ireland. The man laughed in my face. He told me what I already knew only too well – no travel to Ireland!. I was praying all the while and asked the man to hang onto my passport until the ban on travel was lifted. He looked at me as if I was an idiot and explained that the ban might continue for years. I pleaded. With a sigh of exasperation, he took my passport, placed it in a buff envelope and pushed it into a cubby hole behind him.

When I got home I told my parents and Jo what I had done. There was no little derision! I paid no heed but climbed to the top of the house where all the suitcases were stored. I selected a case which would be suitable for my journey to Ireland and brought it down to my bedroom. This caused even greater merriment. I continued to pray, convinced that I would have to really stir up the faith that was in me [2.Timothy 1:6]. I acted as if the passport complete with visa was already in my hand, bought a nice dress for the party and told Ted that I would be with him for June 29th.

War changes everything and the grand ideas of a big dance with a marquee on the lawn at Thorndale had gone with the wind. Ted and I did not mind. We only wanted to be together. May had now come. No sign of the visa but my suitcase was getting fuller. I told everybody that I was going to Ireland in June – and was laughed to scorn. In the end I just became an embarrassment to them.

One Saturday afternoon, Jo and I were alone in the house. I was sitting by the kitchen window writing out a prayer on the back of a holy picture when the doorbell rang. Jo came back from the front door and said in a puzzled voice:

'Miss Joyce, there is a man who wants to see you.'

'Are you sure?' I didn't have visitors who just turned up at the front door like that.

I went into the drawing room, and there was an unknown man who introduced himself as 'Mr Robertson.' Having established that I was Miss Langford he announced that he had brought something for me. I was intrigued.

Out of his pocket Mr Robertson took the buff envelope which I had last seen at the consular office. He handed it over and I ripped it open. Inside was my passport. I flicked through the pages. There was the precious visa for Ireland.

How was it possible?

'Don't ask any questions', said Mr Robertson. I know you are going over to become engaged. At Speke airport you will be met by a man who knows who you are and will identify himself'. I was young enough, and uninhibited enough to give Mr Robertson a big hug!

I went down to the travel agent who was equally amazed and booked me onto a small plane. My astonished parents took me to the airport where I was met at passport control by a man who clearly knew all about me. "I understand that you are going to Dublin to become engaged, Miss Langford. Good Luck!' When I boarded the plane I discovered that I was the only 'unofficial' passenger. All the others were members of the Japanese diplomatic corps flying across to take up residence in Dublin.

When I get to heaven there are a lot of things I want to ask the Lord about. High on the list will be the story behind 'Mr Robertson' and my miracle visa!

Engaged at last

It was wonderful to be with Ted again. For the twenty-first birthday, Uncle Edward put on a smallish party at Thorndale at which he made a speech saying how pleased he was to have me in the family. All the Donovans seemed happy about the engagement – the exception being brother Cecil – Dom Bruno of Ampleforth. I just knew that Cecil did not approve of me and Ted told me that he apparently considered me 'too worldly'! I wondered whether Cecil was regretting that his brother had not entered Ampleforth and did not want Ted to get married at all.

I returned home and went back to working for Daddy in the Evergloss factory. Ted had given me a beautiful platinum engagement ring; bagatelle diamonds set around a single large bright stone. I constantly left the glove off my hand so that everybody at work could see that ring.

Evergloss was now a real family business with fourteen year old Brian working there every day alongside my parents and me. At the outbreak of war, Brian had spent some time in Wales as an evacuee. Like so many other children, he had been sent away from the city to a small village to escape the bombing. His Welsh village was very remote and there was nothing much there except a pub, a few houses and a small school. Brian boarded with a husband and wife and after some time my parents began to receive upsetting letters from him. The schooling was apparently virtually nil and in the evenings the teachers all went to the pub. There was literally nothing for the pupils to do so they hung around the pub as well. Daddy was very concerned about the nightly pub jaunts and made a radical decision with which Brian was happy. He was brought back home to work in the factory. When the war was over, the plan was to get private tutors to prepare him for university.

Phoney war had well and truly turned into real war! At first, I found it all rather exciting. I had read about the exploits of young women in the First World War: the handsome young men going off to fight, and the bravery of the first pilots. It was heady stuff. One night my notions were changed radically. I had gone to the theatre with my old school friend, Julie Jeffers. While we were watching the play we heard the noise of enemy aircraft and knew that bombs must be dropping. Astonishingly, we were not afraid and when we came out we could see the burning buildings.

Neither of us had ever seen large fires and we decided to go 'rubber necking'. There was no danger from the flames but, unbeknownst to us, enemy aircraft were still in the area and we were sitting targets. Suddenly the planes zoomed in with tremendous noise and strafed the passers by. Julie and I instinctively threw ourselves flat in the gutter. When the planes left and it was safe to stand up, we were two badly shaken young women. That was the last time we stopped to look at blazing buildings. We went home and told our families what we had seen. War had really started on the home front and everyone was in hourly danger of their lives.

Bombs

Sometimes the frightening moments had their funny side –in retrospect! One afternoon I had gone to Julie Jeffers' hairdresser sister for a permanent wave. 'Perms' in those days were a far cry from modern hairdressing. Little swatches of ones' hair were laboriously fixed to metal cylinders full of boiling water - which involved the additional hazard of getting a nasty burn on your head. The cylinders were then attached to a helmet like apparatus fixed to the ceiling of the salon and you had to sit beneath this contraption for quite a while.

That particular afternoon it had taken about an hour to get all my hair attached to the cylinders. Julie's sister had just finished getting everything into place when the air raid siren went off. This was the cue for everybody to disappear down to the air raid shelter – apart from those irreversibly attached to the ceiling! Julie's sister told me that she hoped I would be alright and disappeared with the others! I was left alone in an empty salon with the prospect of a bomb dropping on top of me. It was terrifying and I can only imagine that my prayer life increased enormously! Fortunately the whole thing proved to be a false alarm – but one never took chances when the sirens sounded and nobody would have dreamed of staying in the salon if they could help it!

The Evergloss business was doing well and Julie Jeffers soon came to work with us in the office and eventually moved in with us. Julie had arrived at work one morning in a dreadful state because her father had gone to pieces during the previous night's bombing and told his family "You'll not see morning – that's for sure!" Daddy was very worried about her and suggested to Mr Jeffers that she come to stay at our house and travel to work with us in the morning. Luckily he agreed.

The bombing was truly terrible. Every evening we would get home and grab a meal, hoping that there would be enough time to swallow our food and get down to the shelter before the air raids began. I made a mark on the wall every night we had an air raid – on one occasion there were marks on 64 consecutive nights. As night fell, the bombers arrived and did not turn back to Germany until 3.30 or 4.00am so as not to get caught here in daylight. We thought it was wonderful if we managed three hours sleep. Some days I was so tired that I wondered if I would live to see my twentieth birthday!

With all that time down in the shelter I was able to write to Ted everyday and received a daily letter in return. All letters were censored, and it was not unusual to have pieces cut out of ones' correspondence with a razor if anything was mentioned that was considered to jeopardize national security. Ted and I had a code. If I wrote: 'The cat, Jemima is sitting on my lap as I write' it meant we were in the middle of an air raid. 'Jemima' certainly spent a lot of time on my lap during 1940!

William Joyce – known as Lord Haw-Haw – was making German propaganda broadcasts to England and Ted was able to pick up that station in Dublin. Sometimes Lord Haw-Haw mentioned bombing in Bootle and Ted was so worried that he used to ring me. It was wonderful to hear his voice.

Each morning it was a case of waking up - even if sleep had been very short – and praising God that you were still alive! Mercifully, I had the grace to continue to get to daily Mass, no matter what time I got to sleep – and even if I had been awake all night! The church was never actually hit, but there were a number of occasions when the parish priest would have to move all the rubble away from the door in order to get in. I did my best to help him. I tried to say my rosary each day and continued to use Father Valentine's little book of meditations. I had worn out two copies and was now on my third.

On Tuesday evenings, fair weather or foul, I trotted along to the Church to take part in the perpetual novena to St. Anthony. He had provided me with a fiancé and I was now asking him to make sure that Ted and I could get married. By this time the family knew it was useless to say anything and on Tuesdays the mealtime was adjusted to suit me. Afterwards we would all go down to the shelter.

With the constant raids and the lack of sleep it was obvious that we could not carry on like this. My mother came to the rescue. One evening she came home to tell us that she had found a farmhouse north of Liverpool in Mawdesley and rented three rooms. She and Daddy would have one, Brian another and Julie and I would share the narrow single bed in the third room. The plan was to go to the office every day as normal, come home to Bootle to eat our meagre supper and then drive out to the farm for the night. We would return home to Liverpool in time for breakfast before going to the office. We literally slept at Mawdesley and nothing else. I was sorry that Jo refused to come out to Mawdesley with us. She was like one of the family but she insisted on staying in Liverpool and going down to the shelter during raids.

In one of his letters Ted told me that brother Cecil was due to be ordained at Ampleforth during 1940 but none of his family would of course be able to travel over from Ireland. I told my parents and Mummy decided that in some way the Langford family must get up to Ampleforth to be with Cecil in the absence of his own relations. She decided to drive up to Yorkshire with Brian and me and somehow she managed to get hold of the necessary petrol – almost impossible in those days of stringent petrol rationing! I can only imagine that she got it through the black market or by mixing petrol with white spirit to make it go further!

She decided that we would leave Liverpool at two in the morning – but had not reckoned on checkpoints along the route. Civilians were not supposed to have sufficient petrol to drive the hundred miles from Liverpool to Yorkshire so we had to come up with a good story to explain our journey. Fortunately my mother was a quick thinker. At every checkpoint she made up something about just driving to the next village or next town for some very good reason. Sometimes we came across soldiers along the road who were in need of a lift. Once or twice these turned out to be important officers. We could sail through the checkpoints if we were driving military personnel and did not need to explain ourselves at all!

At 6.00am we arrived at Ampleforth. Cecil was delighted to see us and found us wonderful seats in the Abbey. We must have been in that Abbey for about six hours and it was the longest and most boring ceremony I have ever attended. But I was so pleased to be there for Cecil and to receive his first blessing as a newly ordained priest. I hoped that our presence might make him think a little better of my engagement to Ted and he was certainly exceedingly grateful to my mother for making it possible for us to be with him. I have no recollection of the drive back to Liverpool and can only imagine that I slept the whole way.

Sudden death

Life continued in its usual way with Liverpool suffering appalling bomb damage. We were spared the worst because we spent our nights in Mawdesley. One particular Tuesday night in October 1940 is forever etched on my memory. I was about to leave the house for my perpetual novena at church when Daddy came out with a cryptic remark which I have never been able to understand. "You win!" he said: To this day I have no idea what he meant. He added "I'll take you!"

The thought of my father actually taking me to church was beyond belief but this was clearly his intention. I got into the car, speechless, and Daddy drove to the church – neither of us saying a word. When we arrived he told me that he would wait outside. That night I made my novena with particular fervour and when I came out Daddy was still there. We drove home in silence – but this time it was an easy silence.

Back at the house we grabbed a hasty meal – no time even for a bath. As the five of us hurried down the drive the sirens started – bombers were obviously arriving far earlier than usual and we bundled into the car at top speed. Mummy always drove at night because my father's sight was not good enough for night driving. As she was about to start, Daddy suddenly remembered something he wanted in the house. He gave me the keys and told me to go and fetch it. I was surly and ungracious – which I have lived to regret!

I did what he wanted and dashed back to the car. Mummy drove off as fast as she could. The bombers were now well overhead and flares were dropping as we left the city. Suddenly I noticed Daddy slumped down in his seat. I thought he had fainted. Mummy pulled into the side and we all got out. My mother flagged down a passing car and two young men stopped and came across to help us lift my father out of the car and carry him to the grass verge. We laid him down and he showed no sign of returning consciousness.

The two young men told Julie and me to go and ring for an ambulance. We ran down the road for a long way before spotting a telephone box. I dialled 999 and got through to the operator who asked me to insert two pennies – normal practice in those days. Neither Julie nor I had any money on us. This was desperate. Fortunately a passing stranger handed over two pennies and we got through to the emergency services. Could they send an ambulance urgently? No, they couldn't; all the ambulances were out on call – the usual story during raids.

We rushed back to the car only to find that it had disappeared. One of the young men was waiting for us and told us that my mother had decided not to wait for an ambulance but had driven my unconscious father back into Liverpool with Brian and the other man. The second 'good Samaritan' had waited for Julie and me and we leaped into his car and drove off back into the bombing. It was an appalling raid with lots of roads blocked off. All I could think about was the hospital where Daddy had been taken and the awful possibility that we might not be able to get to him. We made it eventually and our kind helper left us at the emergency department – a scene of orderly chaos with casualties being carried in and doctors and nurses moving smoothly and speedily from one patient to another.

Where was my father? Where were Mummy and Brian? Eventually we caught sight of them. Brian was crying and Julie started to weep too. I could think only: "Thank God they got Daddy here – now he can get some attention!" My mother looked at me and spoke gently: "Daddy will not have any more suffering over the war. He won't have any more anxiety about the bombs!" I could think only "Thank God he is safe!" I looked across at Brian and Julie who had tears running down their faces. Only then did the truth dawn on me. My beloved father was dead.

I could not take it in. My mother uttered the saddest words I had ever heard: "Joyce, I am a widow". My parents had adored one another – and they were still comparatively young although they had been married for twenty years. Daddy was forty-six and Mummy only thirty-seven.

Someone had to take action and I knew that it had to be me. The raid was still in progress and we had to get to safety. I asked Julie if her father would allow us to spend the night in the cellar of their house. She managed to get through on the phone – and the Jeffers opened their hearts to us and said of course we could come. I wondered if my mother would be able to drive but it was Hobson's choice – she had to do it! When we got to Julie's house, her parents had cleared two cellar rooms for us and were very sensitive to our need for privacy. Mr Jeffers just made sure we all had cups of tea and said to me privately: 'I can recommend a good undertaker" – the words seemed obscene!

Mummy was beyond anything. She was obviously in shock and had not shed a tear. I knew that it was me who would have to break the news to the rest of the family. I did all the telephoning I could. It seemed unreal and as if somebody else was using my voice. Hours later I managed to get through to Ted in Dublin. He assured me that somehow he would manage to get over somehow to support me at the funeral'. When I finally finished the phone calls I went down to the cellar and lay down. For the rest of the night I heard my mother's footsteps as she walked up and down that cellar floor.

Next morning she went straight to the Catholic Church and asked the priest to say a Mass for her husband. Then we began to talk about the funeral and Mummy told me that the previous week Daddy had been ruminating over something to do with his mother – Granny Langford. Out of the blue he said that he would like to be buried with her. Had he had a premonition of approaching death? Had that also been the reason for his strange remark to me and his offer to take me to church for the novena? I was never to know.

Meanwhile Ted was frantically trying to get a visa to come over for the funeral. Travel between England and Ireland was somewhat more relaxed and we hoped to be able to manage it on compassionate grounds. My mother knew a great friend of the British Ambassador in Dublin and he wrote a persuasive letter making a very good case for Ted to be allowed to travel. The letter was sent, care of Ted, with the suggestion that he take it to the British Embassy himself. On the day of Ted's visit, the Ambassador was away. He was confronted, instead, with the press attaché, the future poet laureate John Betjeman. Ted presented his letter. The press attaché opened the envelope, read the letter, and as Ted watched aghast, he tore it up and dropped the pieces into the waste paper basket. It took me a long time to forgive Sir John Betjeman for that.

This was the first funeral I had attended. It was the funeral of my father and I was not to have the support of my fiancé. It took place in the Anglican Church where Granny Langford had been buried. When the coffin was lowered into the grave the vicar picked up a lump of earth and handed it to my mother. She looked at it blankly, not knowing what to do. The vicar whispered loudly: 'Throw it on the coffin'. Mummy did as she was told. For ages I could hear that awful hollow sound of earth hitting wood. Up to that moment my mother had been numb, unable to weep. The sound of earth hitting the coffin released her and she began to sob.

Picking up the pieces

We had joined the ranks of millions all over the world who were grieving for loved ones. My mother took over the reins of the flourishing Evergloss business and just had to cope as best she could. She was certainly courageous but was unable to eat – she lost weight and just existed. I can remember poor Brian sitting in the office and crying. He was only fourteen. An awful thought flickered in and out of my mind – I would never be able to marry Ted because I was vitally needed in the firm.

Daddy's death somehow did not seem real. My office looked out on the road where he had always drawn up in the green Humber; he would smile as he got out of the car and raise his hat to me and I would salute! The car was now being driven by a young member of the workforce. One day I spotted it drawing up in the usual place and lifted my hand to salute. Only at that moment did it really come home to me that Daddy would never be coming back.

The four of us continued to drive out to Mawdesley every evening but I had a feeling that the owners of the farm did not feel very sympathetic towards my mother. It was Daddy who had really got to know them and been able to understand their strong Lancashire accents.

One morning we arrived back in Bootle to find our home badly damaged. It had not suffered a direct hit but all the windows were gone – in my bedroom hundreds of tiny splinters of glass were embedded in the beautiful walnut headboard and many more in the wardrobe. There was no way that we could stay there and my mother took immediate action. She decided that we would leave Mawdesley altogether and move into a small flat as a temporary measure while we looked for something permanent. My mother wanted to move across the Mersey to a place with the oddest name – Noctorum – I was sure it must go back to Roman times.

The 'temporary' flat was one of several in a large house in Princes Road. The attraction was twofold: the house had its own cellar in which we could take refuge - houses with cellars were hard to come by in the battering Liverpool was taking. It was also closer to the factory. I would rush back to the flat from work, grab something to eat, get a bath if possible – you were never sure whether or not there would be any water – and jump into a pair of slacks. Slacks had become part of normal casual dress for women and they were definitely the most sensible thing to wear during raids.

Mummy and Brian and I would then join the other flat dwellers in the cellar; it had a brazier in the middle which probably burned coke so we were gloriously warm, even in December. There were a couple of mattresses on the floor but some nights it was so crowded in that cellar that there was hardly room even to sit. I had the experience of falling asleep standing up against a wall because I was so worn out.

5

THE CHRISTMAS RAIDS 1940-1941

> 'Nothing can happen to me that is not for the good of my soul'
> **Joyce Donovan**

Christmas 1940 was approaching. We were all exhausted and I was longing to see Ted. My mother offered to finance a trip to Ireland over the holiday period to give me a breather – she was the one who really needed that breather. I was overjoyed and had no trouble getting a visa this time. It was not my only precious document on the trip!

Ted was now working for a Dublin firm of civil engineers for the princely sum of ten shillings a week [fifty pence in today's money!] It didn't seem much of a salary for somebody with two degrees who was hoping to get married. But if Ted had started work two years earlier he would have received nothing at all. Uncle Edward would have had to pay the firm for providing Ted with an apprenticeship. A wage of ten shillings had to be an improvement.

The two of us had decided that we wanted to start married life in England but where was Ted to find a job? It was theoretically possible to travel from Ireland to England to take up reserved work – but where was the employer?

It was at this point that Daddy's sister, Aunt Mabel, came up trumps. Aunt Mabel lived in a large house outside Chester and a number of bombed out people had been billeted on her. Among them was a senior man in Shell Oil, Mr Imrie. Aunt Mabel talked to Mr Imrie about Ted and me and I was invited to meet him. Mr Imrie was obviously keen to help and he shared with me some restricted information. Apparently an oil refinery was being built and civil engineers were needed. If Ted wrote to apply and mentioned the name of Mr Imrie there was a good chance that he would be given a job. Mr Imrie gave me a piece of paper with all the names and addresses and I tucked it carefully away in my bag, ready to hand over to Ted.

My passage was booked out of Liverpool for the night December 20th. Mummy and Brian drove me to the dockside and were then going out of Liverpool so I knew I didn't have to worry about them.

I was thrilled to be getting away from the bombing and overjoyed at the thought of seeing Ted again. There was one bubble of sadness. Grandma Nettie had taken my engagement very badly despite being on such good terms now with Uncle Edward and his family. I suppose she felt that she had been left out of it all when she had been so kind to me over so many years. I probably did not handle things as sensitively as I might have done and she was definitely miffed.

The ship was full to overflowing but Mummy had booked me a berth in a first class cabin with three other girls. Those less fortunate were travelling steerage and had to stay up all night. There was a rail to prevent us mingling!

I went below to meet my cabin mates. They were a mixed bunch. One girl had just lost her fiancé who had been drowned when a convoy had been torpedoed. She was in a state of shock and very angry with Ireland for not coming into the war and lending a hand! I don't remember much about the other two girls.

Our scheduled departure time was six but wartime schedules often went out of the window and the sailing was late. We had moved away from the dockside and were a little way down the Mersey when the siren sounded. During an air raid all ships in the Mersey had been told to stop engines – but we nevertheless kept moving for a little while– anything to get away from the bombers. Then we just stopped still in the river.

The sirens were going full blast with that awful intermittent wail that brought fear to my heart. I climbed to the top deck and for the first time was able to watch the German 'pathfinders'. These were very fast planes which dropped thousands of flares to guide the following bombers. I knew that the huge bombers could not be far behind and went below. The four of us made our way to the stateroom just to be with other people.

The bombers came across in wave after wave. We felt that all hell had been let loose. There was the awful 'crump' and thud from direct hits on the battered city. The bombers were over the Mersey and a ship was hit - we could hear the screams of her passengers. There were enormous thuds as bombs hit the bed of the river and our ship rocked.

It was intolerable just to sit and wait and not know what was going on. I suggested to one of my companions that we go up to the top deck and we slipped away. What a sight awaited us! Fire and devastation on both sides of the river: Liverpool on the one side, and Wallasey and New Brighton on the other. I knew the Dockland well and could see familiar places in flames. The direction of our factory seemed to be red with flames. I thought of all those thousands of gallons of white spirit for making our polish!

For the first time I saw shrapnel and it was a shock. I had always imagined shrapnel as small pea sized bits of metal but large chunks of the stuff were falling onto our ship. There was a direct hit on an ammunition boat a quarter of a mile off – it looked like thousands of exploding fireworks and we could hear the screams of her crew.

Our own anti-aircraft guns were blazing away but didn't seem to be hitting anything. The bombers were coming across in very close formation. They seemed to be dropping 'clusters' of bombs which were falling out of a sort of 'basket' in the air and scattering. Thousands of white 'spots' appeared on either side of the river. When the 'spots' turned red we knew that somebody's home was going up in flames.

Although there was no way of knowing it at the time, we were experiencing the first night of what came to be known as 'The Christmas Raids'; three nights of devastating attacks on Merseyside in which 365 people lost their lives and thousands were left homeless.

After the bombers came another kind of plane – much larger, and not so fast. They were dropping things that looked like large metal boxes which floated down suspended from green silk parachutes. The 'metal boxes' were landmines and when they hit the ground or the seabed there was a violent explosion. A landmine could weight up to 1,000 lbs and destroy a block of flats with an ear splitting roar. I had heard of landmines, and witnessed their devastating effect but never before had I seen them in action. They actually looked rather beautiful as they floated down. One hit the seabed nearby and our ship rocked. I was nearly numb with fear. How I scrambled down from the top deck I will never know.

Back in the stateroom things were getting panicky. A little old lady sitting in the far corner said quietly but firmly: 'I think it is time that we all knelt down and prayed'. We knelt obediently – no atheists in foxholes! And the old lady produced her rosary. I, too, had a rosary – an amethyst one that Ted had given me for an engagement present and which I wore around my neck. My neighbour said: 'I am not a Catholic but please may I share your rosary?' It took a bit of manoeuvring to get it off and as I worked the rosary over my chin my teeth were chattering with fear. Suddenly a thought came to me which I believe to have been one of the greatest graces of my life: 'Nothing can happen to me that is not for the good of my soul'.

December 21st

The bombers eventually left to make the long journey back to Germany. Dawn broke and we clambered out of the stateroom and up onto the decks. What devastation! Smoke and flames were billowing on both sides of the river; familiar landmarks had disappeared and ships were lying on their sides.

Rumour was rife. We were leaving in ten minutes! We were leaving in an hour! We were going back to the dock! Hours passed and nothing happened. By midday we were still in the middle of the Mersey and as the afternoon closed in I am sure the same thought was in each one's mind: 'The bombers will be back tonight!' This time they would need no pathfinders to guide them – the burning and smouldering buildings would be more than sufficient

Dusk was beginning to fall. At about four o'clock I was back on the top deck, leaning over the side when I found the purser beside me. We began to talk and I asked him what was really going to happen? Would we be sailing for Dublin tonight or not? 'If I tell you' said the purser: 'will you keep it confidential?' Of course I would.

His news was far from encouraging: 'No ships are allowed to leave the Mersey till the minesweepers have cleared all the floating mines. We are going to move out of the centre of the river and find haven'. My heart sank.

Ted had been due to meet me on the quayside at Dublin that morning. He would have no clue what had happened to me and would be dreadfully worried. My mother and Brian were waiting for a phone call to assure them that I had arrived safely. They had heard nothing and would also be fearing the worst. Here was I marooned on a ship in the Mersey that was going to 'find haven'. I had no means of contacting anybody.

There was nothing to be done. I went below deck and people seemed to be in good spirits. There was apparently a rule that all the meals were free if you had to stay on board more than a certain number of hours. Passengers were laughing and joking about their free meals! The engines started to tick over and people were telling one another that we were about to sail. We began to move, and a resounding cheer went up. I did not cheer.

I returned to the top deck to await developments; to await the arrival of the bombers. Suddenly there was an unearthly explosion. The ship began to list and I clung to the rail in terror. Later I learnt that the bombers had dropped hundreds of magnetic mines. These lay quietly on the bottom of the river until a metal hull went over one of them. The mine would then shoot up and explode. One of these magnetic mines had hit us amidships. We began to list.

I flew down to the stateroom. Flying glass was everywhere; there was pandemonium and people were panicking. One woman couldn't stop screaming and another slapped her face. The ship gave a tremendous lurch. I knew beyond any doubt that we were sinking.

I also knew that I could not swim very far. Where were the lifeboats? There had been no lifeboat drill for the hundreds of passengers and the crew began to panic as well as the passengers. Luckily for the crew, they had life jackets. No life jackets for passengers. I saw crew members throwing suitcases into the water and jumping in after them wearing their jackets.

Now we were listing badly. On one side, half the lifeboats were beneath the water; on the other, the boats were so tight against the ship that they could not be flung clear. The crew managed to release a single one. Water was rising up the main entry way to the stateroom. Down below we could hear the screams of stokers trapped in the boiler room.

Up I went to the deck again, one of my cabin companions with me. I had to get away from that ship. I had a handbag with a long handle which I strung round my neck. For some unknown reason I also took off my shoes. Some instinct must have warned me that they would be a hindrance.

My cabin mate spotted some rope on the listing deck. We managed to tie that rope to one of the stanchions and slide down the side of the ship into the freezing water. Floating towards us was a large piece of debris. We climbed aboard. Nobody needed to tell us that we had to get as far away from that doomed ship as quickly as possible. When she finally sank, the suction would pull down anything in the vicinity. My last memory of the stricken ship is of a tiny girl walking serenely along the deck. She must have been about six years old.

My companion and I were eventually pulled aboard a little tug which was already full of survivors. There were other rescue ships in the vicinity – all of them full. Just as we thought that the worst was over...the air raid siren went! The bombers were coming back! The thought uppermost in my mind was not my own survival but a continuing concern for Ted and my mother. I thought to myself: 'When we get to the dock I can walk to the Adelphi Hotel and phone them.'

The little tug landed us on the quayside. Dry land at last! What happened next is incredible but absolutely true. In our drowned rat state, covered in oily water, we were told that we would have to remain in the dockyard and would not be allowed past the guards at the main gate. Our passports were stamped out of the country but none of us had the necessary entry visa to prove that we were eligible to come back into Britain!

Meanwhile the bombers were doing their worst. We were directed to an air raid shelter on the dockside. I knew that it could save us from nothing except shrapnel and we would not have a hope in the event of a direct hit. It was dark in the shelter and we were freezing cold and wet; our spirits at their lowest!

I found myself beside a man who began to paw me. I felt so helpless. I tried to get his hands off, but he was very bold. I began to cry. The kindly woman beside me said:, 'Don't cry *now*. You have been brave so far'. I hadn't been brave at all. I had just acted out of instinct in order to survive. In the end I asked the kindly woman to change places with me.

A policeman put his head inside the shelter and was very surprised to find us there as the shelters were still being completed. He said cheerily: 'I hope everyone has their gas mask!'

We were all supposed to carry these sinister looking objects at all times for fear of a gas attack. Another policeman told us brightly that we shouldn't be in the shelter at all as there was an unexploded landmine a few yards away. Our next visitor was one of the port officials on air raid duty. He asked three of the men to volunteer to go round to one of the dry docks - Princes Dock. A ship there had the wherewithal for hot drinks and sandwiches. Off went three very willing volunteers. The port official eventually reappeared with good news: 'If you like to take the risk and crawl half a mile to Princes Dock, you will be guided to the ship where there are hot drinks and sandwiches'.

Half a mile is nothing on a bright sunny day. It is another story during an air raid when one dare not raise ones head for fear of shrapnel. I crawled on my tummy all the way round to Princes Dock where a man guided us to the ship. No lights – not even a cigarette was allowed. We crawled a little further until we were under cover. Then came the blessed and wonderful sound of the 'All Clear'. I went into the toilet. It seemed like days since I had been! I was the only one with a handbag – sopping wet but still hanging around my neck. In that handbag was a lipstick. I shared it with the other women, and it lifted our morale!

Meanwhile I continued to worry desperately about getting news to Ted and to my mother. I had been 'missing' for over twenty-four hours and they would be frantic. It was now safe to leave the ship and I walked along the dry dock. A little way along I encountered a man who turned out to be the captain of a ship which had been hit while in dry dock. I told him that I desperately needed to get to a phone to try and contact my family. The captain knew a place where there had been a phone. He took me to see if it was still there, only to find that the 'place' was a heap of rubble. The captain and I started burrowing. Half and hour later we found the phone. Miraculously, it was still live! The first person I got through to was a good friend of ours in Liverpool, Ron Parkinson. Kind Ron said: 'I will come for you immediately. You can have my bed'. When he arrived, he did not seem to have any problem getting me out of the dock gates despite my lack of an entry visa to Great Britain!

At Ron's house I managed to get through to Mummy. It was an odd conversation.

'Where are you Joyce?'

I told her that I was with Ron Parkinson.

'But I left you on the ship!'

'The ship went down'!

She told me that she would come over as soon as the air raid wardens would allow her to move.

I now had to get through to Ireland. This was going to be tricky as long distance calls were only permitted in emergency. It took ages to get through to the long distance operator because so many cables were down. I asked her if she could get me a call to Ireland. 'No calls allowed to Ireland. Only emergency calls'

'This is an emergency. I have just been shipwrecked.'

She sounded really surprised and put me straight through to Ted.

Poor Ted: He had arrived at the quayside on the morning of the 21st to meet the boat. No boat and no news. Ted spent the 'missing' hours praying hundreds of rosaries and going back and forth to a telephone booth to phone his home to see if I had contacted them. He spent the best part of 24 hours on that dock. Finally, he decided he had better return home and arrived just as my call came through. I had gone through fire and water to try to get to him and now expected some great commendation.

I only remember Ted saying: 'Well, when *are* you coming? I felt angry for ages.

I still had a soggy valid visa for Ireland in my passport. I also had the precious piece of paper from Mr Imrie. But transport to Dublin seemed impossible. Mummy contacted Uncle William Langford and put the problem to him. Uncle William had 'contacts' and told my mother that he would try to wangle a seat on a plane to Dublin. He also advised me to go down to the shipping company (if it was still standing!) and ask what I was to do about compensation for my lost suitcase and its contents. I thought the idea was crazy, but I obediently went down to the office and reported to the man behind the counter. I told him which ship I had been on and when it had been hit. The man behind the counter listened to me, and went away. When he returned he told me that the ship was in good order. It had certainly not been hit! I explained that I had been on board. The man stuck to his guns! Eventually I was given a form to fill in. Seven years later I received my compensation!

23rd and 24th December

Uncle Will was as good as his word. He wangled a ticket for Christmas Eve on a plane from Manchester to Dublin. My mother booked me a room in the Midland Hotel for the night of the 23rd and a kind friend drove me to Manchester.

Little did I know that I was driving into Manchester's worst night of bombing. I walked up to the hotel reception desk and as they handed over the key to the room the air raid siren sounded. I never even saw my hotel room. The guests were all directed to the lower ground floor: the men's massage and sauna room where I bagged one of the long couches.

We were a motley crew in that underground sauna room: a small community united by fear. Among us were some famous names from the world of theatre. There were the six members of The Crazy Gang who were incredibly funny and had such unusual patter. I saw Tommy Trinder who could fill the London Palladium any day of the week. And Elsie and Doris Waters: the most famous female double-act in the history of British music hall and variety. None of them were in the least bit funny that night and no one cracked any jokes. The bombing was savage and more or less non-stop. On the nights of 22nd and 23rd December Manchester suffered appallingly; 700 people were killed and thousands left homeless.

On the morning of 24th December I presented myself at Manchester airport. For some reason, top brass were called and I was asked to explain my reason for travelling from Manchester to Dublin. I told them about my ship going down in Liverpool which left them singularly unimpressed.

My bag was searched exhaustively - they even took my lipstick from its holder, which destroyed it. The searchers came upon my framed photograph of Ted, which I had thrown into my case for some reason. They opened the frame and removed Ted's photograph. Beneath it they found a photograph of an unknown woman which bore the name and address of a Berlin photographer complete with signature.

I was moved into another room for exhaustive interrogation. Who was this woman? I had not the first idea! [I later discovered that she was a friend of my mother who had spent her honeymoon in Berlin!] Worse was to come. The next thing they found in my handbag was the precious paper with all the names and addresses Mr Imrie had given me for Ted: exact details of the oil refinery! It really did look extremely fishy. I talked urgently to God and my main prayer was HELP! Suddenly the men seemed to lose interest in me. I was allowed out of the room, waved through passport control and allowed to board the plane. Perhaps I had been lucky because it was Christmas Eve and all the men wanted to go home. They even left me with the vital piece of paper from Mr Imrie!

The little plane arrived in Dublin in the late afternoon and Ted and his family were there to meet me. Nobody, including me, realised that I was still suffering from shock. Whenever I tried to talk to Dorothy or Freda about the shipwreck, they would say: 'Don't talk about that! Let's see if there is a good picture on at the Metropole'. Sometimes they tried a different tack; 'Let's go to the seaside'. Anything to stop me talking!

Ted was delighted with my details of the oil refinery. He wrote to Shell mentioning Mr Imrie and received the promise of a job in England, starting in January 1941. He had the promise of an Irish passport with a visa for England so all seemed set fair on the employment front.

But what about our marriage? I kept on remembering that in June 1940 Daddy had said that we had to wait a year. Could we get married in June 1941? I had not dared to broach the subject with Mummy because of all that she had on her plate and the fact that I was still badly needed in the firm.

In the New Year I returned to England to find my mother in the throes of moving into a lovely modern house in Beryl Road, Noctorum. It had a beautiful landscaped garden – which did not stay beautiful for long. One night an oil bomb exploded on the garden shed. It burnt itself out, but oil spread across the garden and ruined it. I can still see us carting sacks of sand through the house to mop up the mess. The rotten sacking kept on giving way and the bags disgorged their contents so that we were left with a huge pile of sand on the hall floor.

The oil bomb had a brass head and we left it in front of the house. The following morning I heard Mummy calling sharply out of her bedroom window to the milk-boy: 'Put that down - that is *my* bomb!' I looked out to see the boy holding the brass head. Mummy relented: 'Alright, you can have it - *if* you leave an extra pint of milk today'.

Marriage

Ted arrived in England to begin his new job and came to visit us. We broached the subject of our wedding with my mother and she agreed that we could get married in June 1941. One morning in February she said suddenly out of the blue: 'I think we are all going to be killed - you and Ted can get married before June'. I talked to Ted and we decided to get married on April 19th.

It would have been unreasonable to expect my mother to come shopping with me for a wedding dress so Julie Jeffers came instead. A white wedding was ruled out because it was only six months since my father's death – and a white dress would anyway have taken too many of the precious clothing coupons.

I bought the first dress I tried on. It was ice blue with some small bands of maroon sewn across the top. To go with it, there were maroon suede gloves, maroon peep-toe shoes and a perky little maroon hat with a veil - all the rage in 1941. Ted arranged for me to wear some beautiful Talisman roses with lily of the valley on the day. He also insisted on having a wedding ring for himself – very unusual for men in 1941.

A few days before the wedding there was a particularly bad air raid and we all took refuge under the stairs. The wardens came round and told us we had to leave our home and go to a house further up the road for shelter. People dashed out of their houses with whatever they could lay their hands on. One lady had a precious vase; another was carrying her fur coat. Brian had a coat hanger – he must have fallen asleep with it in his hand. My mother had the best thing of all - a bottle of whisky! When we got to the house she was belle of the ball!

Travel restrictions between England and Ireland had tightened up again. None of Ted's family were able to come to the wedding except for Cecil at Ampleforth who was going to marry us. This would be the first time that Cecil had celebrated a marriage and he managed beautifully. He was staying with us the night before the wedding and I overheard him going over the ceremony by himself. He sounded rather nervous and I hoped that he was not going to drop one of the rings down the grating at the foot of the altar!

We were to be married at St Anne's Church, Overbury Street which was on the Liverpool side of the Mersey. On the morning of the wedding I had to phone around to see if everyone was all right. Stranger still, I had to phone the presbytery of St Anne's as one did not know from day to day which churches would be left standing: I spoke to a maid.

'My name is Miss Langford, and it is arranged that I get married in the church at eleven this morning. Would you please tell me if the church is still standing?'

'Just a minute, Miss. I will go and have a look'.

I prayed that the church was still there.

The maid came back to assure me that the Church itself was fine 'But the back has been blown off'.

Ted and I were going to be married in three quarters of a church!

My father's brother, Uncle Ernie was supposed to give me away. Uncle Ernie was a security officer and at the last moment there was a spy scare in his firm and he had to step down. I had to find somebody else at short notice – in the end our bank manager agreed to do the necessary.

Our wedding day

When I arrived at the church on the arm of the bank manager, the first thing I saw was my mother standing outside and signalling frantically. Ted and his best man had not yet arrived. The bank manager and I would have to drive around the block a couple of times! Eventually the two young men made a belated entrance and I was able to 'arrive'. It transpired that the car that had been picking them up had failed to start. Ted and his best man had to push it! Not quite the send off one imagines for a bridegroom on his wedding day!

Mummy had arranged for a lovely wedding breakfast at the Adelphi Hotel. After the ceremony we walked down the aisle to the back of the church – what was left of it - and climbed into the waiting cars. Suddenly I had a most dreadful black thought.

'I have made the greatest mistake of my life'. I felt that I was covered in a pall of gloom. I kept saying to myself 'There is enough grace in the Sacrament', Looking back now, I believe this to have been a demonic attack and I did not have the necessary experience of spiritual warfare which would have enabled me to deal with the problem. That sense of disaster certainly clouded the day for me. Inside, I kept talking to the Lord, and saying: 'Your grace will be there. I have promised to love, honour and obey. No one will ever know how I really feel'.

Many people say that their wedding day was the happiest of their lives. I feel sorry for them. Marriage ages like good wine and gets better and better. In comparison, the wedding day itself is candy floss and trappings. I would not put the clock back for a moment. Sorrow and suffering, the joy and the laughter, trust and understanding: these are born day by day through sacrificial love. Each one trying [and failing!] to put the comfort and pleasure of the other before one's own comfort and pleasure. During the first year of our marriage Ted and I never went to a film or on an outing that we honestly enjoyed 100%. We were both trying to work out what the other wanted. It was a time for laughter and honesty when we discovered that one!

When we became engaged Ted and I had grandiose ideas about our honeymoon. High on the list of destinations were Rome and Egypt. War dispensed with all such plans. In the end we managed only three days in a hotel – all the time that Ted could take off work. In wartime most hotels were commandeered for one thing or another. The only one we could find was a rather dismal place in Blackpool.

We would have liked to pretend that we had been married for years. Our 'cover' was blown at the reception desk of the hotel when we had to produce identity cards which still indicated that we were two single people with different names. In those days, comparatively few people went away for a few days together before they were married so we got quite a lot of shifty looks.

Worse was to come. My mother and Jo had really enjoyed themselves filling up my suitcase with rice. No confetti in those years of paper rationing – but they had certainly had a ball with the rice! As we walked into the dining room that evening grains of rice were still dropping out of our clothes. We had collected as much of the beastly stuff as possible. I had put it down the hand basin in the bedroom and poured very hot water onto it.

Ted had managed to get tickets for the theatre and when we came back to the hotel afterwards we found our bed beautifully turned back – but the hand basin was overflowing with a huge 'rice pudding'!

That night God gave us an immense grace. We knelt beside our bed and promised God and one another that we would never go to sleep without making up a quarrel. What a grace this has been. We have been married nearly sixty years - and we have never gone to sleep without making up a row even though we have sometimes had to stay awake until four o'clock in the morning!

6

LIVERPOOL, IRELAND, SWEDEN 1941-1948

'I don't think that we can live this Gospel message the way Our Lord wants it, without a community around us. The ways of the world are so alien to all His teaching'

Ted Donovan

'I don't think that we can live this Gospel message the way Our Lord wants it, without a community around us. The ways of the world are so alien to all His teaching'. What in the world could Ted be talking about? The word 'community' sounded perfectly awful. I had a vision of a convent full of miserable nuns. Ted seemed to have a vision of families who would live near one another with prayer as their centre. They would support one another spiritually and in any other way possible. I asked Ted not to talk about this idea to anybody else 'They will think you are crazy'!

In 1941 we were an immature young couple, and years later we agreed that we would have parted many times over, had it not been for our conviction that marriage was 'forever' and our refusal to go to sleep without making up a row.

Despite the fact that I was now married, the 'apron strings' had not been cut between me and my mother. During the early years of our marriage she was far too dominant in my life and was able to manipulate me emotionally. I would nearly always report something to Mummy before I told Ted. In hindsight, this was dreadful and it took a long time for me to make the necessary break. In a similar way, it has taken me years to allow my own children to 'be' without benefit of my 'advice'!

Ted was working on the construction of a Shell refinery near Ellesmere Port which would process crude oil shipped from the USA while I was still going to work for the Evergloss polish business. As newly weds, we were fortunate to be able to rent a house in Noctorum further along Beryl Road from my mother and Brian. Our house, Brook Hollow, was far too big for us but we were very green and had no idea about the sort of house that would be suitable for a young married couple. At least I did not have to do housework. These were the days when it was normal for a middle class family to have help in the house and I engaged a housekeeper.

In June 1941 our first baby was on the way. There can never have been a more ignorant and uninformed mother-to-be. I had never seen a newborn baby, never held one and did not know the first thing about antenatal care. My mother had told me nothing about the actual process of giving birth - anything like that would have embarrassed her dreadfully. To top it all, I had no idea that my childhood diphtheria had left me with a leaking heart valve which would be strained by my pregnancy and by the additional pounds which I would be unable to lose afterwards.

It would be inaccurate to say that I suffered from 'morning sickness'. I was sick morning, noon and night! Every morning I managed to drive to work through the Mersey tunnel but was usually feeling rotten. I had a regular passenger in the mornings - people gave lifts in those days - and I told her about my pregnancy. She recommended a doctor in West Kirby and I went to see him but he never tested my heart and it did not occur to me to tell him that I had had diphtheria.

During my pregnancy, there was one particularly bad air raid during which I was thrown right across the hall. My leg was cut and I was a mass of bruises but my main concern was for the baby. Fortunately there did not seem to be any problem but our house was in a bad way and we knew we would have to get out that night. In mid-air raid it was seriously dangerous to leave one's house but anything was better than staying put.

Ted decided that we should try to get right away from Noctorum and drive thirty miles to Aunt Mabel in Chester, collecting my mother and Brian on the way. They decided to travel in their own car and the journey to Chester was grim. Huge pieces of shrapnel were falling onto the road in front of us and the two cars had to keep stopping at checkpoints although the sentries always waved us through. When we eventually reached Chester, we discovered that Aunt Mabel already had a full house – but she opened her heart and her home to us and found us a corner. We collapsed into bed and slept like logs.

The following morning, Mummy and Brian had to go back to the factory and Ted needed to get to work in Dingle. I decided to stay put for a few days. After the shock of being thrown about in our hall I thought that the baby and I needed a bit of quiet. A few days later I went back to Beryl Road and was shocked at the state of the house. There was filth everywhere, no glass left in the windows and the curtains up the trees! Our new housekeeper had had enough and gone off to stay with her daughter in Devon. I was going to have to manage on my own.

My mother and Brian decided to hold a council of war with Ted and me. Mummy's house was not in such a bad way as ours but we decided that for the time being the two families should join forces and take a house together a long way out of Liverpool – just to try and stay alive. We settled on Birkdale about twenty miles north and Ted and my mother found a large house. The first and second floors were fully furnished and available for rent. There was even a grand piano!

We were going to be six in all as I had acquired a new maid. Ted's sister Freda had managed to find me a maid who was willing to travel over from Ireland.

She was Catholic of course – and Mummy and Brian had a housekeeper who could not stand Catholics! There is no doubt that we should have arranged to live as two separate families and the fact that we failed to do so put an unnecessary strain on our marriage and created all sorts of difficulties.

Food was on everybody's mind during the war and I had a great hankering for scrambled eggs. The 'ration' was supposed to be one egg per person per week but it was months since we had so much as set eyes on an egg. We had smelt them when a goods train full of eggs got stuck in a railway siding!

In my pregnant state I thought endlessly about scrambled eggs and one day my mother told me that she was going out and wasn't coming home until she found some eggs. She was gone for ages and finally marched up the stairs bearing a basket containing a dozen eggs (no egg boxes in those days). Where had she discovered so many eggs? She told me not to ask.

There were six people in the house and twelve eggs, which meant two for each person. How were we going to eat them? Mummy got the maids to come upstairs, and it was decided I would cook the precious eggs myself - two each in whatever way anybody wanted. Down I went to the kitchen in eager anticipation. I cracked one egg – bright green! A second one – just the same! Eleven out of the twelve eggs were bad! I can still smell the sulphur. There was one egg left. If this last one was edible it was agreed that I should have it. I cracked that egg. It wasn't green so I scrambled it but it tasted powerfully of straw!

In 1941 delicacies such as roast chicken had become a mere memory. One day I was alone upstairs when I heard a funny noise. The front door was open and I looked over the banisters to see if somebody had arrived. 'Somebody' had indeed arrived and was perching at the bottom of the stairs – it was a chicken – a real live chicken! I nipped downstairs, out of the back door and round to the front. In I came, shutting the front door behind me. The chicken was now trapped. Clearly it had strayed and was hopelessly lost. We could have roast chicken for dinner!

At this point Mummy and Ted arrived home together. They proved themselves pillars of morality and assured me that the chicken did not belong to me. It was somebody else's chicken and must be returned from whence it came. After years of hunger my conscience was strangely dulled and I stuck to my guns: 'It's a lost chicken. How can we possibly find out where it comes from?' Ted and my mother argued one way and I argued the other. Stalemate! Meanwhile the chicken remained trapped on the stairs! Mummy appeared to be coming round to my way of thinking: "Alright, we will eat the chicken. But I hope you won't mind what the neighbours say when my housekeeper and your maid tell everybody that we have been eating a stolen chicken!"

Ted and I got the stupid chicken into a basket and started on a tour round the houses to find out where it came from. No luck. Finally we decided to go to the police station. We were sure that the chicken could still be ours if it was not claimed within a few days. I cheered up a bit and kept reassuring myself that the chicken had wandered for miles and was really and truly lost. The officer in the police station solemnly wrote down all the details. He took the bird and told us that we could come back for it in three days. My parting shot was 'If that chicken lays any eggs, they belong to us! Greed to the last! Three days later we returned to the station. We saw the same policeman. Had anyone claimed the chicken? No! Please may we have our chicken? No! Then came the awful truth. The police superintendent had taken the chicken home and eaten it for his own dinner. It would never have laid any eggs. My 'chicken' was a cockerel!

Pamela

It had been arranged for our baby to be born in a nursing home in West Kirby which was run by three maiden ladies who were nurses - the Misses Hamm; the eldest Miss Hamm being Matron. They sent me a list of things to bring to the nursing home and one of the items amazed me: Castor oil! 'How cruel' I thought 'to give castor oil to a small baby'. Little did I know!

Ted and I had arranged to move into a nearby hotel a few days before the birth. The doctor speculated that the baby might be late and we wondered how to manage if we had to stay in an expensive hotel for longer than a very few days. We certainly could not afford it. Fortunately things started to happen on the second night. Ted drove me to the nursing home at top speed and then left me. In those days it was unthinkable for a father to have anything to do with the birth of his own baby.

How can one describe the experience of childbirth? The labour was long and terribly painful and there were no pain killers. At ten minutes to midnight on the Feast of the Annunciation, 25 March 1942 our daughter was born. She weighed 5lbs 8oz and she was beautiful - blonde and pretty from the word go and without a wrinkle in sight. The castor oil had done its work and helped the baby on her way! We called her Pamela.

There was a strict rule in the nursing home that fathers and other visitors were not allowed after 10pm and here was Pamela arriving at midnight. Matron Hamm broke all her rules and phoned the hotel. She asked Ted if he would like to come right away. Would he! She told me afterwards that she felt I needed his support because I was such a very young mother. When Ted saw the baby he was speechless. We just couldn't believe that we were the parents of this precious baby - she was indeed an incredible gift. Pamela was perfect - apart from a tiny brown birthmark under her right arm. The doctor told us not to worry, but just to keep an eye on it.

I spent a fortnight in the nursing home and was not allowed out of bed for ten days so I lay and gazed out of the window at the daffodils. In the mornings Matron Hamm used to come to my room and bathe Pamela in a little papier mâché basin. On the morning before I was due to leave she said to me: 'I am going to let you bathe your baby yourself this morning. You have watched me do it but if you are nervous or need anything, just ring this little bell and I will come'.

I lifted our precious baby, and started to undress her - babies wore lots of clothes in those days. When I got her naked, I discovered something appalling. Her head did not seem to be properly attached to her little body. It lolled! I was frozen with horror. I did not bathe Pamela. I did not even put a sponge on her. Carefully and tremblingly I dressed her again and crawled back into bed, rigid with fear. I was beyond words. Ted came in, took one look at my face and asked me what on earth was the matter? I explained that our baby's head was not properly attached to her body. Ted rang for Matron, and told her the dreadful news. Matron Hamm laughed and explained to me about tiny babies and their lolling heads.

My final meeting with Matron Hamm was a most blessed occasion. Pamela was dressed and Ted had come to collect us both. We walked down the lovely long stairway and Matron Hamm was waiting for us at the bottom. She addressed Ted: 'Mr Donovan, sit on that chair. Mrs Donovan, hand your baby to your husband and come into my study".

I followed Matron Hamm and sat nervously on the edge of a huge chair. She addressed me firmly: 'Mrs Donovan, you are very young and I want to give you some words of advice which I hope will stand you in good stead throughout your life! When you came in here you had a very close and wonderful relationship with your husband. Now there is a third member of your family. Like all young mothers, you will have a tendency to put the baby first, and neglect your husband. The correct order is for your husband to be the first member in your family, not the baby.

At no time should your husband ever feel that he is playing second fiddle to your daughter. The day will come when this baby and all your future children will leave home. You may be left with very little if you have not maintained a deep relationship with your husband and given him first place in your life.' Her advice was extremely wise and I have followed it – sometimes to the disapproval of my children!

When we got home the baby certainly received a lot of love but I was totally inexperienced in anything to do with caring for a tiny infant. I felt extremely nervous. My mother gave me one piece of advice which was a gem. She told me to make as much noise as possible so that the baby would get used to sound. Every time we went near Pamela's room we pulled the chain of the loo! Years later when Ted and I were in Canada we went to play bridge with a young couple. When we arrived there was a note pinned to the front door: 'Please don't ring the bell, baby asleep. Knock lightly'. When we went to the bathroom there was another note: 'Baby asleep, please do not flush the toilet'. I forgot, flushed the toilet and the baby woke up and bawled. We were never invited again!

As Pamela was so tiny, the doctor told me to feed her every three hours, night and day. This left me exhausted. No sooner had I finished one feed than it seemed to be time to start the next one. Every time she cried I rushed to pick her up until Ted put his foot down and told me to leave the baby in her cot. When Pamela cried he let me make sure that there was not a pin sticking into her but I then had to put her back down. The baby cried and I cried too. Ted was a brute! But when Pamela discovered that I was not going to pick her up each time she wailed, she changed her tune and we had fewer broken nights.

Anthony and Liz

It soon became apparent that the double ménage in Birkdale was far from being a bed of roses. My mother was still grieving for Daddy, and was very lonely. She hardly gave us a moment to ourselves. My dependence on her was frustrating for Ted and we realised that something would have to be done.

When Pamela was a few months old I discovered that I was pregnant once more. Ted and I were delighted and I expected my mother to be equally pleased. But when I told her about my pregnancy, she was far from enthusiastic and merely reminded me that I was going to be busy – as if I didn't know! Her negative attitude hurt and I was hypersensitive.

Ted's job at the underground storage depot in Dingle had come to an end and we were due to spend Christmas 1942 with the Donovans in Dublin. While we were in Dublin, Ted approached his old firm and was not only given a warm reception but received the offer of a job. We decided that this might be the moment to leave Liverpool. I knew that Mummy would be grieved, but we had to make a break for the sake of our marriage.

We duly packed ourselves up and bade farewell to my mother and Brian. In Dublin we wanted to settle reasonably close to Uncle Edward who had sold the huge family home, Thorndale and moved himself and Dorothy and Freda to a smaller house at

Rathgar. Ted and I duly searched for accommodation in the Rathgar area and found a dear little house to rent which suited us perfectly. We settled in and I was able to get a maid from Mullingar called Marcella Murtagh.

The downside of all these new arrangements was the fact that I was beginning to feel extremely ill. I had not felt like this during my first pregnancy – despite the constant morning sickness. I was very much afraid that something must be seriously wrong and consulted one of the leading gynaecologists in Dublin. He examined me carefully and at long last the leaking valve in my heart was correctly diagnosed. No wonder I had been feeling so awful!

There was every likelihood that the birth might prove complicated and the gynaecologist encouraged me to employ his 'number one private nurse'. She was to be with me for the birth in the Leinster Nursing Home and to remain with me at home afterwards.

In the middle of March I learnt that the baby would have to be induced. The birth was, indeed, complicated and anaesthetics could not be used because of my heart condition. In the end, all turned out well and on 22 March 1943 Ted and I were overjoyed to find ourselves the parents of a baby boy. Our son was born with bright red hair and he was just as gorgeous as Pamela. We named him Anthony in fulfilment of my promise to St Anthony who had 'arranged' our marriage. He was baptised in St Andrews, Westland Row as I had been 22 years previously. My mother came across for the ceremony.

The 'number one nurse' came home with us for three weeks and I was far less well than I had been after the birth of Pamela. A heart specialist was consulted and offered a sorry prognosis. I would never be able to lead a normal life; I would only be able to go upstairs once a day and we were not to have any more babies.

Ted and I listened to all this with trepidation but agreed to ignore the gloomy warnings. We decided to put our trust in God and after a few months began to pray for another baby. By the spring of 1945 she was on her way. This time I dearly wanted to have the baby at home and consulted the same gynaecologist. He agreed to a home delivery on condition that 'number one nurse' should once again be in attendance. November 6th was the Feast of all the Saints of Ireland. At three o'clock on the morning I went into labour and number one nurse alerted Ted. She got him to heat gallons of water on the cooker, told him that it would be ages before anything happened and packed him off to early Mass. Half an hour later doctor and baby arrived together! We called her Elizabeth but always shortened it to Liz. Years later she told me that I only called her Elizabeth when I was cross with her.

It was a great help to have the nurse in the house afterwards. I made a reasonably good recovery but found it very hard to get to sleep. 'Number one nurse' told me not to worry – she had a solution! Every night she gave me an injection and the experience was amazing! I had no idea what was in the syringe and only later did I discover that she had been giving me morphine. I cannot imagine how she obtained the stuff, but I feel sure that it had nothing to do with my gynaecologist!

Life in Dublin

Back in Liverpool the Evergloss polish business was flourishing and my mother had now come to terms with our move to Ireland. Although Brian was still very young he was now running the Liverpool end of things and Mummy used to come over to see us quite frequently. She was keen to persuade Ted and me to start a branch of the polish firm in Dublin but we decided against it. On her frequent visits she stayed at the prestigious Shelbourne Hotel on St Stephen's Green, and then decided to buy a house south of Dublin in Baltinglass which cost a mint of money. One way or another the cash seemed to be flowing a bit too freely!

Mummy's visits gave her an opportunity to visit her own mother. Grandma Nettie was still living in Dublin and although my own relationship with her had taken a turn for the worse when Ted and I became engaged, it had improved again on the arrival of her great grandchildren.

Ted and I took the family to see Grandma Nettie from time to time and on one occasion she introduced us to her friend Gertie who was 'fey' and read palms. Ted and I found Gertie fascinating and had not the slightest idea that palmistry was against the law of God. We thought Gertie was great fun and decided to hold a party to which we would invite friends and relations who wished to have their palms read.

During the party Gertie read Ted's palm - and her reaction was eerie: 'If I didn't know you were married, I would say this is the hand of a priest'. No one apart from me, the Abbot of Ampleforth and Ted's brother Cecil had ever known of Ted's desire to become a monk. To me Gertie said: 'You are going to travel a great deal'. 'Poppycock, I thought!' Little did I know that I would be setting up home in six countries! To one man she said: 'My goodness, you are putting away a lot of money!' Unbeknownst to Gertie, the man was cashier of a bank and we laughed. Unbeknownst to anybody at the time, he was also an embezzler and a lot of the bank's money was indeed being 'put away' into his own pocket!

During our four years in Dublin Ted changed his job a number of times. By far the most interesting period was spent in the employ of a remarkable man, Professor James Bayley-Butler. Bayley-Butler had qualified as a medical doctor and a biologist but was best known as Professor of Zoology at University College, Dublin.

The professor was certainly a genius, even if he was mildly odd. He would have at least six projects on the boil at any one time and would be working full speed on one of them – only to move suddenly to another. Ted was able to cope with this and his flexibility was sheer gift to his boss.

Professor Bayley-Butler was widely known for his expertise in dealing with 'bugs' and he had handled the serious infestation of Westminster Hall by death-watch beetle. We accordingly 'christened' Ted's boss 'Buggy' and he became a good friend of the family. When Buggy decided to remarry, Ted was his best man. Buggy's bride was pretty and plump and would have been in her mid-forties. As the happy couple were coming out of the church a Dublin lady of the streets glanced at the pretty bride and gave her verdict: 'Well saisoned, like meself!'

We appreciated our friendship with Buggy and I was delighted to discover that his connection with my family went back a lot further than I could ever have imagined. One day Buggy was reminiscing over lunch about the dashing young captain with whom he had hoped to go into partnership after the First World War. I pricked up my ears when I heard the name of that captain. It was none other than Fred Langford – my father!

One of Buggy's most useful inventions was a waterproofing solution which was to prove a godsend to the army. Officers relied heavily on paper maps in order to direct troops and in bad weather the maps became rain sodden and thus impossible to read. Buggy offered his waterproofing solution to the American army who were interested but there had to be a 'proving'.

Buggy was nothing if not a showman. He invited senior members of the American forces to his house along with several distinguished journalists. Buggy soaked a paper map in his waterproofing solution and allowed it to dry. He had instructed his maid to prepare a good Irish stew and in the presence of his guests he poured the Irish stew onto the map. He then produced the cat to eat it up and when all the stew had disappeared the map was found to be as good as new. The American army was delighted – and they were not the only beneficiaries of Buggy's magic solution. I used it myself to waterproof the babies' cotton panties!

Sweden

In 1945 war came to an end leaving Europe in tatters with millions of lives lost or damaged irretrievably. Dublin was in the doldrums and for the next two years life was hard for everybody – including civil engineers! Ted was now twenty-five and felt that he needed more experience in working with reinforced concrete. The Swedes were world leaders in the field so Sweden would be the best place for us to go. We spent months praying about this important decision and I typed endless letters for Ted as he searched for a suitable opening.

If we were going to move to Sweden we would obviously have to learn Swedish. Ted visited the Swedish Consul in Dublin, and asked whether he knew any Swedes in Dublin who would be prepared to teach us the language. The Consul turned to his blonde secretary: 'Miss Jonsonn, would you teach this gentleman and his wife Swedish?'

Miss Jonsonn appeared dumbstruck but obviously felt that she could not really refuse. In order to give her the opportunity to meet me before committing herself, Ted invited Miss Jonsonn to come to supper to talk to us both. Little did we imagine the train of events that would result from that invitation!

We had a pleasant evening together and discovered that Miss Jonsonn's first name was Majsan. She was 26 years old, very friendly and self-confident but there was no doubt that she was unhappy in Dublin. She had found it hard to break into a social circle and she was also finding it difficult to get baths in her lodgings! We came to an arrangement. If Majsan would teach us Swedish two nights a week, we would give her supper and a hot bath on each occasion and include her in our circle of friends.

My brother Brian was coming over from Liverpool for a large dance to which we were taking a party. I asked Majsan if she would come as Brian's partner and she seemed pleased at the prospect. Brian duly arrived and was introduced to Majsan. They certainly got on very well indeed. To our great surprise, Brian promptly proposed marriage to Majsan and was accepted. My mother was livid and expressed herself strongly! Majsan was older than Brian; she was a foreigner and she was not a Catholic – this last objection despite the fact that Mummy had herself long been away from the Church! I think my mother's real objection to the marriage was the fact that she would no longer come first in Brian's affections.

While Brian and Majsan were announcing their 'surprise' engagement, our own plans for a move to Sweden were not making much progress. Ted realised that he would have to make an exploratory trip to Stockholm but kept very quiet about it. Dublin was like a village and news of an exploratory trip and a possible change of job would have spread like wildfire. Ted did not want anybody to know until everything was fixed.

He took a few days leave from his job and set off for Sweden. The trip was highly successful and Ted was offered a job in the centre of Stockholm. He returned to Dublin, handed in his notice and it was at that point that we then decided to break the news to our families. Some people thought we were mad, but we were convinced that we were doing the right thing.

I asked Marcella, our maid, if she would like to come with us and she agreed. So we were a party of six setting off for England to cross from Tilbury to Gothenburg on a lovely Swedish ship – alas the crossing did not prove quite as 'lovely' as I had imagined. The journey took just under three days and Marcella and I were as sick as dogs. Ted was wonderful and took care of Pamela 5, Anthony 4, and Liz 2 while I did absolutely nothing. The food on board looked marvellous, but never a bite passed my lips. I felt that it would be a blessed release if that ship went down and me with it! It was wonderful to set foot on dry land at last – even with the prospect of the very long train journey from Gothenburg to Stockholm.

It proved a lifesaver to have a future sister-in-law who was Swedish and had relations living in Stockholm. Majsan's brother and his wife had been thrilled about Majsan's engagement and very generously invited us to stay with them until we found a place of our own. Their house was not very large but they completely rearranged it to provide adequate accommodation for five Donovans and Marcella.

We had realised that we would not be able to do much about accommodation until we arrived in Stockholm and quickly discovered that the Swedish housing situation was appalling. During the long years of war there had been little or no building work and the population was at bursting point. We trailed from house agent to house agent and when we told them that we were looking for accommodation for six people, you could see them trying not to laugh! We made a further unpleasant discovery which was the existence of 'backhanders'! In the unlikely event of our being able to find a flat to rent there would be additional money to be handed over – a 'backhander' which was known as 'key' money and could be as much as £100 – a fabulous sum in 1947!

Eventually we managed to secure the loan of the summer home belonging to the Methodist Church in Sweden which enabled us to stop imposing on Majsan's family. When we arrived at the home I had twelve nappies for Liz and no soap with which to wash them. It looked as if I might have no water either. Our water source was an outside well and every drop had to be heated on a wood burning stove. We were very much afraid that that well might run dry but it never did. Ted and I prayed fervently over it and our prayers were answered!

Winter was coming and the 'summer home' was ill equipped for a Swedish winter. By the grace of God we discovered a house to buy on a small housing estate about fifteen miles outside Stockholm. It was the most beautiful place one could imagine, but out in the wilds. All the houses on the estate were different.

Ours was built on a slope and had a spiral staircase. Alas, it had no sewer system; so we could not pull the chain! Instead we used a special loo which had to be emptied into a huge container. Each week men with a cart would collect the full container and leave us with an empty one!

The temperature dropped and we discovered that, in this country of vast forests, wood was rationed! It was delivered to us in three foot pieces which Ted and I spent hours sawing into stove sized logs! Water was also at a premium. We dared not use precious water from our well for washing nappies and clothes when we needed it so badly for drinking and cooking and bathing. Fortunately there was a huge copper boiler in the basement which enabled us to solve the problem. When the snow arrived, Ted and I spent hours passing snow through the basement window and putting it into the copper to melt.

In order to travel to Stockholm every day Ted had to walk a mile to the railway station. I also did my share of walking because the shops were a mile in the opposite direction. Marcella refused to walk that mile to do the shopping so I did two miles a day there and back – at least I lost weight and my command of Swedish improved!

While Majsan had started to teach Ted and me to speak Swedish in Dublin, we needed a lot more practice if Ted was going to hold down his job. We decided to converse in Swedish over dinner which led to some very stilted conversations! We also enrolled in a language school in Stockholm, only to find that the English/Swedish class was full and we would have to join the German/Swedish class. Neither of us spoke a word of German and our hearts sank. On our first day in the class I was about to cry when a kindly hand touched me on the shoulder. A friendly American voice said: 'Say, do you speak English?' The words were music to my ears! Dan and Kay Browne had just arrived in Sweden from the United States. The four of us were able to persuade the school to make special arrangements for the teacher to make home visits - sometimes to the Browne's and sometimes to Ted and me. My need for a working knowledge of Swedish was less urgent than Ted's, but he was adamant that I should learn a few new words every day. There was one word with which the children and I quickly became familiar: Kalle Anka – the Swedish for Donald Duck!

If we had found house hunting a dismal business, church hunting was little better. We had managed to find a Catholic Church when we first arrived in Stockholm, but were only able to get there on Sundays. Majsan's brother and sister-in- law were non-believers like most of the people we met in Sweden, and our insistence that we get to Mass every Sunday seemed to them little more that humorous. They could not understand anyone wanting to go to church at all – let alone every Sunday! God certainly used this situation to deepen my prayer life. I used every waking moment to turn to him and I did the same when I awoke in the night.

When we found ourselves on the housing estate fifteen miles outside Stockholm there were no churches anywhere around us. On Sundays we had to travel to one of the very few, very poor Catholic churches in Stockholm. These were staffed by elderly priests, who looked really badly fed. Their churches were bitterly cold and I feel sure that they didn't have a bean for heating. The temperature inside was not much higher than outside – where it frequently fell to 30°C below! In those unheated churches one really had to wrap up warmly to protect against frostbite!

These were the days when one had to fast from midnight in order to receive Holy Communion. Every Sunday morning we got the children up early to give them breakfast and leave the house at 6.10. No breakfast for Ted or me. We walked the mile to the station, carrying or pushing the little ones, and took the train to Stockholm. We would hear Mass, be defeated by the Swedish sermon and miss the train back by 10 minutes. We would eventually get home at 10.20. Ted could not even afford to buy us a cup of coffee to help us on our way.

Marcella also had to get to Sunday Mass. I had an arrangement that she would start out for the station and meet us on our way home. As we passed one another, I would give her my season ticket and she would put her finger over my photo to con the men at the ticket barrier. I told the Lord that if he would get us out of this situation, I would never again take Mass for granted. We were in complete spiritual isolation and did not know a single fellow Christian! It was now that I came to share Ted's 'vision' of a Christian community life in which neighbouring families could share their faith with one another.

Going to confession in Swedish was an interesting religious experience! The priest did not speak English but could manage in German and French. Ted and I knew no German and very little French. We eventually devised a solution. The priest would ask us questions in French and we would do our best to answer. How long since we had last been to Mass? We struggled to get there every week!

The first time we went to confession, the priest gave us each the Litany of the Sacred Heart to say as a 'penance' afterwards. We had been used to having several Our Fathers or Hail Marys for penance. On this first occasion, the priest came to meet us afterwards and we were able to tell him that we did not know the Litany of the Sacred Heart. We talked for some time and he told us that in nine years in Stockholm he had never before met a couple who were both cradle Catholics and had each gone on to marry a Catholic spouse.

In December 1947 Brian came to Sweden to meet the family of his fiancée and was planning to spend Christmas with us. December 13 was the start of the Christmas festivities and there was great excitement. A beautiful blonde girl drove through the lighted streets of Stockholm in an open carriage drawn by six white horses. She was swathed in white ermine, with a crown of lighted (electric) candles on her head. This was to celebrate the feast of St Lucia, the feast of light, which used to occur on the shortest day. This had been December 13 until the calendar was changed in the sixteenth century by Pope Gregory XIII.

During the run-up to Christmas, the streets were beautifully decorated with overhead lights and the shop windows were like fairyland. Each home seemed to have a six sided star in the window which was lit from first thing in the morning until last thing at night. It was a wonderland but until Christmas Eve there did not seem to be the slightest indication that the celebration was anything to do with the birth of Christ. On Christmas Eve we all went to the midnight Mass in one of the cold churches of Stockholm and found to our surprise that it was packed to the doors!

As a family we prayed together and Ted and I also prayed for guidance about the future. It was becoming increasingly clear that we had not done our homework in terms of Catholic education in Sweden. We had been able to enrol Pamela and Anthony in a little play school which was a bus ride away but we needed to discover some form of proper Catholic schooling for Pamela. We made exhaustive enquiries but our findings were grim. There was a convent where they would teach children in French but they could take Pamela on only one day in the week – Saturday! We agreed to Saturday attendance - and that school laid the foundations of Pamela's lifelong love of French.

After only six months in Sweden we became aware that the political situation was threatening. People were talking about 'When the Russians arrive...' rather than '*If* they arrive' which was very alarming. The Irish Ambassador told us that Americans were being advised to go home if they possibly could. He encouraged us to do likewise. We had three small children and were responsible for Marcella but how could we ever raise the money for six fares from Sweden to Dublin. Out of the blue a solution arrived. Ted had inherited from his mother a part share in a coalmine in Wales. Britain's Labour government had nationalised the mines and compensated the shareholders. Ted's 'compensation' would carry us home!

7

Dublin again
1948-1952

We left Sweden in such a hurry that our furniture was still on the high seas when we docked at Dun Laoghaire. Fortunately my mother's house at Baltinglass was empty so we were able to go straight there and move back into our old home at Rathgar when our belongings eventually made their appearance. Ted was able to return to his old job with Delap and Waller so everything was working well. Our only sadness had been the need to leave Sweden before Brian and Majsan's wedding. But we had no choice.

Very soon after my return in 1948 I had to undergo urgent gynaecological surgery in a Dublin hospital. There I became friendly with the girl in the next bed, Mona Quinn from Dundalk. I soon realised that Mona and her husband Larry were real powerhouses of prayer. Ted had once told me that I 'collected' people who had the ear of the Lord. Mona and Larry have certainly been among them.

That Dublin hospital was very poor and the food was indescribably awful – they even made the rice pudding with water instead of milk. We had to rely on our visitors to bring in so-called 'extras' – which included tea! It took Ted and me a few days to cotton on to all this, but in the meantime my generous fellow patients ensured that I lacked for nothing.

There was wonderful camaraderie in that ward despite the fact that some of the women were close to death. After 'lights out' we were supposed to be silent. Instead we recited a complete rosary – all fifteen decades of it - which must have taken nearly an hour. That rosary was followed by other prayers which I found supportive and uplifting. When we had finished praying we shared experiences. Some nights I had to put cotton wool in my ears to stop me hearing the funny stories – it hurt my stitches to laugh so much.

One of the senior nurses had a cruel streak. She must have been about forty-five - which seemed old to me in my mid-twenties – and she treated the women very harshly. Sometimes it was obvious that she was hurting them deliberately. I was astonished at their bravery and lack of complaint under her 'ministrations'.

It was my turn to suffer when the time came to have the clips taken out of my scar. The sadistic nurse arrived in the company of a little assistant who had the task of holding the bowl. As each clip was pulled out the skin was broken. I squeezed my eyes shut but the tears rolled down silently. My tormentor kept saying: 'You are not very brave, are you? Let's see about this one!' Eventually she departed with the promise that she would: 'leave the rest till tomorrow'. As she moved off I wept into my pillow. I would so much rather have got it all over with in one go. Half an hour later the little nurse who had held the bowl tiptoed across and whispered: 'All the clips are out. She always says she is coming back tomorrow so as to worry people!'

Ted was a daily visitor but there were two days towards the end of my stay when he did not make an appearance. Instead he sent a very loving letter explaining something about pressure of work. This satisfied me - I was not very bright! When the day arrived for me to come home, Ted came to collect me and we drove off. A few blocks away from the hospital he drew up and told me that he had some serious news to give me about three year old Liz: 'She has scarlet fever, and is in the isolation hospital. I wasn't able to come to see you for fear that I might be infectious myself. I didn't tell you because I didn't want you to fret'. I was completely stunned.

Ted had arranged to take me straight to the isolation hospital where I would be allowed to stand at the door of the ward and could at least catch a glimpse of Liz. When we got there, we hurried along to the ward and peered through the door. Three-year-old Liz was about seven beds down, sitting up in a large cot. I called to her and she looked me straight in the face and immediately looked away. My daughter was refusing to acknowledge me. I felt devastated.

It was not for some time that I learnt the full story. When the scarlet fever had been diagnosed Liz had been ordered to the isolation hospital in an ambulance. When it arrived, she had the impression that her father was allowing two strange men to put her onto a 'carry-bed' and take her away without doing anything to stop them! The men had taken her to a 'strange place' where there were lots of other children in beds. When the nurse unpacked Liz's clothes she found that Ted had packed one of his own vests by mistake. The nurse held up the vest for the other children to see: 'Look what Elizabeth's Daddy has packed!' They all laughed.

As far as Liz was concerned, her father had deserted her and her mother wasn't there either. No wonder she wouldn't even look at me when I eventually appeared. It was a bitter reminder of my own miserable experience in the Liverpool isolation hospital when I had diphtheria and had been told that my parents had deserted me. I had been eight years old at the time but Liz was only three! It was a wretched experience for a tiny child.

Settling in

Thanks to the sale of the Welsh coalmine which had paid our fares from Sweden we were now in a position to buy a car. Up to now we had relied on a tandem which we rode with three children on board! It would not be allowed today but we never had a spill. We even used that tandem to take ourselves to dances – myself in a long evening dress and Ted in white tie and tails! These were the days of petrol rationing and everybody used bicycles. It was not uncommon to see a senior surgeon or a Member of Parliament peddling along – complete with top hat!

We purchased our car for the princely sum of £450 and it opened up all sorts of wonderful avenues. In the holidays I was able to take the children and their friends to the sea every day – weather being no deterrent as they would be getting wet anyway. The biggest decision was always where to go. We had such a lot of lovely places around Dublin – Seapoint, Dun Laoghaire, Blackrock, Greystones, and for longer trips there was Brittas Bay. Sometimes we wanted to be sure of a fine day for a picnic on the beach so I would phone the police in a particular place and ask them about the weather. They were always helpful but the answer was often along the lines of: 'Ah, Madam, you would be all the better if you went five miles further on. It's a grand soft day here, thank God'. A 'soft day' was Irish for 'pouring rain'!

**Brian, Majsan, Pamela, Anthony Liz,
me and mother**

**Grandma Nettie, Mother, Pamela me –
four generations**

Pamela was now six years old and preparing to make her First Holy Communion in the church in which my parents had been married. It was a joy to prepare her white silk dress and her little headband and to receive Holy Communion with her for the first time. On the afternoon of the great day Pamela was allowed to choose a special treat and decided on a visit to the zoo. We were friendly with the zoo superintendent who was great with children. He would always allow our three to go behind the scenes and fondle any baby animals which were not likely to be dangerous. I think he stretched it a bit on the day of Pamela's First Communion. We have a photograph of her with Anthony nursing a lion cub, which is practically as big as himself!

GRASPING THE NETTLE

Anthony with lion cub and Pamela

We all loved the Dublin zoo and I took great delight in studying the marvellous colours the Lord had chosen for birds and animals. I used to come home and try to copy them for the girl's dresses. Clothes rationing was still in force and it was a battle to keep them all warmly and attractively turned out. We had no central heating and had to rely on open peat or coal fires. I decided to buy raw wool and to knit the girl's underwear instead of buying it – cheaper and far warmer. I looked out for attractive fabrics at low prices and was able to create attractive dresses for Pamela and Liz as well as for myself. One of my particular enjoyments was smocking. I developed a real craze for it. Ted used to say that he expected to come home and find that I had been smocking the curtains!

We were concerned to find the best schooling for five year old Anthony and heard about a new school for boys which had been started by the Jesuits. We promptly enrolled Anthony and he wasted no time in letting us know what he thought of the place. Every morning he screamed his head off as we struggled to get him into his uniform and out of the door. We imagined that the loathing would wear off but it showed no signs of doing so. Anthony hated everything about that school and it was obviously wrong for a little boy to be so miserable. We made further investigations, and discovered a suitable school in Donnybrook run by the Dominican nuns. Pamela and Anthony both went there and were happy and Liz eventually joined them.

The Donnybrook convent was not only a blessing for the children but also to Ted and for me. It was here that we met Sister Bernadette who was to have such an influence on our spiritual lives. Ted and I very much wanted to deepen our relationship with Jesus and to bring our children into relationship with him. Sister Bernadette recognised this and took us beneath her wing. Under her guidance, we began to say the Divine Office, the daily public prayer of the Catholic Church, which is recited by priests and by members of some religious congregations. The Office enriched our lives beyond words with its powerful words and the awareness that we were praying 'with' the Church across the world.

She also introduced us to the Third Order of St. Dominic: the secular institute which enables lay people to associate themselves with the great spiritual 'family' founded by St Dominic in the thirteenth century. My childhood friend, Father Ferdinand Valentine, had been a Dominican and I felt very much at home as part of his spiritual family.

Another gift I received from Sister Bernadette was an 'introduction' to a spiritual writer who delighted my heart. This was Columba Marmion [now Blessed Columba], an Irishman with a French mother who had died only twenty-five years previously. Columba Marmion had belonged to the great spiritual 'family' founded by St Benedict in the sixth century and had become Abbot of the Belgian monastery of Maredsous. I revelled in Father Columba's writings and everything about his life captured my imagination. During the First World War Abbot Marmion had sent his young monks from Belgium to Ireland to complete their monastic training. In order to keep in touch with them their Abbot had been obliged to travel across war-torn Europe in all manner of disguises. On one occasion he had left occupied Belgium disguised as a jockey and arrived at Tyburn Convent in London in the guise of a cattle dealer!

Artist's model

One afternoon in Dublin a man approached me to ask if he could paint my portrait. I thought he was trying to pick me up and I cut him dead. Somehow he discovered my telephone number and rang up. He was nothing if not persistent! The man began his phone call with an apology for his abrupt approach in the street and went on to introduce himself. The persistent man was none other than the distinguished

Irish painter, Tom Nisbet. His request to paint my portrait was perfectly genuine and he wished to exhibit it in the National Gallery of Ireland. I was very flattered by the request but explained that I would have to consult my husband and would contact Mr Nisbet when I had done so. Ted was in favour so I rang Tom Nisbet to arrange a date to visit his studio.

What was I going to wear for the great occasion? I decided that my glamorous black off the shoulder evening dress would be ideal. It would look stunning with all the family jewels I could purloin from Grandma Nettie. Mummy and Ted preferred a striking emerald green creation so I took both along to the studio. Tom Nisbet liked neither. 'Bright red', he insisted. 'I want to paint you wearing bright red!'

I had nothing suitable so it was time for a shopping trip. I acquired a bright red wool dress with a horseshoe neck and added a green jade necklace and earrings set in gold. The ensemble met with Tom's approval.

I enjoyed sitting for a distinguished artist and was very pleased with the result – although Ted was disappointed because the picture did not show me smiling. The experience inspired me to try my hand as an artist and I decided to apply to the Royal Hibernian Academy. I was accepted and it was arranged that I should attend on two evenings a week. On the first occasion I was helped to set up my easel by a kindly man wearing a black seaman's jumper. He said only: 'Good evening' and of course I thanked him for his assistance. The following week my kind helper was there again and so it went on. Should I tip this kind man sixpence for his trouble? I consulted Ted who advised repeatedly against tipping. Surely I should express my gratitude in some tangible way.

When I had been attending the Academy for some while, Tom Nisbet invited me to accompany him to a prestigious event, hosted by the President of the Academy, a distinguished Irish painter who had been a pupil of Sir William Orpen. I dressed myself up to the nines and Tom and I swept up the beautiful horseshoe staircase of the Academy, flunkeys on every side. At the top stood the host in all his regalia, surrounded by officials. Tom introduced me and the President turned. My jaw dropped. Thank God I had not tried to tip him! My kind helper had been none other than the President of the Royal Hibernian Academy, Sean Keating.

Canada

By the autumn of 1951, we had been back in Ireland for three and a half years. The previous year it had become apparent that Uncle Edward was ailing and the future looked bleak. A nurse moved into the house to help Dorothy to care for her father and we knew that it could only be a matter of time. In November 1951 Uncle Edward died at the age of 79.

The family were obviously grieved but Grandma Nettie was absolutely shattered. She and her brother had become increasingly close after their long estrangement and his death left a big gap in her life. She had become increasingly isolated in her huge house where she lived with one maid. I felt that she should have moved long since into something smaller but she insisted that she had come to that house as a bride and there she would remain!

As far as our own situation was concerned, Ted's job with Delap and Waller was totally secure but his salary was never going to enable us to give the children the sort of education we wanted. It was time for a mammoth decision about our future. Should we remain in Ireland or would it be better to emigrate?

Ted made a number of enquiries and we eventually decided that Canada would be a suitable place in which to build a future. Fired up with the prospect of a new life ahead, we decided to book passages. We had no idea what would be awaiting us at the other end in terms of job or accommodation but we were young and optimistic. We knew that Canada welcomed immigrants – even those who did not have jobs.

When we broke the news of our impending departure to our families we decided not to tell them that a job was not already lined up. It would certainly have smoothed Ted's path to have had letters of general recommendation from Irish people with clout and influence. But if Ted had requested such letters it would have been only a matter of hours until half of Dublin knew that the young Donovans were sailing off into the blue without a job to go to - far better to allow our families to 'assume' that a job was ready and waiting. We would be praying hard that it was!

It did not take us long to discover that passages on ships to North America were hard to come by in early 1952. Europe was still trying to recover from the rigours of war and North America beckoned invitingly to those who wanted to escape the 'old world'! Eventually we managed to secure five berths on a cargo boat, *Irish Oak*, which accepted only twelve passengers. We bade farewell to family and friends – including Marcella who declined the opportunity to accompany us.

We sailed on a day of terrible storms and throughout the voyage the weather remained frightful. The captain told us that it was the worst crossing he had ever experienced. The ship was riding high in the rough seas as it had little cargo on board and the journey lasted nearly a fortnight although it was supposed to take eight days. Fortunately I had stocked us up with Dramamine so the Donovans did not fall prey to sea sickness and were the only passengers to appear for every meal.

We were blessed in our captain and purser who were obviously fond of children and were very kind to our three. They thought up all kinds of games for nine year old Pamela and eight year old Anthony and allowed them into all sorts of places which were normally closed to passengers. The adult passengers were less fortunate and found the voyage extremely boring. Those who had not succumbed to seasickness passed the time playing cards. Ted and I tried to join in but the only card games we knew were cut-throat bridge and whist.

One day I was alone in our comfortable cabin when I was suddenly overcome with a terrible sense of fear about the future. I knelt down to pray. The thought came to me: "You are alright at this moment." It was followed by words from the twenty-third psalm "I lack nothing". That was certainly true. We were well fed, comparatively comfortable and we had a roof above our heads – even if it was a roof that creaked appallingly as the ship rolled! Panic abated and peace returned.

At long last Nova Scotia appeared on the horizon. It was a thrilling moment. We were sailing into the Bay of Fundy which has the highest tide in the world – a difference at the head of the bay of sixteen metres between high tide and low tide in a single day. Fortunately our Swedish experience had prepared us for the colossal drop in temperature – outside it was twenty degrees below. Just as well that we had hung on to our Swedish winter clothes. We disembarked by way of a steep gangway which we negotiated nervously to set foot in North America for the first time.

8

CANADA
1952-1956

The next stage of our journey from the town of St John's to Montreal took seventeen hours by train. We climbed aboard, only to discover that this was no ordinary train! Our railway carriage was upholstered in finest leather and contained pale blue armchairs. On the walls were panels of glass etched with scenes from early Canadian history. I asked the railcar man if all Canadian trains were like this. 'Oh no, Madam,' said he. 'This is the royal train, which was used last year when Princess Elizabeth and Prince Philip toured Canada. It is being taken all over the country and this week it is our turn to use it!

The high prices on the train staggered us. Fortunately we had invested in food vouchers before boarding and these had not been too expensive, but we were certainly in for some surprises when it came to the food itself. Boiled eggs arrived broken into a glass and were eaten with a long spoon and rich fruit cake was served to us with ice cream.

This was indeed a new world – and a world of contrasts! Outside it was twenty below while the train was heated to eighty degrees - I nearly died with the heat but soon came to realise that an indoor temperature of eighty was considered perfectly normal in Canada. People expected to peel off layers of clothing when they came into a house and it was quite normal to wear a sleeveless dress at home in the depths of winter.

At long last we arrived in Montreal and at the exit to the station we had our first encounter with 'magic eye' swing doors which open when approached. The children had a ball going in and out and it was a joy to hear their laughter.

We had booked ourselves into a 'Tourist Home' right in the centre of Montreal and very close to the huge cathedral of St James. We found ourselves in one very large room, containing a double bed and three small singles. On the first morning we all went to the Cathedral for Mass and never did a couple pray more fervently. It was a short and simple prayer: 'Father, HELP!' We knew hardly a soul in Canada. We had very little money and, most worrying of all, we had NO JOB!

After Mass the first priority was breakfast. Across the road was 'Murrays' where the prices were high but the children were hungry – they all seemed to have hollow legs! At Murrays we discovered the Canadian dish of all dishes – pancakes with butter and maple syrup - comparatively cheap and certainly cheerful!

The first priority had to be Ted's job. He told me that he was going to look through the Yellow Pages and visit some engineering firms in the city to see if he could land anything. Off he went, and I promised that the children and I would stay in our room and pray! At lunchtime we went to an expensive snack bar where we filled up on soup and in the evening Ted arrived back with good news: 'I have the offer of three jobs, which shall I take?' I answered like a shot: 'The one that pays the most!' My 'vision' was limited to the cost of feeding three hungry children!

Ted accepted the best paying job so one problem was solved. The next was accommodation. In fourteen days our furniture would be arriving from Ireland and where would it go? We had one 'contact' in Montreal. A man named "Bill" who was the brother of the Canadian Consul in Dublin. When we were departing Dublin the Consul told us that his brother lived on the outskirts of Montreal and he had given us the phone number. We had accepted this casually and as a polite way of saying "goodbye". We had no real intention of contacting brother Bill.

Things looked very different after a single day in this expensive city and we plucked up the courage to telephone. First thing the following morning Bill was on our doorstep. He took one look at our multi-occupancy room, asked what we were paying and told us it was far too much. Bill piled us into his car and drove off around the enormous city in search of an apartment to rent.

Two hours later we arrived in Westmount and I spotted a large apartment block on Sherbrooke

Street overlooking a park. The sign outside read: *Apartments for rent – No dogs, No pets, No children!* Despite this discouraging beginning I felt prompted to ask Bill to stop. He was very reluctant and told me that I had better go inside by myself if I was really determined to try my luck.

Through the front door I went and discovered that the block was owned by a most unusual lady. She welcomed me, listened patiently to my saga about three children sitting outside in the car and my conviction that God would help us. She asked how much money we had, where we were staying and how much it cost. I answered all her questions like a little girl and she responded in the same way as Bill: 'That price is ridiculous. You must leave the Tourist Home immediately because I have an apartment for you here! Your children will certainly make some of the tenants mad, but I am the boss!'

I explained that our furniture would not be arriving for fourteen days which might present a problem. "Fiddlesticks" said this extraordinary landlady. "I have some bits and pieces in the basement that you can use and I can lend you bedding and sheets till your own things arrives'. I didn't even ask to see the apartment but returned to the car to share our good news. Bill was transfixed! He said that he and his wife would feed us that night and take us to the new apartment the following afternoon.

Our new apartment was perfectly adequate and had the added advantage of being only a couple of blocks from a Catholic Church and a Catholic school. We promptly enrolled the children.

Two weeks later our furniture arrived. We discovered to our sorrow that the Dublin firm to whom we had paid a small fortune had done a shabby job of packing and crating our possessions. Everything was a mess and I sat down and wept!

Canadian life

It did not take us long to discover one of the greatest Canadian outdoor sports - ice-skating. We bought skates for the whole family but Ted and I found it very hard to remain upright – let alone skate anywhere! One morning Anthony asked me what I would give him when he could skate around the school rink without falling. Imagining that the children would be having just as many problems as Ted and me, I recklessly promised to hand over a dollar! That afternoon, Anthony informed me that I owed him a dollar - and proceeded to skate round and round the rink to prove it! The boy was a natural skater – completely fearless. I was proud to give him his dollar.

Anthony was equally fearless on skis. One Saturday Bill and his wife invited us to join them at their place in the Laurentian Mountains at St Sauveur where there was excellent skiing. The children were thrilled but Ted and I felt slightly nervous. We had acquired skis during our six months in Sweden and brought them to Canada but had little confidence in our abilities.

When we arrived at our destination, Bill paid his entrance fee for the ski lift while the Donovans remained on the lower slopes doing gentle runs.

After a while Anthony came and asked if he could have money for the ski lift. We explained that the upper slopes were for experienced skiers and that in a few months he might be able to cope with steeper slopes but for the moment he had to stay with us. Anthony was most insistent, and assured us that he *knew* he would be able to go down the mountain with the experienced skiers. He was utterly confident and we knew how quickly he had learned to skate. We gulped, counted our pennies and paid out the enormous fee for a day ticket on the ski lift.

Up went Anthony. When he reached the top my heart was in my mouth as I watched him poise for 'take off'. He swooped down that slope with the ease of a pro, swaying this way and that to take in the curves and contours of the mountain. The boy had no fear; he never had a fall and spent the entire day going up in the lift and swooping back down the slope. Eventually he became so proficient that he didn't need poles at all and 'wore out' the underside of his skis.

I got into a daily routine of packing Ted and the children off to work and to school and then going to the nine o'clock Mass. Ted was able to go to Mass at midday. These were the days of obligatory fasting from midnight if one wished to receive Holy Communion so Ted left the house without a proper breakfast.. There was slight mitigation in the form of porridge which had the consistency of water. Ted started the day with a bowl of this revolting gruel and then went hungry until lunchtime.

Fortunately I was able to produce something considerably more appetising than watery porridge when he came home at night. I had always enjoyed cooking and the children soon wanted to bring their friends home for meals. I had the bright idea of encouraging Canadian children to broaden their culinary experiences by tasting some typical examples of Irish and English cooking. Alas, I was to discover to my cost that Canadian kids were interested only in hamburgers, chips, coca-cola, frankfurters and ice cream – 'foreign' food had no appeal whatsoever!

Notwithstanding the youthful passion for frankfurters and ice cream the shops seemed to be crammed with delicious food. There was a widespread craze for getting hold of unusual recipes which had a definite element of one-upmanship. I had a friend who was a particularly good cook and justly proud of her recipes. She gave the impression of being happy to share them with others but confided the fact that she always omitted an ingredient when writing down a recipe for an enquirer. I have always felt honoured to be asked for a recipe and it seemed terrible that this friend's unsuspecting friends would spend hours and days trying to follow faulty recipes! Her deception took my breath away!

With so much fattening food on tap, it was no great surprise to discover that everyone in Canada appeared to be diet conscious. I discovered that each bathroom possessed a set of scales and made a point of weighing myself in my friends' bathrooms, only to discover that a number of them were pulling the wool over their eyes! I knew my own weight to the last ounce but on some sets of bathroom scales I 'appeared' to be ten pounds lighter! The owners were obviously deceiving themselves that their diets were working!

Next door to us lived Mr and Mrs Harterre. She was a psychiatrist and he was the director of a big meat packing enterprise. Mrs Harterre was a butterball but desperate to lose weight and I was 'pleasingly plump' and also wanting to shed my extra pounds. Mrs Harterre lent me her diet cookbook and we came to an arrangement. I would use the diet book to prepare three meals a day for her and she would provide me with all the meat I needed for my own family. What a gift! I faithfully prepared every single meal for Mrs Harterre in accordance with the diet book and a meal for my own family. Little by little, I shed my extra pounds but Mrs Harterre didn't seem to be changing shape! Eventually the cat came out of the bag. Every afternoon she was 'topping up' on a couple of large choc bars! In my innocence I had never even suspected.

Food was not the only area in which I was naïve. One afternoon I was walking down the road in my warm black astrakhan coat which had been a gift from Ted. A car slowed down on the opposite side of the road and the driver waved. I imagined that I must know the man so I waved back. Perhaps this was a friendly neighbour offering a lift. The man beckoned me across. When I reached the passenger door he leant across and opened it. I peered inside, racking my brains to try and remember who this could be. In the end I had to own up: 'I am sorry. I just cannot remember your name'. 'Never mind, honey', said the man: 'Step inside and we'll get to know one another!'

I hastily backed away and laughed all the way home! Nobody had warned me that life in Canada was not quite the same as life in Dublin! In Montreal a 'friendly' man in a car might have something else on his mind apart from a good turn to a neighbour!

Liz

The time had now come for six year old Liz to prepare for her First Holy Communion. I knew that her First Communion dress would involve a big outlay but had not bargained for the wonderful community spirit of Canada. One day I was coming out of church when a lady I hardly knew approached me: 'I know your little girl is making her First Holy Communion, and I wonder whether you would allow me to lend her a dress. I have this long white dress which has only been worn once and I would be so happy if you would allow your daughter to wear it'. That sort of thing just did not happen in Ireland or in England.

We had similar experiences when people found out that we were looking for anything at all. Someone would say 'Don't go and buy it. We probably have just what you want in the attic!' We reckoned that this generosity must be a survival of the frontier spirit that bonded people together and enabled them to survive when they first landed in North America – many of them with little more than the clothes they stood up in.

Liz's 'borrowed' First Communion dress was exquisite: white organdie with pleats top and bottom. Some kindly Episcopalian friends had taken a shine to our kids and I showed the wife this beautiful creation.

One day she appeared with a little white organdie bag for Elizabeth to carry on the great day. This presented a problem. The nuns at the convent were adamant that none of the girls should carry handbags because it might distract them. I was in full agreement but at the same time I did not want to hurt my kind Episcopalian friend who was planning to come to see Liz in all her glory! I puzzled and prayed and eventually came up with the answer. With great care, I stitched the little bag onto Elizabeth's dress so that it was too firmly attached for the nuns to remove but could be snipped off afterwards!

Pamela, Anthony and Liz

Liz was due to make her First Confession on a Thursday. On the Friday our three children were all to receive the sacrament of Confirmation and Liz would then make her First Communion on the Saturday.

Ted and I were not happy about all the children being confirmed together. Pamela and Anthony were ten and nine but Liz was only six. We did not want any of them to receive confirmation until they were well into their teens and could make a comparatively mature decision to follow Jesus. Despite our reservations, the custom of early confirmation seemed to be so much taken for granted in Canada that we did not feel able to register a protest.

One morning at around the time of her First Communion Liz failed to come out of her bedroom. I went in and saw her lying rigid on her bed. I felt her forehead – it was very hot. My heart lurched. Had Liz succumbed to the dreaded polio? Trying to remain calm I said: "Are you alright, darling? A tear rolled down Liz's cheek. My whole being was filled with fear. I tried not to panic and said gently: 'Lift up your head, darling." Another tear rolled down. She replied: 'I can't move my head.' I knew that a stiff neck and a temperature were among the early signs of polio.

Ted rang the doctor while I wiped Liz's fevered brow with a wet towel as tears coursed down her face. 'Mummy', she said: 'You are going to be very angry'. Angry? With a child with polio? I said 'Of course I won't be angry – the doctor is coming, and you will soon be better'. Liz repeated that I was going to be very angry. 'Why?' I enquired. 'Because I have done something you forbade me to do.' What on earth could the child have done? A few more tears rolled down her cheeks and out came the sorry tale! 'I have taken chewing gum to bed, and it is stuck to the back of my head!' I investigated.

Sure enough, Liz's head was anchored to the pillow with two great blobs of rock hard chewing gum! We had to cut it away and a chunk of her hair was removed as well. As I was performing the 'operation' on my tearful daughter, the doctor arrived – and was kind enough not to laugh!

Moving to Kingston

On the spiritual front, I had been feeling the need of a director but few of the priests in French-speaking Montreal could converse easily in English and my command of French was far from perfect. One day I was praying about this matter of a spiritual director and trying to 'listen' to the Lord.

It was as if I heard him say: 'Pick a dead one!' What a funny suggestion. Was this a 'nudge' from God or my vivid imagination? The following day Ted received his quarterly copy of the *Ampleforth Journal*. It contained a flyer about Abbot Columba Marmion whose writings had helped me so much in Dublin. Apparently the books were reprinting and I decided to try Abbot Marmion as my 'dead' spiritual advisor! I ordered his trilogy: *Christ, the Life of the Soul*, *Christ the Life of the Monk* and *Christ in His Mysteries* and found them exceedingly helpful – although *Christ, the Life of the Monk* might seem an odd choice for a wife and mother! One way or another I was an extremely busy wife and mother! Ted was studying for his Masters degree in engineering and on top of everything else; I was typing and retyping his dissertation.

After a year and a half in Montreal Ted arrived home one evening to announce that the firm had asked him to move to Kingston, Ontario, a hundred miles south west of Montreal. Ted had been asked to become resident engineer at the first Terylene factory to be built in Canada. Neither of us was very excited at the prospect of such a move, but there was little choice. If Ted was going to keep his job with the firm he had to go to Kingston more or less straightaway and try to find a house to rent. We broke the news to the children and hoped that the schools in Kingston would be of a reasonable standard. Ted set off and was able to find a suitable bungalow.

There was no doubt about the suitability of the bungalow when we arrived in August 1953. With the arrival of winter it became chillingly clear that the building was insufficiently insulated – icicles were discovered inside the front door! Something had to be done immediately and we were lucky to find a more suitable house which had been built around 1800. In Canadian terms a house that was 150 years old was rare. Strangers would knock at the door and ask to look around this 'antique' – we were happy to welcome them although their enthusiasm surprised us. In Ireland we had buildings that went back a thousand years old and were still in use – a house dating from 1800 seemed almost modern!

Some aspects of that old house were very positive. On the debit side, it lacked a good many modern conveniences. The kitchen was lousy and had an ancient pot-bellied stove which jutted out into the middle of the room. We could afford only to lay new linoleum and paint the walls. I could have accepted that kitchen more easily if I had been less aware of the modern kitchens in the houses of some of my friends. At least we had a little car which was not in its first youth but enabled us to get around and take the children on outings.

My first summer in Canada had nearly killed me and I had been warned that it would take me a year to adjust to the heat because of the leaking valve in my heart. We moved to Kingston during our second summer but I was not really feeling much better. Fortunately I acquired a wonderful doctor in Kingston who was a Catholic and a real gift from God. The cardiologists in Dublin had told me to take my pulse night and morning. I had faithfully continued to do this; – and been duly depressed by any irregularity. Dr Koster of Kingston did me a great favour in forbidding me to continue taking my pulse. I obeyed him and felt the better for it.

Dr Koster also came to my rescue by encouraging me to have a comparatively simple operation which should have been carried out years previously. From childhood I had suffered from sore throats and tonsillitis and these recurred in Kingston with the added complication of a constant high temperature. This persisted for six months while Dr Koster tried everything possible to bring it down. Eventually he insisted that the tonsils be removed. I was admitted to the local hospital where a surgeon who was a friend and a Catholic would carry out the operation.

When I came round from the anaesthetic I was told that I had spent four hours on the operating table because they had been unable to stop the bleeding I awoke to find a piece of cotton wool attached by string to my cheek and going down into my throat where a swab was attached to the source of the bleeding. I felt as if I was going to choke any minute. The surgeon explained that I had to keep that swab in place for as long as possible: 'Just try to keep it there for an hour'. I was horrified - and also very thirsty although swallowing was impossible.

At the end of the first hour the surgeon coaxed me into allowing the swab to remain for a further sixty minutes: 'I know that you are a brave woman with great powers of endurance!' Good psychology! The choking sensation was frightful and I was burning up with thirst. The hours passed and at the end of each one the surgeon reappeared and persuaded me to keep going. On the positive side, Ted was with me all the time and he engaged a private nurse to wet my lips with iced water throughout the night.

Opposite my bed was a crucifix at which I gazed and gazed as I tried to endure the terrible sensation of choking, coupled with burning thirst and a high temperature. The words of the Lord during the crucifixion were vividly present to me: 'I thirst' [John 19:28}. Deep within my spirit I seemed to feel the thirst of the Lord for souls. From that day forward I have sensed within me a profound desire to evangelise others in order to assuage the Lord's deep thirst for souls.

In the end, I managed to keep that cotton wool in place for more than twenty-four hours but the moment finally came when I could stand it no longer. I was convinced that I was about to choke to death and sent word to the surgeon. True to his promise, he came running and gently removed the swab. Mercifully, the bleeding had ceased. After that ordeal it took me a long time to get my strength back. I learnt subsequently that the surgeon had been afraid I was going to die on the operating table.

Spiritual developments

Ted's worksite was outside the city on the shores of Lake Ontario and although he had to leave early in the morning, we were at least able to get to Mass together. Our little church had rough wooden floors and the parish priest told us that a Russian émigré called 'Catherine' had insisted on scrubbing these regularly. We discovered that the 'émigré' was in fact Catherine de Hueck Doherty who had founded the Madonna House Apostolate in nearby Combermere. This apostolate was to grow into the worldwide 'family' of Madonna Houses in which laymen and women and priests live a life of poverty, friendship and hospitality and serve the local area. Catherine had also pioneered the Russian concept of 'Poustinia': the provision of small hermitages in which individuals can spend twenty-four hours in solitude, fasting and prayer. Unfortunately we were never able to meet her, but I believe Catherine Doherty to have been one of the great Christian women of our time. Her life was a great adventure which took her from the wealth of Czarist Russia to the poverty of a refugee when she arrived in North America.

In Kingston Ted became chairman of a Bible Study Group and was able to take part in an annual silent retreat for men at a Jesuit retreat house. I wanted to find a similar retreat for women but the only religious house which could offer such a thing was 135 miles away in Alexandria Bay. The director of this centre was prepared to host a retreat if I could find the participants and arrange a priest to lead us. Collecting people wasn't easy until I discovered that I had been going about it in the wrong way.

A priest I did not much like telephoned me to ask how I was getting along. I gave him my spiel about unsuccessful attempts to invite people to take time away from the hurly-burly to attend to God. He responded bluntly: 'No wonder you haven't got anybody – that's a rotten way of going about it. You want to say: 'How would you like a weekend away from housework, kids and cooking meals? How would you like some time to wander in the woods, read that book you can't get around to and talk to God about a special request?" I changed my approach and people signed up fast. I had learned a valuable lesson about starting from where people are 'at' in their own lives.

We still needed a few more people to make the retreat viable so I decided to contact the Archbishop of Kingston to ask if he would announce a silent retreat for women from his pulpit in the Cathedral. I made an appointment to visit the Archbishop and his response was discouraging: 'Mrs Donovan, I don't approve of retreats – women should be home looking after their families and cooking meals! All they need is to go to Mass on Sunday!' I was shocked at his attitude and told him so. I asked if he was forbidding me to arrange the retreat. He told me that he was not actually forbidding it - but neither was he prepared to help in any way!

One of the priests in his residence told me subsequently that the Archbishop continued to remember my visit and various other Donovan undertakings. From time to time his Grace would apparently lean across the table during meals to enquire what the Donovans were 'up to'! Perhaps I had approached him in the wrong way. According to my priest friend in the residence, the Archbishop had a dry sense of humour. I was told that one of the altar boys lost his bike and had prayed to St Joseph for its return - without success. When word of this unanswered prayer reached the Archbishop he had muttered: 'Foolish boy – he is praying to the wrong saint! Joseph lost the Child for three days!'

With or without the help of the Archbishop, forty-five women eventually signed up for the silent retreat in Alexandria Bay. I had arranged for a well known preacher to lead us but at the last minute, this man was told by his bishop that he could not come. A different priest was assigned to us and I was indignant - and still more indignant when I had heard the first talk. This new priest seemed to be concentrating on his memories of being a university chaplain and telling funny stories - not much 'spiritual' input! I discovered afterwards that God certainly knew what he was doing in sending us that particular priest. Most of the participants thought the retreat had been a roaring success and it became a yearly event. Bad luck, good luck, who knows?

From my point of view, the best thing about that retreat was a new friendship with a young woman called Pomona Pefanis. Pom was sheer gift – and just as 'odd' as me. She had been baptised in the Holy Spirit and was eager to read Scripture. She had come on the retreat with the encouragement of Father Hendrick, a Dutch priest from Amsterdam who had suffered in the dreadful Dachau concentration camp. Fr Hendrick said little about his experiences in the camp but revealed that his greatest suffering had been the experience of watching men being tortured for breaking 'rules'. This horrified me and also made me think more deeply about the crucifixion of Jesus. I subsequently discovered a book by a French doctor, Pierre Barbet, *A Surgeon at the Foot of the Cross*. It brought home to me the appalling reality of crucifixion and for years I used that book during Holy Week.

Pom had been born in South Africa to parents in the diplomatic service who had moved to Canada when her father was appointed South African High Commissioner in Ottawa. Pom had lived in style until she married her husband Sarandi and moved to Kingston but she was delightfully classless and had no time for the apartheid regime. She told me that she had created a 'diplomatic incident' in Cape Town when she acted as sponsor for a black South African who was being received into the Catholic Church.

When Pom's parents were posted to Ottawa they brought with them their superb cook. In the world of first class diplomatic cuisine the cook at the South African High Commission stood head and shoulders above the rest. Invitations to dine with Pom's parents were the passport to an evening of culinary delights. One young guest was unaware of an unwritten rule which precludes guests at an Embassy or High Commission from requesting a recipe. This young person dined several times at the South African High Commission and was pressing in her demands for the recipe for a delicious creamy dessert. Pom's mother explained that the recipe belonged to the cook in the hope that that would put an end to the matter. The guest failed to take the hint and continued to press for the recipe. Pom's mother finally told her that she would have to ask the cook herself. She took the young lady downstairs to meet the queen of the kitchen. The cook was obviously displeased but the young lady seemed blissfully unaware of the fact. She produced paper and pencil and demanded a list of ingredients. "Eggs, cream, butter and milk" said the cook coldly. The guest interrupted: 'How much milk do you use? The cook fixed her with a steely eye and her answer put paid to any further questioning: 'Weeell – I use about a mouthful!"

Pom was the best friend I ever had. She was a very special person and our relationship might have become too close and excluded our husbands but fortunately this was never the case. We spent a lot of time together because we both loathed housework – Pom had never had to do any and I had been blessed with domestic help in Europe. We decided that the best way to get through the dreaded chores was to do them together. We would join forces in one or other house and do the cleaning together which left us with time to pray and read Scripture.

Schools and schooling

Ted and I were the only Irish couple in Kingston and when the Irish Ambassador and his wife paid a visit we were invited to receive them. I did a lot of cooking and the visit seemed to go well. The following day a huge box was delivered to my front door by a local florist. When I opened it, I was delighted to discover a beautiful bouquet of flowers - a 'thank you' from the Ambassador.

That night Ted and I were attending a charity ball in aid of the local hospital. I had decided to wear my old black velvet evening dress with a heart shaped top and yards of material in the skirt. It was a romantic creation but somewhat elderly. The flowers gave me an idea for improvement. I cut down the stems until only the flower heads remained and sewed them around the hem of my black frock. The result was dramatic and my 'creation' received a mention in the local press. Readers must have imagined that Mrs Donovan had a very

Ted and I – Charity Ball

wealthy husband who could afford to splash out on *fresh* carnations in the depths of winter.

Although our finances were certainly improving, we were very far from being wealthy. We did, however, decide that we could afford to invite my mother to come for a visit and offered to pay her fare. Mummy accepted the invitation and the children were overjoyed at the prospect of seeing Granny again – Pamela, especially, because she was 'favourite grandchild'; my mother made no bones about that!

Pamela was now thirteen and had greatly enjoyed her schooldays in Montreal where her education had been in French. She had had to revert to English in Kingston but was anxious to pursue her French schooling if at all possible. We knew that we could now afford to send Pamela to boarding school in Montreal but wanted her to come home for weekends like the other children. Kingston was too far away for this to be possible and we talked the situation over with my mother during her visit. We then came up with the wild idea that my mother should remain in Canada and get a job. She was only in her early fifties and very outgoing and gregarious. We were sure she would land any job for which she applied. Mummy liked the idea of staying in Canada, especially because she could see a way of solving our problem over Pamela's education. She would apply for a job in Montreal and rent a flat where Pamela could spend the weekends with her grandmother.

This idea met with everybody's approval and kind friends in Montreal helped my mother with flat hunting while she turned her attention to the job-market. To our astonishment, my mother landed a job as a bookkeeper. She must have managed it on charm alone because she could hardly add two and two without using her fingers! Somehow she managed to hold down that job and I imagine that she must have brought a lot of joy to her fellow workers because she was immensely kind to everybody and always full of stories. Pamela went to school at the Villa Maria and was able to go to Granny for weekends which delighted both of them.

Anthony and Liz remained at school in Kingston and Anthony had now been trained as an altar boy. I recall an occasion on which he was asked to serve at a solemn Mass for the dead which was a complicated business in those days before the Second Vatican Council [1962-5]. On this occasion the Archbishop of Kingston was presiding with several priests in attendance and Anthony was the only altar boy. In the 1950's priests wore square black headpieces as they processed to the altar where they would remove these 'birettas' and hand them to the altar boy – Anthony - who piled them up on a table. I was in the congregation and have never been more distracted in my life. The requirements of an altar boy seemed to defeat Anthony and he was constantly in the wrong place at the wrong time! His greatest moment came at the end of the service when the priests turned to leave the altar and collect their birettas from the server. The Archbishop was alright – he was the only one with a mitre and Anthony returned it in good order. As far as the priests were concerned, our son handed out birettas like newspapers, regardless of which headpiece belonged to which man. Each priest attempted to don 'his' biretta only to find that it didn't belong to him at all and was either far too large or much too small. They gave up and walked away from the altar with the ill-fitting birettas clutched in their hands.

Anthony was doing well at the Cathedral school but we knew that we were going to have to make some serious decisions about his future education The Cathedral School had shortcomings in terms of discipline – we were particularly concerned by the fact that one of the pupils had hit a nun and knocked her down. We were also concerned because of the anti-Catholic feeling in Kingston at that time. The Catholic children were not permitted to take part in some of the leisure activities. This frustrated Anthony who was a normal lively boy and wanted to join in everything. We also heard that boys in the town had been accused of something that made no sense whatsoever to us – 'glue-sniffing'. We were baffled beyond words and did not realise that we were having our first encounter with the drug scene!

Ted and I prayed hard and came to the painful decision that it would be in Anthony's best interests to go to England and continue his education at Ampleforth. There was a waiting list for the school, but Ted's brother, Dom Bruno, told us that he would speak to the Abbot and to the Headmaster. Ampleforth told us that they would accept him, but only after a year at a suitable preparatory school in England. This was Elston Hall in Nottinghamshire which could apparently bring Anthony up to the required standard.

The prospect of sending Anthony so far away left me feeling that my heart was being torn out of my breast. I tried to keep the feeling to myself because Anthony liked the idea of going to England and I was assured by several people that he would be receiving the best education in the world. But others told me that they could not consider sending their own sons so far away.

We needed a great deal of money to rig Anthony out. We obtained this in a somewhat surprising fashion. When we had first arrived in Montreal Ted and I had taken part in the Dale Carnegie course on 'Effective Speaking and Public Relations'. We had done well and had gone on to train as Dale Carnegie teachers. The fees from running our own courses in Kingston enabled us to equip Anthony for Ampleforth.

We booked his passage on a liner out of Montreal and the twelve year old set off on his long journey. Anthony seemed very young to travel alone but we gathered from his letters that a kindly priest had befriended him on the voyage and he arrived safely. From then onwards, his letters home were sometimes far from happy. It was clear that Elston Hall left a good deal to be desired and I cried myself to sleep on many a night and agonised about whether or not we were really doing the best thing for our son.

Meanwhile, nine-year old Liz was doing well at the Cathedral school. She was a happy, bright, cheerful little girl and receiving good marks – but after our experience with Anthony and the entrance exam we were wary of 'good marks'. One day Liz came home and announced that she had come second in class but was not going to be moved up the following year. We were very angry and went straight off to visit the school inspector. He told us that Liz was not being moved up because it would upset the numbers to have one more little girl in the next class. We argued with him but the man was adamant. We knew that this bright little girl was going to be bored silly if she was held back a year. Something had to be done – and that 'something' was drastic and was going to involve us in yet another move.

9

BOSTON
1956-1957

If Liz was going to get a good education it looked as if we would have to find a private school for her as well as for Anthony and Pamela. There was no way that Ted was going to be able to finance private education for three children so he was going to have to find a better paid job. The only viable possibility was a job in the United States and that would mean yet another move!

We agreed that Boston would be the best place to start job hunting; not only was it a centre of learning, but there were strong links with Ireland. As Ted's 'secretary' I wrote 64 'job-seeking' letters which resulted in the offer of two interviews and a third which came about through the kindness of a friend. Ted took some holiday leave and we left Liz in the care of friends and travelled overnight to Boston.

We booked into the cheapest room in the prestigious Parker House Hotel at the foot of Beacon Hill. Ted set off for his appointments while I took a nap and then decided to find a church, although I was sure that it was far too late for Mass. I walked into St Anthony's Church to find Mass in progress with a large congregation in attendance. Most people went forward to receive Holy Communion which indicated that they had been fasting since midnight. After nearly three years in Kingston it looked as if we might at last be moving into a fervent Catholic community.

Ted returned to our hotel with the offer of a job in the Cambridge district at a good salary. Now we had only to discover somewhere to live and find a suitable school for Liz! We rented a temporary apartment in Boston which would at least give us a roof over our heads - but had no idea where to start the hunt for a school.

Back in Kingston, Ted handed in his notice and we packed up and terminated the rental of our old house. April 1956 found us driving to Boston and as soon as we reached the city we decided to stop off at the local Catholic Church to give thanks for a safe journey and ask God's help in finding accommodation and a really good school for Liz. Coming out of the church, we found ourselves alongside a middle aged couple. The woman had noticed the Ontario number plate on our car. She said a kindly word to Liz and explained that she came from Ontario. We launched into our saga about coming to Boston to seek better schooling for our daughter. The woman leapt to our assistance. She had a daughter who would be happy to help us because she knew all about schooling in Boston. We exchanged addresses and the following morning the daughter arrived at our door in a huge station wagon. Talk about God moving fast!

She told us about a particularly good school run by the Society of the Sacred Heart: it was very expensive and apparently had a waiting list a mile long so we hadn't a hope. She suggested that we drive around the grounds: 'So that you can at least have the pleasure of seeing how lovely they are'.

The grounds were indeed superb and we were about to drive past the front door when Ted asked our kind friend to draw up. He reminded us that Jesus had told us to *ask* and Ted was about to take him at his word! He wanted us all to pray that we could get Liz into this school if it was the will of God.

Our driver was a little taken aback but she agreed. Ted, Liz and I got out of the car, rang the doorbell and asked to see the headmistress. In due course Mother Hill arrived. This was a woman who exuded holiness and we could see at once that she was interested in our story and interested in Liz. She told us about their long waiting list and their astronomical fees! We didn't think we had a hope and then, out of the blue, Mother Hill came out with: 'Of course, we will take Elizabeth. The fees will be adjusted to whatever you can afford, and Elizabeth can start tomorrow!'. We tottered back to the car in a state of shock. Our astonished driver took us out to lunch to celebrate!

The next hurdle was permanent accommodation. We had been given the address of friends of friends and on our second morning in Boston I telephoned to announce our arrival and ask for help. The wife came straight round to see me and was duly appalled at the sum we were paying for our temporary accommodation. She was determined to get us out of there and offered to drive me to visit 'apartment agents'. I had memories of the extraordinary way in which we had 'found' our apartment in Montreal and decided to try the same tactics in Boston. I persuaded her to forgo 'apartment agents' and just to 'drive around'.

When we reached the Belmont area I asked her to stop. We were not far from Ted's workplace and en route to the Sacred Heart Convent. We walked up and down the roads but could see no 'To Let' signs. My driver was becoming increasingly sceptical when I suddenly spotted a 'duplex': a property on two levels - each one quite separate from the other. On the ground floor level there were no curtains, which indicated that the property was being decorated.

To the astonishment of my driver I marched straight up the path and knocked on the door. The lady who opened it seemed rather nervous when I asked her if by chance the lower level might be available to rent. First she told me that her sons dealt with any business matters but then relaxed and admitted that the lower level would be going on the market in a couple of weeks. But her sons were adamant that there were to be no children and no dogs. We had three children and a big friendly golden retriever!

It looked hopeless - but I was praying hard in the knowledge that the Lord likes to work in 'hopeless' situations! To cut a long story short, the woman and her sons agreed that we could have the duplex at a reasonable rent – children, dog and all!

Boston is such a beautiful city – a real joy by day and by night. We discovered that one could buy tickets for the Boston Symphony Orchestra for a dollar on the day of a concert - and we revelled in the Boston Pops Orchestra conducted by the American musical icon Arthur Fiedler with his mane of white hair.

In order to be sure of getting to Mass each day we went along to the parish church in Belmont - only to find that the earliest Mass was at 7.30 - far too late for Ted who needed to get to the office early. We decided to go and talk to the parish priest and made a point of praying before we knocked at his door.

Monsignor Sheridan had arrived in Boston from Ireland many years previously. He was thrilled to discover that some 'real' Irish people had moved into his parish. There was no shortage of Irish Americans whose great-grandparents had emigrated – but we were the real McCoy! We chatted away: the man was obviously very gregarious and a great story teller.

When Monsignor Sheridan finally finished speaking, we explained our problem about the time of his first Mass. The Monsignor summoned one of the three curates. When he arrived, he introduced us. 'Meet Mr and Mrs Donovan and their daughter Elizabeth'. The Monsignor addressed the curate with all the authority of the head of the house! 'From tomorrow morning the first Mass will take place at 7.00am. You will be saying it!'

Life in Boston

It was reassuring to know that Liz was in a first class school and, as far as I was concerned, that

Sacred Heart convent became an 'open door' for all sorts of things. The nuns took a real interest in our family and one of them asked another mother at the school, Anita Wingard, to take this 'young woman from Ireland' under her wing. Years later Anita told me that when she was first asked to befriend me she had imagined that I came from the bogs!

On Wednesdays I joined a group of mothers and friends who were helping to make church vestments. It was the custom for some young married women to donate their wedding dresses to the convent so that these could be made into vestments for the priest to wear at the altar and I sewed away at the beautiful silks and satins while listening to the fascinating conversations around me. The sewing ladies opened my eyes to a whole new world of luxury lifestyles and 'coming out' balls in New York: I was stupefied at the amount of money spent on such entertainments for teenage daughters. One of the women in the group made friends with me and took me to lunch. Years later I discovered that she was the aunt of President Kennedy and another of the ladies had been at school with Rose Kennedy, the President's redoubtable mother.

One day I overheard one of the ladies say to another: 'See you here on Friday at 3pm for the talk'. The following Friday was a 'First Friday' of the month with its special dedication to the Sacred Heart of Jesus. When I learnt that there was to be a talk I thought: 'Goody-goody' and took myself along. I discovered that the ladies in the vestment making group also belonged to a lay association,

'The Children of Mary' who have a particular dedication to the Mother of Jesus. They met once a month for a talk in the chapel followed by Benediction and a very swanky tea. Two ladies sat at each end of a huge table, serving tea and coffee from silver teapots and coffeepots. The headmistress would make a point of coming along to pay her respects.

One day I realised that some sort of enrolment ceremony took place periodically in the chapel, when some of the ladies in the group became 'Children of Mary' and received a medal. I wondered when I, too, could become a 'Child of Mary' and consulted the Headmistress. She looked puzzled and asked me whether 'my sponsor' had not told me about that. It was my turn to look puzzled: 'What is a sponsor?' The Headmistress explained that 'my sponsor' was the person who had invited me to come to the meetings. 'Nobody invited me, I just joined in!' The headmistress looked amazed and then laughed: 'Don't worry! There is a committee meeting next week and I will have you included in the next enrolment.

A few days later I was called into her office and she looked troubled: 'I feel very unhappy about what I have to tell you, but the ladies have decided that you have to go back to the beginning and start a year's probation because you just 'turned up' and did not have a sponsor. I decided that I didn't want to be enrolled after all but would just continue to attend the meetings.

The Headmistress continued to take a great interest in us and certainly did not confine her attentions to Liz. She had heard all about Pamela and decided that she wanted her to leave Montreal and join Liz at the convent in Boston. We were not at all sure how Pamela would respond to such a suggestion because she had been so keen to pursue her education in French. A move to Boston would also have implications for my mother who would be unlikely to want to stay in Montreal if Pamela decided to move to the United States.

There was only one way to sort this out. Ted and I went up to Montreal to discuss the whole thing. Rather to my surprise, Pamela leapt at the opportunity of moving to Boston and my mother was keen to come too.

We knew that Pamela had a place waiting for her at the convent so the next step was to find an apartment for my mother. Apartments in Boston were hard to come by but we eventually found a gem in Battle Street, close to Harvard Square – complete with a tiny turret in the sitting room. After she moved in, my mother discovered that she had lovely neighbours, one of them being the sister of T.S. Eliot and the two became firm friends. This lady had a beloved cat that was adept at negotiating the elevator. All the tenants knew that they had to open the elevator door when the cat wished to enter and press the button for the correct floor so that it could disembark!

With the move to Boston and Ted's new job, we could stretch our finances to cover private education for three children. We had not, however, bargained for 'extras' – the new tennis racket, the replacement for a lost blazer and the collection for Reverend Mother's Feast Day. Sometimes it was really hard to make ends meet. Visits to the hairdresser became a thing of the past and we often had to turn down invitations because we just did not have the money to return hospitality. Ted was working overtime and even with that 'extra' money we were often down to counting dimes! But however dire our straits, Ted remained determinedly optimistic and had bottomless trust that God would take care of us. I have never met anybody who trusted God so consistently, however dire the situation.

In England Anthony had now moved from Elston Hall to Ampleforth which was an improvement. But his continuing absence was a real grief to me although I tried not to let it be known. In February 1957 I concocted a huge birthday cake for his fourteenth birthday - rich wedding cake mixture topped with marzipan and royal icing and costing a bomb to crate up and mail. But it was worth every dollar and the cake arrived at Ampleforth in good time for the birthday on 22nd March. Anthony wrote to tell me that he kept the cake in his locker and chopped off hunks with a penknife – I never learnt whether anybody else was allowed a bite!

The following summer Anthony at long last came home for the long holidays. It was wonderful to have him back and we tried to do everything to give him a really good time. All sorts of kind people were eager to entertain him including Monsignor Sheridan who had become a good friend. One day he arrived at the door with a request: 'Would Anthony like to pack his bag, and join me for a few days at the White Mountains?' Would he! Anthony was thrilled! Monsignor Sheridan could not have been kinder and took our son all around this beautiful mountainous area of New Hampshire with its waterfalls and wonderful mountain views. The pair stayed in hotels and Anthony was particularly delighted that Monsignor Sheridan always allowed him to choose whatever he wanted from the menu – the perfect holiday treat for a fourteen year old with hollow legs!

Monsignor Sheridan was very good to me as well as to Anthony. I had become a member of the Dominican Third Order in Ireland and renewed my membership in Boston. I discovered that the Dominicans were running a theological course at Emmanuel College based on the great theological treatise Summa Theologiae, compiled by St Thomas Aquinas in the thirteenth century. Alas, the course was open only to graduates and the application form had to be countersigned by someone who would vouch for the applicant's academic ability! Ted would be alright as a graduate of Dublin University but I didn't think I had a hope. I shared the sad news with Monsignor Sheridan over a cup of tea. 'Don't worry, Darling', he said: 'You 'graduated' over afternoon tea!' He took my application form to his friend Cardinal Cushing who countersigned it and I was accepted.

Mother's illness

Soon after her arrival in Boston, my mother went down with something that appeared to be a tummy bug and kept her off work. She couldn't eat and we invited her to stay with us until the 'bug' departed. A doctor friend examined her and prescribed medication but she was unable to keep down any food and the doctor told us that she should be admitted to the prestigious Lahey Clinic. The fees were astronomical and Mummy had neither medical insurance nor the necessary funds. We gulped, drove to the clinic and explained our circumstances. They were extremely kind and told us not to worry about the cost – they would bill us later!

Pamela was terribly upset by the illness of her beloved grandmother and this was affecting her work and making her miserable at school and at home. One of the Sacred Heart nuns suggested that she might become a weekly boarder and I had to say that we simply did not have the money. Mother Oswald was not deterred: 'There is a spare bedroom in the West wing and I have a white blazer someone left behind' – weekly boarders wore white blazers while the day girls had grey ones. Mother Oswald made Pamela extremely welcome and never charged a cent!

Meanwhile, at the Lahey Clinic, Mummy became a sort of day patient. I took her to the clinic every morning for a variety of tests and examinations and brought her home at night. She never told me the details of the tests but I am pretty sure that they were unpleasant! She certainly wasn't getting any better and her pain was increasing. I was given pain killers for her with strict instructions to give one pill every four hours. She begged me to increase the dosage and it was incredibly hard to have to deny her and to witness her suffering.

The clinic was able only to discover a slight curvature of my mother's spine and this was certainly not the cause of the continual pain. One night she was in agony and Ted decided that we had to get her into the local hospital as an emergency admission. This hospital did a better job of controlling her pain by increasing the medication. They decided that there was no alternative to an exploratory operation, to which my mother agreed. I asked a kindly priest to look in casually just to 'make contact' and the nurses told me that he had visited and spent some time with my mother.

On the day of the operation I decided to stay in a nearby church but after an hour could bear it no longer and felt that I could pray just as well in the hospital. As I reached the ward I saw my mother being wheeled back to her bed on a stretcher, still unconscious. The surgeon called me to one side, and warned me that the news was bad. He told me that as soon as they had opened her stomach they had seen that there was widespread cancer. There was nothing to be done so the surgeon had sewn up the incision and that was the end of the 'operation'. I asked how long my mother was likely to survive and was told: 'Not more than three months'.

I sat by my mother's bed in a state of shock, waiting for her to come round. When she opened her eyes, she held my hand and asked me about the operation I lied, and told her that everything had been fine. Ted and I prayed about the situation and then talked it through with Monsignor Sheridan. We decided that my mother should not be told the truth about her condition and we should go 'one day at a time'.

A few days later she was transferred to the Deaconness hospital where I visited her each day.

One afternoon I was sitting beside her bed when she announced that she wished to return to England to visit Brian! How could we afford it and would she ever be well enough to travel? Unbeknownst to Mummy, Ted had already undertaken to cover all her medical expenses and these were terrifying and getting larger by the minute! Now she wanted a plane ticket to England.

We cast around for charitable help and one of Ted's colleagues told him about Red Feather Services who apparently provided charitable assistance. I found my way to their headquarters and was shown into the office of the President who was a gracious lady in her sixties. I realised that I was off to a good start when the President expressed interest in my English and Irish background. The highlight of the President's life had apparently been a meeting with the Queen of England and she proudly showed me the signed photograph she had received.

I was duly impressed and then launched into the story of my dying mother's desire to fly to England and the mountain of bills stacking up in the Donovan household! The President was a real answer to prayer. She gave me cash in hand to cover my mother's plane ticket to London and assured me that the hospital had an emergency fund for people who could not pay the bills. I was to go to the hospital administrator and explain our situation. He would certainly grill me but the hospital would not be able to force us to pay! The administrator did indeed grill me but there was no way that we were ever going to be able to pay the bills and there was nothing to be done about it!

We had of course kept Brian briefed about my mother's situation and arrangements had been made to admit her to a nursing home quite close to Brian and Majsan. We drove her straight from the hospital to the airport and were allowed to accompany her into the departure lounge and onto the aircraft. "Alyce" said Ted: 'You look like a bride today and I am going to carry you onto the plane!" We knew that we would never see her again.

I sat holding her hand while Ted moved away to leave us alone together for a few final moments. At the last minute my mother turned to me: 'Joyce, I have something to tell you before I leave. A strange thing happened the day before I had this operation. A young priest came to see me. He held my hand, as you are holding it now and he heard my confession. Then he asked me if I was afraid about the operation and I told him that I was. He asked me if I could feel him holding my hand and I told him that I could. Then he told me that Jesus was holding my hand in just the same way but that Jesus would never let it go'. My eyes were swimming and my mother looked me straight in the face and said her final words to me 'Jesus is still holding my hand. He will never let it go'.

My mother defeated medical prognosis and lived for six months.. She not only left the nursing home, but was able to move back into her own flat in Liverpool's Sefton Park where she was next door to a lifelong friend. This kind woman wrote to me every day to keep me in touch.

One morning after Ted had left for work the phone rang and a beautiful voice enquired whether I was

Mrs Joyce Donovan. 'This is Bell Cablegram service - are you alone my dear, as I have not very good news for you?' I told the woman that I was alone but had been expecting bad news about my mother'. With such love, the operator said: 'I am sorry my dear, but your mum passed away this morning - would you like me to read you the cable, or shall I just send it to you? Is there someone you would like me to phone?' I asked her to phone Ted and he came straight home.

We knew that we would be unable to go to the funeral but Brian was there to represent the family. Pamela took her grandmother's death very hard and so did poor Grandma Nettie who was temporarily in a Dublin nursing home and was shattered at the death of her daughter. Somehow we managed to get together the money to allow Ted and me to fly to Europe. We wanted to visit Anthony and I was concerned about Grandma Nettie. Sadly, we could not afford to take Pamela and Liz with us. We went to Grandma Nettie first and I hoped that the visit might bring her some comfort. Nettie was now back in her large house and still refusing to move into something smaller.

While we were in Dublin, I mentioned that Pamela was very anxious to return to Ireland. The reaction of one of my good friends in Dublin was: "Why not?" She reminded me that our daughter would certainly find herself among friends and that there were plenty of people with whom she could stay during the holidays. Mount Anville, the Sacred Heart Convent in Dublin, would be an ideal school and I made some enquiries. The nuns indicated that they would be pleased to welcome Pamela and as soon as we got back to Boston I put it to her. Pamela leapt at the idea. The move was just what she needed to escape from the sad memories of her grandmother's death and at fifteen she was ready to step out into the wider world.

10

HOLLAND 1957-1961

> One can only hold the hand of another
> as far down as one has been oneself
> **Joyce Donovan**

Ted was working all the hours God made in order to pay our debts and make ends meet. One day in the summer of 1957 the firm dropped a bombshell. Ted was warned that in a couple of months all overtime would be stopped so we would be back to relying on his basic salary. Without that extra 'overtime' we failed to see how we could manage.

As always, we turned to the Lord in our troubles and he did not fail us. One autumn evening, Ted arrived home to announce that there was a good chance of his being picked to join a team which was to be sent to Holland for nine months to build an oil refinery. The salary was good and Ted liked the idea of moving back to Europe. What did I think about it?

I was flabbergasted but as we discussed the possibility and prayed about it we began to see many advantages. Two of our three children were at school in Europe and it would be wonderful to be closer to them. But what of Liz who was happily settled in Boston? Could she join Pamela at Mount Anville in Dublin and would she be happy to do so? I discussed the possibility of the move with Liz and she was in favour. The next step was to write to the Irish nuns to explain the situation and ask if they would accept our younger daughter. In reply, I received the shortest cable imaginable: "Welcome Number 359!" – Liz's school number with which all her belongings would be marked.

It was a major job to pack up, say farewell to all our friends and set off to Europe but November 1957 found us on our way. Ted's firm was not sure whether the proposed refinery was in fact to be built in Holland, Norway or Denmark. While they made up their minds, we were to be accommodated in a five star Dutch hotel!

We flew out of Boston first class and our first stop was Dublin in order to deliver Liz to Mount Anville and find how Pamela was faring. We were happy with the arrangements in Dublin and flew on to The Hague in the assurance that the girls were well placed at Mount Anville and would be coming to join us for the Christmas holidays – first class travel at the expense of Ted's firm! As we came through customs at The Hague, we were greeted by a senior member of Ted's company and a kindly lady who presented me with a beautiful bouquet - my first experience of the Dutch habit of saying everything with flowers! I felt like a queen!

We had been intending to learn Dutch – or, indeed, Norwegian or Danish if the oil refinery was to be built in one of the Scandinavian countries, but soon realised that most people in Holland spoke several languages. We could get along perfectly well with English alone except when it came to the Sunday sermon in church!

The children were due to arrive in the Hague for the Christmas break but just before the holidays we received an agitated phone call from friends in Dublin with whom Pamela had been spending the weekend. Pamela had had a bad cold and our friends had asked a doctor to take a look at her. In the course of his examination, the man had noticed that the mole beneath Pamela's arm was much enlarged. He thought that the problem might have been exacerbated by the heavy woollen school uniform but told our friends that Pamela's parents should be alerted immediately because she might need an operation.

As soon as Pamela arrived in the Hague, I took her to the doctor recommended by Ted's firm and he arranged for her to be admitted to the Red Cross hospital after Christmas. Ted and I were extremely anxious but did not want Pamela to pick up our concern. We set out to make the best of Christmas and take our minds off our troubles.

It certainly was wonderful to be together again as a family. Anthony had shot up and was growing out of all his clothes, and we had to rig him out in new things. On Christmas night there was a mammoth

Christmas dinner followed by dancing. A young Dutchman came up to Ted, clicked his heels, bowed and said in impeccable English: 'May I have the honour of asking your daughter to dance with me?" "You may", said Ted, and Pamela whirled away in the arms of a new beau.

Immediately after the Christmas break I took Pamela to the Red Cross hospital for her operation. The growth was far deeper than the surgeon had suspected and he was afraid that she might lose the full use of her arm and be unable to raise it above her head. He also warned Ted and me that the mole might be cancerous. We obviously did not share this fear with Pamela and mercifully the growth turned out to be benign. The surgeon prescribed exercises which Pamela carried out faithfully and there were no lasting ill effects.

Scheveningen

By the end of January 1958 I was fed up with hotel life – grand and swanky though it was. Ted was bored with the luxurious Dutch breakfast of breads, meats and cheeses and yearned for porridge! He made friends with the head waiter who persuaded the kitchen to produce the porridge – recipe supplied by Ted!

It was eventually decided that the refinery was to be built in Rotterdam and we could at last think about moving into our own home. It was comparatively easy for Ted to commute from The Hague to Rotterdam each day so we decided to stay in the place we knew. We rented a small place temporarily which would at least enable us to move out of the hotel and in March 1958, we took over a very comfortable flat in Scheveningen with plenty of space for the children. It was wonderful to be able to shut our own front door again.

The brand new flat was on the seafront and the owners allowed me to go to a store and order whatever I needed in the way of kitchen utensils at their expense. I got to know the woman who ran the kitchen store quite well and during our first week in the flat she knocked on the door and said that she wanted to ask a favour. Would we allow her to sit on our balcony at a particular time the following week when Queen Juliana of the Netherlands and Queen Elizabeth of England would be driving past in an open carriage? I was delighted to say yes and the lady arrived on the due date with the gift of a beautiful bunch of sweet peas.

As our own furniture had not yet arrived from the storage depot, the two of us had to wait for the procession as best we could. The open carriage eventually arrived, drawn by two white horses and the two Queens looked up at us and waved their white gloved hands. This is the only occasion on which I have seen Queen Elizabeth II. I was sitting on a dustbin while my companion perched on a stepladder!

These were the days of pretty hats and, like most women, I had quite a number. One delightful velvet and feather creation from Filene's basement in Boston needed remodelling. I discovered a middle aged Dutch lady who excelled in 'resurrecting' elderly hats! She was small, bird-like and very anxious to please.

We made an appointment for 'hat surgery' and when I arrived at the shop the milliner had not yet returned from a visit to the doctor. When she came in I said something polite about hoping that she was alright. She explained that she had to go to the doctor every week because of stomach problems. Her eyes then filled with tears and she added, almost as an afterthought'. "I was in a Japanese concentration camp."

This was no time to be thinking about hats! I invited her to sit on the sofa beside me and held her hand as the story came out. This woman and her husband had been in the former Dutch Indonesia at the outbreak of war. Her husband was taken to one camp and she and her baby son to another. They were close to starvation and frequently reduced to eating bark from the trees.

Every day, at a particular time, a train passed by. The women discovered that some of the husbands were on that train en route to road building duties. My companion was sure that her husband was among them. Every day she contrived to be outside her building when the train passed by. She would hold up the baby so that her husband could see that they were both alive. At the end of the war they were released but obliged to travel for miles on foot. Her one concern was to be reunited with her husband. After many months she learnt that he was dead.

She was alone in the world with her baby and then suffered a further horror. Her son was kidnapped by bandits and murdered. The poor woman wept as she told me and my heart was breaking too. She explained that it was a relief to talk as she had felt unable to share her story with anyone.

The milliner was a devout catholic and a woman of prayer but explained that she was unable to find peace. She kept imagining that her little son was "lost" up in heaven without his mother. She had a picture in her mind of the little boy wandering alone. I longed to comfort her and was able to share a little of the teaching of the great theologian St Thomas Aquinas that in heaven there is no sadness or disability. We shall all have glorious radiant resurrected bodies without blemish and we will not be children but in the prime of life. I explained that it was impossible for her son to be 'lost' in heaven. She shared something further which she had never revealed. Alongside her concern for her 'lost' son she had a recurring dream of a beautiful youth the full bloom of manhood. He placed his hands on her shoulders and said: "I am alright, Mother." She had not known what to make of the dream because of her abiding concern for the "lost" baby. We wept together and I am deeply grateful that God worked through me to bring her peace at last and the conviction that her son was living in the radiant presence of God. I look forward to meeting them one day in heaven.

Diplomatic life

It was wonderful to have the children home every holiday – frequently bringing friends with them. We wondered whether the flat would be too cramped for five Donovans and assorted young people. We quickly realised that kids *love* being cramped, and in the 1950's it was quite an adventure to go abroad in the school holidays. Anthony at Ampleforth was in St Wilfred's house with the future Abbot of Ampleforth, Patrick Barry, as his housemaster. One school holidays Anthony arrived home with his red hair curling down onto his shoulders – the 'teddy boy' fashion hit England long before it became known in Holland and Anthony's 'new look' produced a few surprised faces among our friends, many of whom were in the diplomatic service!

When the children had gone back to school, my lifesaver was the American club. As an Irish citizen, I did not qualify for membership but every week one of the American members brought me along as her 'guest' and we had some wonderful outings. Tulip season was perhaps the best of all with the spectacular fields of stunning blooms.

We made a visit to the 1958 World Fair in Brussels! My American friends were obviously keen to visit their own national pavilion which contained examples of the American lifestyle – the drug store, real ice cream, hot dogs and hamburgers – the queue to get in seemed a mile long.

There were an enormous number of 'pavilions' and it was possible to visit only a few in a single day. One of the most spectacular belonged to the Holy See and had been built in the shape of an ark! The British pavilion contained Annigoni's portrait of Queen Elizabeth II as well as a genuine English pub. The British pub suffered a set back in terms of serving 'bangers and mash' – their sausages apparently did not contain sufficient meat to meet European requirements.

One day one of my American friends telephoned me in great agitation. She had apparently heard me mentioning St Anthony as a 'finder' of lost objects and she had lost a valuable emerald ring. The police had been called, but she wondered if St Anthony might do a better job! I assured her that I would 'have a word' and sent up some fervent prayers. The following day my friend telephoned with the glad news that the ring had turned up in her vacuum cleaner! She then enquired, rather sheepishly, whether she should not hand over some money. I assured her that I would have a further word with St Anthony. The following day I telephoned her with St Anthony's 'answer': 'He says: "This one is on me – but next time you ask me to find something please give a donation to the poor!"

Spiritual Life

Ted and I felt that it was about time we made a retreat but it obviously had to be in English so we were going to have to arrange it ourselves. We booked a retreat house in Utrecht and set about finding participants who were likely to be more comfortable with English than Dutch! The retreat leader was a Jesuit who seemed remarkably avant-garde. He invited us to participate in the Eucharist by sitting in a circle with him and receiving Holy Communion in our hands instead of on the tongue. We were also invited to receive the Precious Blood from the chalice which was not part of normal Catholic practice in the 1950's.

Ted and I found the whole experience memorable but very daring. We wondered afterwards whether our 'leader' had not in fact been jumping the gun!

Among the retreat participants was the Indian Ambassador to the Netherlands and his wife and I found them particularly impressive. M. Thivy was a man of obvious holiness with a doctorate in theology from the University of Louvain. In those days it was rare to meet a layman with a theological doctorate.

I kept in touch with M.and Mme Thivy and some while later had occasion to ring Mme Thivy about some activity in which we were both involved. As usual, I spoke to the butler first and asked to be transferred to my friend, adding: 'This is Mrs. Donovan from Ireland'. The butler immediately asked whether I was speaking from Ireland which struck me as a strange question and prompted me to enquire whether anything was wrong. The butler responded quietly: 'His Excellency died last night'. I was flabbergasted and managed only to say: 'Oh!' before replacing the receiver. I tottered into the kitchen really shocked and knelt down to pray before carrying on with some chore. The thought came to my mind: 'I am not that close a friend; I am not a member of the diplomatic corps and Mme Thivy will be surrounded by important people – all I can do is pray." This was immediately followed by the idea: 'Why not go and see how things are!' This would be daring, indeed, amidst the protocol of the diplomatic community and the 40 members of the Indian diplomatic entourage.

I made sure that I had a visiting card and went down to the car and drove off. As I approached the

Embassy I could see television cameras, police and officials. With as much confidence as I could muster, I drove right up to the gate, stuck my visiting card out of the window and said 'Ireland' to the guard who waved me into the grounds where I was directed towards a parking place.

My heart was pounding at the thought of having passed myself off as a member of the Irish diplomatic corps. Then, down the steps of the Indian Embassy, came the Irish Ambassador Brian Gallagher whom we knew well. 'Brian', I said 'Have I done the wrong thing in coming?' 'By no means' said Brian. 'You did perfectly right – go straight in!' The butler showed me into the main salon where M. Thivy was laid out on a bier in Indian dress with four lighted candles around him and his rosary in his hands. Mme Thivy was sobbing but she hugged me and seemed delighted that I had come.

I stayed for a little while and then returned home but decided to go back to the Embassy later in the afternoon. By now the visitors had gone and Mme Thivy was alone with her family and the staff. As I was sitting beside her, there arose a wailing from the Indian staff which reminded me of the biblical account of the mourners whom Jesus banished when he raised the daughter of Jairus from the dead. It was an eerie sound and rose to a crescendo. Mme Thivy turned to me regally and said: "Mrs Donovan, will you please say some of *our* prayers?"

I should have known the *De Profundis*, I should have known all sorts of things, but I was so unnerved by the keening, that I could only manage an *Our*

Father, a *Hail Mary,* and a *Glory Be to the Father.* Mme Thivy then said: 'Would you please take off the crucifix from the rosary in my husband's hands. I cannot bear to do it myself.' I broke off the cross and handed it to her. She kissed it reverently.

On the morning of the Ambassador's funeral I was telephoned by a Catholic priest on behalf of Mme Thivy. She apparently wanted me to come to the funeral and to bring a missal containing the Scripture readings in English. She was particularly anxious that English should be used for the readings so that the majority of people would understand. I arrived to find the church surrounded with police and television cameras but had no trouble gaining admittance. I was then told that Mme Thivy had asked that I sit with herself and her children at the altar. I was astonished but felt deeply honoured to be with her at such a time.

Education

It was becoming alarmingly clear that Pamela and Liz were not doing well at the Sacred Heart Convent in Dublin. Their school reports were awful and some of the things they seemed to be learning about Christianity were antediluvian; especially in view of the excitement and ferment fostered by the forthcoming Council of the Church which had been called by the newly elected Pope John XXIII.

Something had to be done about our daughters' education and Ted decided to write to the Headmaster of Ampleforth. He put the problem before him and the Headmaster wrote back very sympathetically suggesting a change of school and recommending the Convent of the Holy Child at Mayfield in Sussex. He warned us that the waiting list was considerable but it might be worth trying our luck. Ted wrote to the Headmistress, Mother Colette, explaining our concerns, begging her help and sending on the awful reports from Mount Anville! We concealed nothing! Ted told her that we would be prepared to come to Mayfield if there was any chance that Mother Colette could help us. She agreed to receive us.

We travelled overnight to Sussex where we met the headmistress; a handsome woman, her face surrounded by an elegant wimple. Mother Colette was small and precise and seemed very business like. She took us into her office where I sat gingerly on the edge of my chair while Ted and the headmistress discussed the disastrous reports. Suddenly Mother Colette turned towards me and addressed me as if I was a child: 'Stop feeling so nervous, Mrs. Donovan. You can relax – we have decided to take your daughters!' What an answer to prayer! The girls were to be richly blessed at Mayfield and we knew that we had made the right decision.

Ted's firm continued to fly the children home for the holidays and we wanted to take the opportunity to visit various places in France. We decided to make a family visit to Lourdes and it was on this pilgrimage that we received remarkable help from Liz's guardian angel! When our children were very small we had told them all about guardian angels and their importance. This had made a deep impression on Liz who named her guardian angel 'McRory' and nightly made a place for him on her bed. The instigator of the trip to Lourdes had been our friend Niall who had been so moved by the visit he had made to the Shrine with Ted and me in 1949. It was agreed that we would all meet up in Lourdes on a particular Monday morning at 10.00am on the steps of the Rosary Basilica. The Donovan party in fact arrived in Lourdes twenty-four hours earlier on the Sunday and went to a service in the underground basilica of St Pius X – the largest underground church in the world which can accommodate more than 20,000 people.

We were anxious to meet up with Niall but knew we hadn't a hope of finding him in a crowd like that – even supposing him to be already there. After the service the crowds milling about outside were denser than ever. Thirteen year old Liz had not met 'Uncle Niall' since she was two but had heard plenty of stories about him and was eager to see him again. She was still a firm friend of guardian angel 'McRory' and said brightly: "Why don't we all kneel down and pray to McRory to ask him to tell Uncle Niall's guardian angel that we are here?" We had certainly got the point across about the usefulness of guardian angels! I felt a little sheepish about kneeling down among all those people. But we knelt as Liz suggested and asked guardian angel McRory to help. Liz had no idea what Uncle Niall looked like but as we stood up she pointed to an 'unknown' man standing with his back to us: 'There's Uncle Niall!" And so it was!

Another visit to France took us to Lille. We wanted to give Pamela the opportunity to stay with a French family. Her command of French was excellent after her years in Montreal but her accent was French Canadian. We felt that the experience of living in France would be beneficial and Liz could repeat the experiment if it proved successful. Pamela liked the idea of being 'guinea pig' but we obviously wanted to make sure that we sent her to the right people. Friends in Boston put us in touch with the Mulliez family in Lille and we decided to ask if we could just 'drop in' to get an idea of the setup and for Pamela to see what she thought. Ted telephoned M and Mme Mulliez who were not only happy for us to drop in but wanted us all to spend the weekend with them. I had understood that the family were not well off and it seemed appalling to impose upon their generosity. I realised from Ted's end of the telephone conversation that he was accepting the invitation and made frantic 'No, no!' signs across the room at him. Ted put the phone down and told me that it would have been grossly rude to decline the invitation. I was appalled – not least because my French wasn't up to a weekend with a strange family.

The whole visit assumed awful proportions in my mind but in the event the family were charming and more than happy to have Pamela who was very pleased with the idea. M. Mulliez spoke sufficient English and it transpired that he was a major industrialist, a rich man who had entertained Queen Elizabeth II and Prince Philip the previous year. Their large house was set in a beautifully manicured garden in which M. Mulliez's mother had a sort of dower house, while one of the sons who was a surgeon had built his own separate dwelling.

On the Sunday morning, M. Mulliez suggested that he take us to Mass in a neighbouring church which had been built by his brother. I imagined that the brother had been a mason or an architect, but it transpired that M. Mulliez 'church builder' had in fact been a very rich man who said one morning to his wife: 'Ma chere, I think I shall build a new church for the parish!' – and proceeded to do so! The church was the most modern I had seen and dedicated to my friend, St Thérèse of Lisieux – even her statue was modern. I was particularly moved by the backdrop to the altar - the head of Our Lord crowned with thorns which had been painted on hessian by Georges Rouault. The thick black lines were stark and after a time the eyes really seemed to 'speak' to the worshipper.

We had a happy weekend and arranged for Pamela to come back to stay with the Mulliez family. She greatly enjoyed her visit and everything was going smoothly until the night we received an urgent phone call to tell us that Pamela had been taken seriously ill. She had acute appendicitis and an urgent operation was required. M. Mulliez' surgeon son would be glad to perform the operation, subject to our agreement.

Ted and I gave our consent and hurried away to Lille. By the time we arrived the operation had been carried out successfully, but Pamela was still unconscious. We sat by her bed and as she began to come round her first language appeared to be French – Ted and I mumbled appropriate responses in pigeon French until we tumbled to what we were doing and laughed.

Breakdown

Ted's initial contract had been for nine months and although this had been extended to two years, Ted eventually found himself working on a 'month by month' basis. This was dreadful, and meant that we dared not plan ahead at all because we had no idea where we might be when the children were due to come home for the holidays. Ted was magnificent but I became increasingly depressed and unable to sleep. I knew that if we had to go back to the States we would be unable to bring the children over more than once a year and I was already missing them dreadfully during the school terms.

The day came when I broke down completely and had to be taken to hospital where I spent the next five weeks. I have no memory of this time but understood subsequently that my nervous breakdown had been triggered not only by the intolerable strain and anxiety but also by pills which I had been buying from our local chemist.

Ted told me later, that I would have been allowed to come home much earlier if there had been anybody in the flat to look after me. Ted had to be away all day in Rotterdam so there was no choice but to remain in hospital. The whole experience of breakdown was bitter and sorrowful but there is no doubt that it has enabled me to reach out to those suffering intolerable stress. One can only hold the hand of another as far 'down' as one has been oneself – and I went very far down.

Eventually I was able to leave hospital and move into a convalescent home. One morning my wonderful hairdresser arrived with a bunch of sweet peas and prepared to spend the entire morning 'resurrecting' my hair. Mr Peters spoke perfect English, French and German and was a real artist. On this occasion he bleached my hair 'the colour of pearl' - a considerable feat in the late 1950's. The whole thing had been arranged by Ted who knew that a new 'hairdo' would provide a much needed boost.

Back home, the depression was still with me although it was now under control. I felt unable to trust in God to the extent that I feared I was losing my faith. It was obvious that I was in urgent need of spiritual help but there was no one in Holland to whom I felt able to turn. From most people I could conceal my inner anguish - but not from Ted. He telephoned the Dominicans in London and arranged for us to go over for the day so that I could talk to the Prior.

In the event I met instead Father Simon Blake to whom I poured out my anguish about the children; the uncertainty over Ted's job and my fear that I had lost my faith and that God was angry with me. Simon Blake was a wonderful listener. He asked me if I thought that a father would be angry when a child could not manage the spoon and spilt the food down its front. Of course not! "You know", said Simon Blake: "Maybe the spoon is just too big for you at the moment." The Lord used that man to bring me peace and I returned to Holland in the certainty that although the strain and anxiety were very great, I had not lost my faith.

Ted consulted with the doctors about my condition and they told him that it was vital that I return to an English speaking country. Ted explained to his boss that we had to go back to the United States but the man was furious and insisted that the doctors must be mistaken. It now came to light that Ted was going to be very hard to replace and the company did not in the least want him to leave Holland – despite the contractual insecurity we had suffered. Fortunately the president of the company had a soft spot for our family and supported Ted in his insistence that he return to the USA. The president promised that when Ted got back to Boston a job would be waiting for him.

11

BACK TO BOSTON
1961-1963

'He will not break a bruised reed or quench
a smouldering wick'
Matthew 12:20

It was not going to be as simple as we had imagined to return to Boston. As Irish citizens, the Donovan family required entry visas in order to get back into the United States. We put in our applications to the American consulate in Rotterdam, only to learn that a medical examination would be required. Liz was home on holiday at the time so we all went down to the relevant department - Ted to one section and Liz and myself to another. We had the unpleasant experience of being herded into a large room by a warden-like nurse who instructed all the women to: 'Strip to the waist". After each had been examined we were allowed to dress and were shown into another room where there were a number of posters. One of them filled me with horror: '*If you have been admitted to a mental hospital within the last six years you cannot gain entry to the United States'*. I had only just come out of mental hospital! The form I was asked to complete included the dreaded question. 'Have you ever been admitted to a mental institution?' I could choose to lie, but I knew that I had to be truthful.

With a heart of lead, I wrote: 'Yes'. The forms were collected up and we waited in line to be shown into the doctor's office. When my turn came, I discovered the doctor to be a friendly young American. He looked at my papers and asked about my stay in the mental hospital. I told him everything – the exact truth; all about the pills I had been taking, my intense worry about Ted's job and my anguish at being parted from the children. He said to me: 'I am going to tear up this form, and you are going to sign another one. You are going back to Massachusetts, which is my home state, and you are going to relax and grow flowers and get well'. I signed the new form and received my visa. May the Lord bless in abundance that young doctor who had such a warm heart. I will always remember his look of compassion as I told my story.

Although we could have flown first class, we liked the idea of a sea crossing and decided to sail on the 'New Rotterdam' which had just completed her maiden voyage. The Irish Ambassador and a number of other friends were at the quayside to bid us farewell.

Ted and I had a suite, which consisted of a sitting room with easy chairs, a double bedroom with twin beds instead of bunks and a bathroom. I was fascinated to discover that a steward was to be in attendance on Ted while there was a stewardess for me. I had had no idea that such grandeur existed on board ship! The breakfast menu provided a choice of sixty six items – I could hardly believe that it was possible to have so many choices at breakfast time. At our table, a wealthy man from Kuwait chose to start the day with onion soup sprinkled with parmesan cheese which was followed by steak and eggs! That sea crossing had every conceivable luxury and amusement laid on but I could not really enter into it all. I was in a continual state of worry about the future and still suffering the after effects of my breakdown.

We had wanted to be sure that we could get to Mass each day and the helpful travel agent told us that there were usually several priests sailing to the USA. Upon embarkation, we were most disappointed to discover that there were no clerical collars on board. We hoped and prayed that a priest might join us at Southampton, our first stop. Various passengers embarked but we didn't spot a priest until that evening in the bar. Lo and behold, there was a black garbed man. 'Are you a Catholic priest?' we enquired. 'Sure, I am: Father Twomey from Texas – No, I forgot! I've just been made Monsignor Twomey! And this is my friend'. He introduced us to a second priest and told us that they had arranged to celebrate Mass each morning in the ship's theatre. The two commandeered Ted to act as their altar server and asked him to take round a basket and a box of hosts so that members of the congregation could put a host in a basket if they intended to receive Holy Communion. The first morning it seemed to take Ted ages to go round the room with his basket – some members of the congregation apparently thought he was taking up a collection and had to be dissuaded from putting money in the basket!

We arrived in Boston to discover that Ted's firm had arranged for us to spend two weeks in the Sheraton Plaza – one of the grandest hotels in the city - which gave us time to draw breath and decide on our next step. We were now in a position to buy a house because I had received a legacy. Grandma Nettie had died while we were in Holland and left me sufficient money to purchase a modest house – the first home that we would be able to call our very own because we had always lived in rented accommodation.

We obviously wanted to find a house that would be convenient for Ted's work in Cambridge, but apart from that we had no particular area in mind. We consulted an estate agent – a realtor as they are known in the United States. She was very high-powered and obviously wanted us to buy an expensive house and take out a huge mortgage! She had several properties to suggest and as she drove us to the first one she seemed to be musing to herself: 'There *is* a place, but I don't think it is the style for you folks – not really the standard you have been used to!' She must have been misled by the fact that we were living at the Sheraton Plaza!

With one voice, Ted and I said: 'Take us there!' and the realtor obediently drove into the Allston district, West of Boston, and stopped before a light green painted clapboard house. Outside was a small grass patch and behind the house stood a magnificent oak tree – which would do a good job of keeping the sun off any flowers I might try to grow! Inside we found a beautifully proportioned living room, a sun parlour which had been converted into a dining room and four large bedrooms and one small one. The icing on the cake was the huge basement. Everything about that house suited us down to the ground but we were suspicious about the price – it seemed far too low! We returned to the Sheraton Plaza, without even looking at the original house the agent had wanted us to see and Ted remarked wisely: 'We need input from someone who is completely uninvolved.'

Ella McMacken was a good friend in Boston who had sound judgement and we knew that we could trust her for good advice. Ted suggested that I ask Ella to walk through the house with me and tell me if there was anything seriously wrong. Ella was delighted to help and we did our 'walk-through' while the rain poured down outside. I was pleased that Ella would be seeing the house at its worst!

She went from room to room and finally gave her verdict: 'There's nothing wrong with this house, the only thing it's on the wrong side of the tracks'. That meant that it was not in a fashionable area so the standard of local schooling would be low and Ella also knew that the local church did not have much to recommend it. Neither of these 'disadvantages' worried me as our children were at school in England and I did not necessarily intend to attend the parish church – although Ella pointed out that I would need to make myself known to the priests if I ever wanted them to come out on a sick call!

Apart from 'wrong side of tracks', Ella could find nothing wrong with the house so we were no wiser about the suspiciously low price. When I went back to the realtor I at last discovered the reason. The house had belonged to the Salvation Army and for some wonderful reason they did not believe in selling in accordance with escalating market prices! Our predecessors had been an Army major and his wife and not only were they keeping the price down but they had left the property spotless for the new owners – we could have eaten our meals off the beautiful parquet floors.

We finalised the deal and in June 1961 we moved in. We found ourselves surrounded by delightful new neighbours and began to make contact with old friends in and around Boston. I also found myself being asked to give talks to various groups; drawing on my experiences of living in several countries and working in different countries. My so-called English accent apparently helped to make me popular and the talks brought in much needed cash.

When we had lived in Boston in 1957 I had worked as a volunteer reader for people who were blind and needed help with their books. A number of those for whom I had read were studying for a PhD and the subjects were frequently so far above my head that I was able to understand hardly a word of whatever I was reading. I was now able to pick up the threads and continue to read to blind people who needed such help in order to master their academic subjects. This led on to the creation of a tape library, but that will have a chapter to itself.

The Passionist parish

On our first Sunday in our new home we had gone to our local parish church and found that Ella McMacken had indeed been right - we just didn't like it! Fortunately there was a Passionist monastery quite close by with more than forty priests in residence because this was a house of studies for younger Passionists as well as a home for their elderly priests. The monastery was also responsible for St Gabriel's parish, some parts of which were very run down, while others were extremely well to do with parishioners living in beautiful old clapboard houses – we decided to join the congregation at St Gabriel's and felt very much at home among such a motley crew.

The Rector of the Monastery, Father Gerard Orlando, was to play an important part in our lives and he became a good friend. Father Gerard was Italian by origin; a big man with a heart to match, a great sense of humour and an evenness of temper which was a gift from God. I think he was the most humble man I have ever met and I asked him to become my spiritual director. One day Father Gerard confided to me that he had not come into a deep personal relationship with Jesus until he entered the Passionist novitiate. This was an eye-opener to me as I had always imagined that priests had a very close relationship with the Lord from the word 'go'. One night Fr Gerard telephoned me about an 'unspiritual' matter. He was doing a crossword puzzle and was stuck over an 'Irish' clue. What was 'Head of the house in Ireland' in seven letters? I knew the answer immediately: 'Himself'! From that day onwards

Father Gerard's phone calls to Ted or myself always began with: 'It's 'Himself'.

Some time after our arrival, a new Passionist priest arrived at the monastery, Father Edward Hennessey who was appointed parish priest. Father Edward was a Canadian from Hamilton, Ontario and was certainly a man of vision who was well ahead of his time. When he took over the parish, he spent his first two weeks going around and finding out about all the different parish organisations. He then closed down the ones which did not have some spiritual aim or activity! The parishioners were dazed when they realised what he was up to! Fortunately Father Edward got away with this radical beginning because he was a man of the utmost charm – when he wanted to use it. He also had real spiritual vision; the seemingly impossible dream of 'parish as extended family' – a true and living parish community.

Father Edward was well aware of the uselessness of trying to teach children about Jesus and about 'living' the Gospel unless parents themselves also had some idea of Gospel values. He therefore decided to teach the parents before trying to teach the children and set up a series of courses on 'Jesus in everyday life': the practicalities of living the Gospel day by day. Parents were invited to come to a preliminary meeting one Tuesday evening and Ted and I were asked to put out chairs. Father Edward estimated that about thirty five chairs would be sufficient but in the event 200 people turned up and we were dashing around trying to find places for everybody. Fr Edward was so staggered that he decided to give the same talk two days later. This time we put out fifty chairs out - and once again two hundred people arrived. This was truly staggering and an indication of the hunger within people but it was also a tribute to the interest that this priest could inspire.

There was no doubt that our parish priest was an exciting person to have around and a man of deep spirituality, but he could also be unpredictable and you didn't always know which way he was going to 'jump'. This caused a certain amount of friction in the parish and I listened to some sad stories from those who had been offended. I decided to try and make peace by standing up for him - perhaps he had behaved in a particular way because he had been up all night on a sick call or he had been feeling unwell. I even suggested to one 'complainer' that he might have ignored her because he had been in an ecstasy of prayer! In the end the parishioners decided that I was not much use as a source of sympathy and gave up telling me what Father Edward had or had not done or said!

I remember getting cross with him myself because of something or other. I told him that if he was ever made a bishop, I would design a coat of arms for him with a motto he might not like. Most people did not speak to him like that and he couldn't decide whether to smile at me or glare – but he was curious and asked which motto I would choose. I told him it would be: 'The bruised reed thou shall not break' – he didn't like that and I can still see him swishing his rosary beads at me!

Alan, one of the teachers who helped Father Edward with his evening classes, was a convert from Judaism. One day he came and told me that he was resigning as a teacher and also leaving the Catholic Church because Father Edward had been so rude to his wife. I could well believe it, and had to think fast because the man was obviously extremely upset. I told Alan that there was a protocol in the Catholic Church which required a teacher who was resigning to tender his resignation in person to the parish priest. Alan gazed at me, wide-eyed while I tried to look authoritative. He trotted off to tender his resignation and no sooner was he out of the door than I was on the phone to Father Edward: 'Alan is on his way to see you and if you are anything other than totally charming to him, you are going to have an entire family leaving the church – remember the bruised reed!' Father Edward said not a word but replaced the receiver. A few days later I bumped into Alan who was on top of the world. He told me that he had gone to 'tender his resignation' to Father Edward who would not hear of it but congratulated him on the great job he was doing and insisted that he continue. He had given Alan a rosary for his wife and a beautiful statue for the children!

At the time of Father Edward's arrival, Ted and I had been feeling that we could do more for the parish and had embarked on a course in teaching religious education, otherwise known as catechetics. This ultimately led us into teaching the basics of religion to young people who came from the very run-down part of the parish where the boys and girls were in the habit of carrying flick-knives. Ted had the junior boys who went to non-Catholic schools, and I had the senior girls aged 17-18 who actually came *voluntarily* to the classes which was most unexpected!

The set books for the course were awful - dull, uninspiring, and in no way geared to making people excited about following Jesus Christ, and getting to know him better. I talked the problem over with Father Edward who gave me carte blanche to teach the girls *anything!* This was marvellous, and I always based the evening around the Gospel of the following Sunday and did my best to apply it to daily life. I had a good bunch of girls but they had some strange ideas – one young lady asked me how much she could steal before she committed a mortal sin. I learnt later that she had been planning to steal 'a venial sin's worth' of lipsticks from Woolworth for Christmas presents!

One evening the teacher of the senior boys was ill, and I was given both senior girls and senior boys to deal with. This was tricky because at that age they wanted to flirt with one another and 'God' was the last thing on their minds. I decided to scrap whatever I had prepared for the girls and told the mixed group that I would instead respond to any questions they wanted to raise – and I prayed that the Holy Spirit would give me the right answers! One of my girls said, tauntingly, to one of the boys: 'Ask Mrs. Donovan *anything* – she will bring it around to God!' This truculent young man came out with: 'Why do we have to go to this silly Confession business?' I took a deep breath and asked him if he knew when the Sacrament of Confession first began. He shook his head. I sent up a quick prayer and plunged on: 'It was when the apostles were huddled in the upper room, scared out of their cotton socks because their Master had been crucified, and they were afraid they might be crucified as well. Jesus appeared in His glorified body, and stood amongst them. He could have said: 'You dirty rats, you might have at least looked after my Mum, but you all ran away'! Instead, he smiled at them and said 'My peace I give to you, whose sins you shall forgive, they are forgiven'.

That led to some interesting questions about confession, but it was not an easy class – and the evening did not improve when one of the Passionist seminarians teaching next door arrived in my room with a problem: 'Joyce, one of the boys in my class has a gun, whatever shall I do?' I told him to go back, and ask quietly for the gun. If the boy refused to hand it over, the seminarian was to come back and tell me and I would go in and ask for the gun myself. I was shaking in my shoes - but the seminarian managed to get hold of the gun and brought it to me! This incident led to 'Himself' using his authority as Rector of the monastery to withdraw all seminarians from teaching in the parish. I asked him why he seemed to be more concerned about his seminarians than about Ted and me – but he just smiled!

From time to time I had to go to the home of one of 'my' girls in the high rise apartments. This was my first encounter with real squalor and with the impossible circumstances in which some families are obliged to live. On my first visit I asked two of the other girls to accompany me. One of them said: 'I saw you on TV last night, wearing that hat!' I always wore a large hat in the summer to keep the sun off but was intrigued to know what she had been watching. She told me the time of the programme and I looked it up when I got home. I had mixed feelings when I found out that she had been confusing me with Zsa Zsa Gabor!

One of our neighbours across the road appeared to suffer from similar confusion where I was concerned! This neighbour considered himself a bit of a ladies man and one day I was standing at the tram stop when he came across and tried to 'chat' me up. A car drew up beside us and the back door opened. 'Here are two of my friends" said my persistent neighbour: "I should like you to meet them because they have never met a little lady who was born in Dublin". One of the men in the car stretched out his hand and I leaned forward intending to shake it. At this point my persistent neighbour gave me a shove. I fell into the back seat and he jumped in beside me, slammed the door and off we drove.

I was extremely angry. 'Don't worry, honey" said my persistent neighbour. We are off to the races for the day. We will stake you and give you a nice dinner and some company." Don't you dare," said I. "My husband is waiting for me in Boston. They all laughed and I knew I was in a tight spot so I began to pray. Inspiration dawned: "Gentlemen", said I "I would have you know that I am a jujitsu expert, and when we get out of this car I will throw the first one of you that comes near me over my shoulder!" That stopped them in their tracks. I then told them that they had made me extremely late and to take me to Park Street immediately because Ted would be waiting for me. They meekly did as I asked and when I told Ted about the incident he was extremely angry. Not so, "Himself" who laughed until the tears ran down his cheeks. He told me that when he was in the chapel he had had to stuff his handkerchief into his mouth to stop the chuckles breaking out again!

Pamela, Anthony and Liz

Meanwhile our children were growing up. Pamela was now nineteen and due to leave Mayfield during our first summer in Boston and we were longing to have her home with us. Pamela was 'pleasingly plump', as I had been, and extremely pretty with darkish blonde hair, and skin that tanned too easily so she had to try and avoid the sun. She did not seem to have a clue about a future career and Ted felt that the children should not go to college or university unless they had some idea of what they wanted to do afterwards.

Out of the blue, we received a letter from Pamela telling us that she wanted to be a nurse; she had never mentioned this before and, more importantly, she had never studied any science subject. Ted wrote back telling Pamela that he did not think that nursing was a good idea and suggesting that he put her through a first class secretarial course so that she would always be able to earn her living. By return, we received a passionate letter from Pamela accompanied by one from her headmistress, Mother Colette; – both letters assuring us that Pamela really meant what she said about wanting to be a nurse.

Mother Colette pleaded with us to give Pamela a chance to 'follow her star' and we capitulated, but felt that we still needed to make sure that Pamela was truly suited to nursing. The best way to do this seemed to be to put her through some sort of careers guidance and we heard of a suitable centre which was run by a nun in Boston who charged a fat fee. Pamela agreed to go through the course when she arrived home in July 1961 and she was put through all sorts of tests. The results showed that she definitely had what it took to become a nurse. But she was still without any science subjects and if she wanted to train in the United States she was also going to need to pass an exam in American history! Quite a lot of study would be required before she could even apply for admission to a nursing school with any hope of acceptance. We found an excellent 'learning centre' which was run by a gifted couple who were Jewish and could teach students *how* to study and how to use libraries. The course was costly but the results persuaded us that it had been worth every cent. Pamela really knuckled down and she came out of the course with 'honours' – the only student to do so!

Anthony was now eighteen and had left Ampleforth. He was a gifted artist and wanted to make a career of his art. While we had been in Holland Anthony had considered architecture but eventually decided against it. Ted and I were doubtful about art as a career choice because artists seemed to make money for their heirs, and starve during their own lifetimes. But our son was very determined so we had to take the matter seriously and investigate the possibilities of art training in the Boston area. We made various enquiries and had high hopes of the school attached to the Museum of Fine Arts which was extremely expensive but refused to interview prospective students without a portfolio. Anthony had no portfolio so I had to try and enrol him in some other way.

I made an appointment to see the dean, and on the designated day went down to the school 'dressed to kill' and sporting a huge black hat. I turned on the charm and the dean did likewise! The upshot was that Anthony was accepted into the school and the dean told me that he was the first student to be taken on without the school seeing a single painting! He certainly justified the dean's faith in him and became an exciting artist.

During the first summer vacation, Anthony and a fellow student earned some money by working at St Elizabeth's Hospital. They were responsible for wheeling patients from ward to operating theatre and dubbed themselves the 'RTS' – 'Rapid Tumbrel Service'!

At the end of his first year, Anthony was awarded the Elizabeth Bartol Scholarship which covered part of his fees for the remainder of the course. He seemed to be doing extremely well until, one evening; he arrived home with an announcement which took our breath away. Anthony announced that he had been seriously reconsidering his future. He now felt that art was really something that should be considered in the nature of a hobby and he had a very different career in view. Our son was intending to return to England to seek admittance to the Ampleforth novitiate. He wanted to become a Benedictine monk.

We were absolutely astounded but we realised that if God was really calling Anthony to religious life we had to do everything in our power to help him to respond to that call.

There was a second bombshell in store for us. Sixteen year old Liz arrived home for the holidays with a similar vision for her future which we had never remotely suspected. She, too, wanted to enter religious life and to become a nun with the order who had been educating her – the Congregation of the Holy Child Jesus. We felt deeply honoured that God seemed to be calling our children into religious life but it was a source of grief that they were intending to be so far away when I had imagined that we would all be together at last in the United States. Liz told us that when she discussed her vocation with the community at Mayfield she had said that she wanted to enter immediately. The nuns had asked her to wait a year and, in the meantime, to take a good secretarial course.

It looked as if Pamela was going to be the only one left at home. In the summer of 1962 she had gained an Equivalency High School certificate which opened the door to entry into nursing school. She chose the school at St Elizabeth's Hospital which meant that she would be able to come home for weekends. With the prospect of Anthony moving back to England in the autumn of 1963, and Liz following him a year later it meant a lot to have Pamela close at hand.

One day, the phone rang and a voice, out of the blue, said: "Joyce - this is Brian here'. I had not spoken to my brother for so long that I said: "Brian who?' It was a joy to hear his voice and to hear that he was passing through Boston airport. Was there any chance that we could meet?

Ted and Liz and I headed straight out to Logan Airport where we met a much older man than I remembered. Brian was obviously doing well as managing director of the UK branch of an American company. He and Majsan had a beautiful house near Henley. They were both flourishing but grieved not to have children. "It appears that we can only breed dogs!" he said bitterly. I could see that my brother was much taken with Liz in all her sparkling brightness – I noticed that she did not tell him that she was planning to become a nun!

Ireland and England

After so many family 'surprises' Ted and I decided that we needed to take a short holiday by ourselves so we headed back to Ireland to spend a little time in the Dublin mountains, one of our favourite haunts. Cardinal Cushing became aware of our plans and asked us to visit the Foundress of the Medical Missionaries of Mary, Mother Mary Martin, at Drogheda north of Dublin. He commissioned us to ask Mother Mary if she would permit one of her nuns, Sister Nativity, to come to Boston to care for seminarians in a house which the Cardinal was opening for those with 'late vocations'.

When we arrived in the Drogheda convent, Mother Mary embraced us warmly. We explained the Cardinal's request to which she responded: 'Let's go and talk to Sister Nativity.' We were introduced to a rosy cheeked nun with twinkling eyes, to which

Mother Mary asked that we convey the Cardinal's request. Ted and I had imagined that some sort of negotiations had already been underway but we soon realised that this was the first Sister Nativity had heard about the possibility of going to Boston! She listened carefully to what we had to say and responded in her deep Irish brogue: 'If Reverend Mother is willing, you can tell His Eminence that I am willing to go and look after the old ones'.

We learnt subsequently that Cardinal Cushing had met Mother Mary when he visited Ireland and been very impressed by her sanctity and her vision of a religious congregation of highly trained medical personnel who could engage in surgery and obstetrics. Prior to 1936 the Catholic Church did not permit women in religious life to engage in either speciality and Mother Mary had had to wait for the fulfilment of her vision but it eventually came about.

Ted's brother Cecil from Ampleforth had been present at the time of the Cardinal Cushing's visit because he was preaching a retreat to the Medical Mission Sisters. Mother Mary had apparently shared with the Cardinal her vision of a really modern hospital in Drogheda and when Cardinal Cushing departed he had slipped into her hand an envelope which she placed in the top of her nursing apron. She thought no more about it until she was undressing during the 'Great Silence' which pertains at night in monasteries and convents except in cases of emergency. Mother Mary evidently considered the contents of the Cardinal's envelope to be an 'emergency'. She rang the convent bell and called all the nuns to the chapel to share the good news. When all were assembled she asked Cecil to make the announcement. Cardinal Cushing had presented the Medical Missionaries of Mary with a cheque for one million dollars!

Ted and I returned home refreshed from our holiday and decided to make a further visit to Ireland in September 1963 when Anthony was due to enter the Ampleforth novitiate. We planned to 'deliver' him to the monastery and to take Liz with us because she and Anthony had always been close and this seemed to be the final opportunity for a family holiday. Pamela was unable to join us because she was in the throes of her nursing studies. We hated leaving her behind and she wept bitterly at the airport when she came to see us off. Fortunately 'Himself' had also come to wave goodbye and he and another Passionist priest took Pamela out to dinner that night and kept in touch with her during our absence.

We had asked Anthony and Liz what they would especially like to do in England, and they came up with a stay at the new London Hilton and a visit to an old fashioned English inn. At the Hilton Liz arranged a lunch party for some of her friends from Mayfield. It was a sort of al fresco lunch held in two of the enormous adjoining bedrooms and the girls went through the food like locusts. Ted and I made ourselves scarce!

For the second part of the holiday we decided to stay in a sixteenth century coaching inn south of London, The White Hart in Lewes. Ted and I had stayed at the White Hart a number of times and found it delightful. Much later, Liz told me of an escapade when Ted and I had gone to bed. On the first night in Lewes, Anthony and Liz sat up talking together in Liz's room. At 3.00am they realised that it would look very bad if Anthony was seen leaving her room because people were not going to believe that they were 'brother and sister'. Anthony took off his shoes and crept out, looking the picture of guilt, only to encounter an elderly couple who gave him a very frosty look which was still on their faces at breakfast the following morning. As a memento of the trip, Liz and Anthony bought Ted a silver sugar shaker in 'The Lanes' in Brighton and for me there was a beautiful black 'highwayman's' hat chosen by Anthony.

Ted and I duly delivered Anthony to Ampleforth into the care of the newly elected Abbot, Basil Hume. Ted expressed concern about a dowry for Anthony and Abbot Basil reassured him: 'There is no dowry – you are giving us your son'. Anthony was going to be joining seven other young men under their novice master, Ted's brother Cecil, Dom Bruno. These young men were choosing a life of austerity and they were certainly going to find it at Ampleforth – that monastery was freezing!

12

THE TAPE LIBRARY
1963-1971

> 'You yourselves are our letter,
> written on our hearts...... not written with ink
> but with the Spirit of the Living God.
> **2.Cor.3:2-3**

In 1963 I returned to reading for the blind, and decided to act as a sort of 'on call' reader as it was difficult to make firm commitments with so much else going on. There was one young man named Walter for whom I read regularly. Walter had been blind from birth and was now studying for a doctorate in psychiatry. He had fourteen readers each week to get him through the necessary work and when he was trying to take something in, he had a habit of walking round and round his room, wearing a circular pattern into the lino!

Walter was a delight to be with, a devout young Catholic without any self-pity. I enjoyed my time with him and would read for stretches of two hours with a ten-minute break in the middle, during which Walter's mother brought us coffee and biscuits – much needed by me after an hour of ploughing through academic tomes of which I understood hardly a word. The only 'fly in the ointment' was Walter's beloved 'seeing-eye' dog, an elderly bull mastiff called Bessie who was devoted to her master and would take him wherever he wished to go. Unfortunately she smelt ghastly and dribbled!

During our coffee breaks, Walter would quiz me about my life at home. I realised that I could provide him with a door into another world and would try to think up interesting things to share with him. One day I told him about the Meditation from *A Surgeon at the Foot of the Cross*, and he was fascinated.

This book had long been my regular Holy Week reading and I had asked permission from 'Himself' (Rev G.A. Orlando) to use it as part of the parish high school religious education course. 'Himself' had agreed, and we had decided that it would make the strongest impact if the Meditation in the book could be read aloud in the chapel in the presence of the Blessed Sacrament exposed in the monstrance. I invited course participants, other teachers and the Passionist seminarians to join me in the lower chapel where they could sit comfortably during the twenty-five minute reading. This was followed by a period of silence during which we allowed the words to touch our hearts as we sat in the presence of the Lord.

Walter asked me if I would read the meditation from *A Surgeon at the Foot of the Cross* on one of my visits to him and allow him to record it. On the appointed day he had the tape recorder set up on my arrival and as I began to read Walter stood up and began his circular walk around the room. When I had finished, he sat down and turned to me a face of great distress: 'It is perfectly dreadful' he said: 'I never realised that the Crucifixion was so awful'. He had of course never seen a crucifix or any of the paintings of the crucifixion with which sighted people are so familiar.

Driving home, I reflected on Walter's situation. Here was a young man living in a strong Christian home who nevertheless had no real idea of the spiritual and physical reality of the passion of Jesus. What must it be like for countless other Christians who were also blind but did not possess Walter's advantages?

For ages Ted and I had been talking vaguely about becoming involved in some particular religious work, when the children were older and we had more time and money. Here, in the lives of so many blind people, there appeared to be a crying need. We prayed about it - and I told 'Himself' of our concern. His immediate reaction was that of a loyal and patriotic American: 'America has everything that is required for handicapped people. There are tapes available for all their needs!' For 'Himself', that was the end of the matter. Not so for the Donovans!

We were quite prepared to believe that America had everything for the spiritual wellbeing of people who were blind - but we wanted to be absolutely sure about it. I spent months investigating the availability of spiritual tapes for blind people; months of letter writing and following up all kinds of leads. It was fascinating to explore the wealth of the catalogue of the American Library of Congress - opera, chess, bird-watching, treasure-seeking – you name it! That vast catalogue nevertheless seemed devoid of anything to do with the Good News of Jesus Christ. The largest library in the world appeared to possess only three religious recordings - the books in question being nondescript titles by little known authors.

I frequently reported to 'Himself', who was beginning to realise that I was not going to allow the matter to rest and that the 'Land of the Free' was not perhaps perfectly equipped in terms of religious recordings for blind people. He promised to make investigations himself, and visited a Jesuit friend in New York who ran a tape library which included the latest books read aloud by famous actors and actresses. 'Himself' had been convinced that his friend would be able to set him on the track of all the spiritual titles available on tape but he returned from New York somewhat crestfallen: 'I guess you are right. There is nothing available on tape which is purely spiritual.'

He was certainly coming around to our way of thinking and suggested that I visit a large rehabilitation centre for blind people which was run by a priest – I shall call him 'Father X'.

'Himself' offered to come with me but for some reason I told him that I would prefer to go alone. At this stage, Ted and I were thinking only in terms of setting aside a sum of money each month which we could donate anonymously to some organisation which would be willing to make religious tapes for blind people. We thought it would be a simple matter of beaming in the money each month. We were to learn that the Lord had something quite different in mind.

I made an appointment to see 'Father X' and arrived at his huge establishment to be greeted by a succession of priests, each one of whom led me deeper into the building - it was like going to see the Pope! Eventually I reached Father X's inner sanctum –an enormous office with a huge desk. Father X did not rise to greet me but merely acknowledged that I had made an appointment.

I explained my experience of reading to Walter and his great interest in the book *A Surgeon at the Foot of the Cross*. I spoke of my sadness at the number of blind people who seemed to be without access to the Gospels, let alone spiritual books. I explained our desire to donate a sum of money each month to enable recordings to be made available. My spiel appeared to leave Father X cold. He informed me that he employed more than twenty sighted people and he doubted whether any of them had so much as read the Gospel of St John. Who did I imagine was going to record spiritual books? The thought flashed through my mind that perhaps Father X's rehabilitation centre was the recipient of Federal aid. This would certainly place a limitation on any reference to religion.

It was clear that no help was likely to be forthcoming from this quarter. Father X was not in the least interested in our concerns. "So you won't help?" I said angrily. "No!" "Right!" said I – without actually stamping my foot although I was sorely tempted!

"Pray, what will you do?" enquired my interlocutor. "I don't know" I replied "But I will pray to the Holy Spirit and you will hear what happens next!" With that I swept out of his office and stormed off home. Constantly before my eyes was Walter's tear stained face as he listened to the description of the Passion!

I had promised to report back to 'Himself' but was too angry to go and see him. I rang him up and launched into a blow by blow account of my exchanges with Father X. I told 'Himself' that I was fed to the teeth with priests. When he eventually managed to get a word in edgeways, he asked me a question: "When did Our Lady appear to priests?' I was stunned, and told him that I was not in the mood for stupid questions and could not think of any occasion when Our Lady had appeared to priests!" His next question was "To whom did Our Lady appear?" Without giving me a chance to respond, he gave the answer: "Our Lady appeared to little children, and I think that the Lord has given you this good idea, because you are only a child. I want you to pray very hard, to wait and to be humble' – and with that he replaced the receiver.

That telephone conversation certainly gave me something to think about. I was far from humble and could well appreciate that much prayer was going to be needed. In my heart I had felt that the possibility of recording spiritual books was a definite 'nudge' from the Lord. When Ted arrived home I told him what had happened with Father X and my subsequent conversation with 'Himself'. We began to pray and resigned ourselves to waiting – and waiting…. whilst I continued reading to Walter and to others.

It took a long time for anything at all to happen. One morning 'Himself' telephoned me out of the blue with the news that he had decided to allow me to tape the Meditation from *A Surgeon at the Foot of the Cross*. I was to come up to the monastery that afternoon where I would find 'Himself' and the tape-recorder ready and waiting.

Afternoon came and I was ready to leave the house when something really horrible happened. I can only describe the experience as a thick dark 'blanket' which seemed to descend upon my spirit and filled me with fear. I sensed evil all around me; it was almost tangible. Negative thoughts flooded into my mind. It had been a stupid idea to try to do anything for blind people – I had been crazy to entertain it. Such an idea could never work out.

I decided that I was certainly not going to be making a recording for 'Himself' that afternoon, but it would be only polite to go and tell him so face to face. I had, after all, been badgering the poor man for months! I locked the house, got into the car and started off for the monastery, still feeling very shaky and frightened. At some level I understood that I had experienced real evil.

I arrived at the monastery, still feeling wretched. There was 'Himself' with his tape recorder machine all set up. These were the days of reel to reel machines which were fiddly to set up and required small deft fingers which 'Himself' most certainly did not possess. "It's all off" said I: "I won't be doing any recording". "What on earth are you talking about? You have been praying and talking about nothing else for months. You have convinced me that it is something from God - and now you come to tell me that 'it is all off'!"

I seemed once more to be enwrapped in the thick dark blanket of fear. I felt totally unable to explain myself and sensed that whatever was troubling me was in the realm of the spiritual. I could only manage to say, pathetically: "Bless me?" 'Himself' looked at me in amazement and raised his hand in what I can only describe as a 'floppy' blessing. I sensed that the power of God was desperately needed. To his considerable surprise, I sank to my knees in front of him, with the request that he give me the full Passionist blessing which calls upon the power of the holy name of Jesus and of His precious blood. I added that I also wanted this endeavour placed under the cloak of Our Lady. I had never come out with anything like this before – but never before had I suffered such a chilling experience of evil. 'Himself' placed his hands upon my head and spoke the powerful words of the Passionist blessing with every scrap of his considerable authority. As the words rang out, I sensed the darkness lifting and light and peace flooded into my soul. "Will you now make the tape?" he enquired – and I knew that I was ready to read. When I had finished, 'Himself' complimented me on the reading and told me that he was going to play the tape to a number of people.

The feedback was positive and Ted and I were given the 'go-ahead'. As far as 'Himself' was concerned, the 'go-ahead' was the limit of his involvement - apart from some useful suggestions about suitable books to record. Henceforth Ted and I were to be on our own. Nobody else was going to run a tape library and we were going to have to stumble along by ourselves as best we could.

The library was going to have to be woven into the warp and weft of daily life. Ted was working full time and although I was less tied down, I still had to run the household and we were both involved in all manner of things including the Dominican secular Institute which had about one hundred members. We had rejoined on our return to Boston and I had now been appointed Prioress.

Early days
Ted and I quickly became aware that people who had lost their sight were frequently possessed of acute hearing. They would pick up the faintest background noise on a tape which would escape the rest of us and would find such noise extremely irritating. With this in mind, we took as our maxim 'Nothing but the best' and became very fussy about the quality of our work. We would not even allow the tiniest "click" during recording when the machine was turned on or off. It took ages to perfect this detail but we knew it was important.

Gradually we began to make tapes available to people who needed them and our clients were thrilled to receive spiritual recordings. Tape machines were a lifeline to people who were blind and we soon became aware that many of our friends and clients were afflicted with faulty machines which went wrong in all manner of ways. Repair shops charged ten dollars just to look at a machine and repairs were very expensive. Ted was now highly competent and could mend the machines himself. He undertook to make repairs free of charge and to collect and deliver the machines – I will never know how he found the time. Our dining room became a workshop and faulty machines seemed to 'breed'! I remember an occasion when guests sat down to dinner in the company of seventeen faulty tape recorders piled around the room!

'Himself' continued to come up with suggestions. One day he said to me: 'You two lay people aren't going to get past first base in this apostolate without the name of a clergyman.' He proceeded to give me permission to sign all letters relating to the library with his own name: 'Very Reverend Gerard A. Orlando CP.

This was incredible! 'Himself' never read a single one of the letters we sent out over his name. From time to time, responses would come in from nuns and laypeople which required a reply from me which amounted to spiritual direction. As time passed, an increasing number wrote with problems and anxieties to which I felt unable to respond adequately. I then made a curious discovery. Time after time, the book I was in the process of recording contained exactly the advice necessary for a particular correspondent. I seemed to become a sort of 'conduit' – passing on the advice gleaned from a particular book.

We had to find a name, and decided on "Our Lady of Sorrows Library" in acknowledgement of the sufferings of so many of our clients. Since the earliest days when I asked 'Himself' to place the undertaking beneath the cloak of Our Lady, we felt that she had indeed given the Library her special care.

Ted continued to make enquiries and was now able to talk to manufacturers and suppliers on their own terms. He discovered a five thousand dollar machine would meet our needs – but where were we to find five thousand dollars? America was the land of the fund-raiser – but I was appalled at the idea of trying to raise funds myself. I did not think that I had the right sort of personality. In the past I had given a few talks to raise small amounts, but the hard-nosed 'big sell' seemed way beyond my powers.

Ted and I talked to expert fund raisers who advised us to think in terms of a raffle with expensive prizes. They told us that there were three major prizes which would apparently tempt people: first prize – a colour television: second prize - a case of whisky and third prize – money. We were advised to have the television and the whisky on display at a suitable venue in order to encourage punters but we refused to buy the prizes in advance which our advisors considered most peculiar.

On the night of the draw the prizes remained unseen because they were still unpurchased - although we kept this fact to ourselves! The crowd at the draw included many of our friends and a number of clients of the library. The first ticket to be drawn belonged to a couple who were blind and wished the prize to go towards the expenses of the library. Second prize was the crate of whisky – and that went to a man who did not drink and also wanted his prize to go back into the funds! The third lucky winner was a young married couple who were so blissfully happy that they did not want the money! The library had now raised the funds for its 'dream duplicator' - and Ted and I had not spent a cent. We felt that the angels must be laughing.

The 'dream duplicator' duly arrived and I signed for it, adding the words 'not examined' which turned out to be extremely fortunate. Ted unpacked the boxes and we discovered to our horror that the 'dream duplicator' was in fact a nightmare. Under no circumstances could it be persuaded to work. We contacted the company, asking them to send an engineer to look at the machine. Nothing happened and nobody appeared. Eventually we lost patience and decided that the time had come for the machine to be returned to the manufacturer with a request for full refund. This suggestion was not well received by the company and after ten days, I decided to take the bull by the horns. I telephoned the head office in New York and repeated my story - with which they were already well-acquainted. When I had finished I offered them a choice. Either they could send a team of experts to our house straightaway or alternatively I would bring the machine down to our front garden that afternoon and leave it outside on the grass for all the passers-by to see. Within three quarters of an hour a team of experts from the Boston office were on our doorstep. They poked and prodded at the machine and – joy of joys – it began to work and continued to do so.

Many people were now using the library but we were entirely dependent on word of mouth to make ourselves known. More publicity was needed and we wanted to be included in the catalogue of the Library of Congress in Washington. We wondered which title to send them and after much prayer, Ted suggested that St Thérèse of Lisieux, known as the Little Flower, might be the person to help us. Ted reminded me that Thérèse was patron saint of the Missions – and we were certainly undertaking a mission! We decided to 'persuade' her to help us by recording her own autobiography to offer to the Library of Congress. I read the autobiography in the translation by Monsignor Ronald Knox with which I was very familiar. Before each chapter I placed the project in the hands of the Holy Spirit and of St Thérèse, asking that I might record her story just as she would wish.

In high hopes, we sent off the recording, only to receive a duplicated letter telling us that the tapes were of 'incorrect standard'. We returned to our prayers and four weeks later posted the identical set of tapes to the same department. This time the Library of Congress informed us that they could not accept the tapes because: 'the speaker has a marked Italian accent – not acceptable!' That one certainly puzzled us. We had one more try – same tapes, same department. No letter arrived but eventually we received a copy of the huge catalogue of the Library of Congress. Included within was the longed for entry: 'Our Lady of Sorrows Library: The Autobiography of the Little Flower: St Thérèse of Lisieux'.

At last we would be able to make the existence of the library known to the thousands of people across the world that had access to the catalogue of the Library of Congress. Word spread and letters began to arrive from every continent. One brief message scrawled on a piece of paper read: 'Please send me an opera'. The postmark was Italian and Ted and I looked at one another in dismay – the writer appeared to have mistaken us for a music library. We did not want to ignore the request, so we sent off a commentary on the Gospel of St John and four months later received it back with four dollar bills and an appreciative note: *"Thank you so much for the opera. I enjoyed it very much, please send another"* At last the penny dropped! The Italian word for work is 'opera' and the 'opera-lover' became an enthusiastic borrower!

'Himself' had arranged for us to use a large room in the basement of the monastery. From there we found ourselves in contact with all manner of clients from bishops who were blind, to the residents of a leprosy hospital in Panama and a man on Molokai in the Hawaiian islands where Father Damian had ministered heroically to patients with leprosy. Among our more distinguished contacts was the Abbot of the Cistercian monastery of Gethsemane in Kentucky where Father Thomas Merton lived. Two of the monks in the community were blind and the Abbot wanted to take advantage of our services. In a letter to "The Reverend Gerard Orlando", he praised the recording of Ronald Knox's translation of *Story of a Soul* which the community had apparently found 'most edifying'. He added that he had: "never thought to hear a woman's voice in our refectory".

Tapes were now on loan to borrowers in nine countries. I had recorded more than 500 titles and we had a number of volunteers helping us. One day Ted asked me to pay particular attention to a letter from England which came from "St Cecilia's Guild for the Blind" and was, as usual, addressed to "The Reverend Gerard A Orlando" The writer was kind enough to describe our library as more sophisticated than their own and he was enquiring about the possibility of copying some of our tapes for "St Cecilia's" clientele. He also wondered if we would allow their Guild to suggest some titles which we might care to include on our own list. I scanned the letter quickly until I reached the signature at the foot of the page. The writer was none other than my old friend and spiritual director, Father Ferdinand Valentine. This presented me with a dilemma. Father Valentine had written to "The Reverend Gerard A Orlando" as one priest to another. Should I reveal my identity or continue to correspond under the usual alias? Ted and I thought and prayed about this and in the end we decided that I should behave as I would to any other correspondent and maintain the 'deception'. We believed that the Lord would understand and 'Himself' was perfectly happy about it – he certainly had no time to become involved with any of our correspondence.

Over the years we loaned a great many tapes to St Cecilia's Guild including some recordings I had made of books by the distinguished English Dominican, Gerald Vann. In one of his replies Father Valentine confided: "I never could stand listening to Father Vann or reading his books but your reader made his work sing!" That was encouragement indeed. "Reverend Gerard Orlando" wrote back to Father Valentine thanking him for his kind remark and assuring him that it would be "passed on to the reader"!

I especially enjoyed recording Father Ferdinand's own book *Whatsoever He Shall Say: The First "Theophila" Correspondence* which takes the form of an exchange of letters between an 'enquirer' – Theophila – and her spiritual director. In the letters from 'Theophila', I once again recognised many of the queries that I had raised in my own lengthy correspondence with Father Valentine. Ted and I recorded the book together. He took the role of Father Valentine and I was "Theophila". Ferdinand Valentine was thrilled with the tape and his response made it clear that he imagined the male voice to be that of "Gerard Orlando".

From time to time 'Himself' asked why on earth I did not reveal my identity to my former spiritual director. I told him that I was refusing to do so because Father Valentine and other priests had written to "Reverend Gerard Orlando" in a way in which they would surely not have written to a lay person. I felt that it would be inappropriate for all kinds of reasons to 'reveal' that the recipient of the letters and author of the responses was in fact a laywoman!

'Go to the fountain head'

In 1968 tragedy struck our family as I shall describe in the next chapter. For a period of time I went through each day like a zombie – just existing and getting through as best I could.

Meanwhile the Library had grown into a sizeable undertaking and we were circulating about ten thousand reels of tape a year. 'Himself' now alerted us to a potential difficulty in terms of our relationship with Boston Archdiocese. We were well aware that the archdiocese was a hive of industry in terms of the number and variety of undertakings and the Cardinal Archbishop apparently liked to have everything under the diocesan 'umbrella'. 'Himself' alerted us to his probable 'designs' on the library once the archdiocese realised the extent of the undertaking. We were going to be snowed under with a mountain of diocesan paperwork when we already had more than enough to cope with.

One day I was alone in the church and sharing with the Lord my concerns about our work if Cardinal Cushing became aware of it. I seemed to hear a 'still small voice' saying "Go to the fountain head". From time to time I had received a 'word of knowledge' from the Lord and I knew that one had to be vigilant about 'messages' as they could come from a variety of sources. I seemed to hear the voice again: "Go to the fountain head". What could it mean? I pointed out to the Lord that He Himself was the fountain head and that I had indeed gone to Him with my problem! A further thought came to me. For Catholics, the 'fountain head' on earth was the Pope, the Vicar of Christ. The idea seemed preposterous – how could I possibly go to the Pope!

Suddenly I recalled that 'Himself' was away on pilgrimage to the Holy Land and would be spending a subsequent week in Rome. He spoke fluent Italian, and I knew that he had been hoping to meet the Holy Father, Pope Paul VI. Did the Lord want me to ask 'Himself' to suggest that the Pope took the tape library 'under his wing' so that the archdiocese of Boston would not be able to take over? At first the idea seemed preposterous but as I thought and prayed about it I came to the conclusion that that must indeed be the meaning of "Go to the fountain head".

That night I wrote a letter to 'Himself', inspired by the thought of St Catherine of Siena who was not given to mincing her words when addressing prelates and pontiffs. I told 'Himself' of my experience in the church – he was still my spiritual director - and suggested that the fact that he was visiting Rome at this time was more than 'coincidence'. In the spirit of St Catherine, I told him that if he failed to mention the Library of Our Lady of Sorrows to the Holy Father, I would consider him 'chicken'.

The following morning the letter went off to Rome by registered post to await the arrival of Father Gerard Orlando. I prayed and continued to hope. Two weeks later, I was in the church when a lady I did not know approached me to enquire whether I was 'Mrs Donovan'. She had received a message from Father Orlando which she had promised to pass on. "Father Orlando has a message for you from the Pope." I rushed home to Ted and we wondered fruitlessly about the extraordinary 'message'. 'Himself' was due back that night and the following day I received a phone call: "I'll give you three minutes to get up to the monastery!" I made it – but when I got there 'Himself' was obviously determined to take his time satisfying my curiosity and was going to enjoy himself at my expense! Eventually he came out with: "I was actually more scared of you than of the Pope!'. It transpired that 'Himself' had managed a few moments conversation with the Holy Father and had confided to him the existence of a 'new and worldwide missionary endeavour: the first of its kind'. Would the Holy Father take it under his protection and give it his special blessing? The Pope confided to 'Himself' that he had a special concern and interest in the needs of people who were blind and he was happy to take the Library under his special protection. The Library of Our Lady of Sorrows Library had indeed "gone to the fountain head" and discovered it to be a source of living water. When we moved away from Boston in 1971, one of the most important tasks was the handing over of the tape library to those who would run it well and faithfully. It had been difficult to find suitable people who were able to make the necessary commitment but we were eventually satisfied that the library had been left in capable hands.

13

THE VALLEY OF THE SHADOW 1963-1968

Ask not what your country can do for you;
ask what you can do for your country.
> **John F Kennedy**
> Inaugural address 20 January 1961

Most people over fifty remember what they were doing on Friday November 22nd 1963 - the day on which the world was stunned by the news of the fatal shooting of President Kennedy in Texas. I was alone in the house when a neighbour came across to tell me that she had heard on the radio that the President had been 'hit' while visiting Dallas. Liz and Ted each telephoned me and I turned on the radio. The news came through that the President was dead and that vice-president, Lyndon B. Johnson had been sworn in as the new President of the United States.

Offices and workplaces closed down and Ted arrived home within the hour. We were totally stunned. The manner of the President's death seemed such an affront, not only to the grieving people of America and of the world but to the very dignity of the presidential office. Ted and I knelt and prayed for President Kennedy and for his family. After a while Ted suggested that we go up to the monastery. Many parishioners had had the same idea.

Everybody seemed to feel that they had known President Kennedy personally, although the vast majority of Americans had probably never set eyes on him. Ted and I had caught a single glimpse of the President in the Sheraton Plaza Hotel. We had been coming down the hotel staircase when we heard a rumour that he was in the building. A kindly plain clothes policeman encouraged Ted and me to stay and 'rubberneck': 'Lady, you and your husband just stand right here, and don't move. The President will come out of that elevator! Today I imagine that the building would be closed for security.

Eighteen year old Liz was to be very closely associated with arrangements for the funeral of the President in a way that was totally unforeseen. In 1963 she was still intending to join the religious Congregation of the Holy Child Jesus and, in accordance with the wishes of her future superiors, she had taken a first class secretarial course. In June 1964 she graduated from the Aquinas Secretarial School as a legal secretary and landed an interesting position in the Chancery of the Boston Archdiocese where she worked for a number of Monsignors. I always imagined that Liz's participation in church bureaucracy must have been a 'learning experience' in terms of appreciating the difference between 'establishment' religion and a real and living relationship with Jesus!

Cardinal Cushing asked all the parishes in Boston Archdiocese to celebrate requiem Masses for the President on Sunday 24th November instead of the usual Sunday liturgy. Ted and I realised that it would be 'all hands on deck' at the diocesan chancery as they had only the Saturday on which to contact their many parishes. It was now Friday night and Ted and I imagined that Liz would receive a phone call asking her to go into work the following day, not only because of the change to Sunday Masses but because the Kennedys were a Boston family. Cardinal Cushing and the Chancery were likely to be involved in the funeral arrangements.

The phone call never came and on Saturday morning Ted and I suggested to Liz that she go into the office anyway to find out whether or not she was needed. Liz demurred on the grounds that she was the youngest person working in the Chancery and it would appear presumptuous to suggest that anybody might need her. Ted insisted that she at least make an effort to offer her services and drove his most reluctant daughter to her place of work, armed with a packet of sandwiches from me in case she had to stay all day.

We half expected to see Liz back on the doorstep, telling us that she had been right all along. But by four o'clock on Saturday afternoon she had not returned and my curiosity got the better of me. I telephoned the Chancery and Liz herself answered. 'Mummy', she said: 'You will hardly believe this, but I am the only person on the staff to have reported for work. I know where the President is going to be buried and even his family do not have details yet. She had taken a phone call from Senator Edward Kennedy and had spoken to Cardinal Cushing who had told her that he was to be the principal celebrant at the requiem Mass in Washington. The Kennedy family had originally wanted the President to be buried in the family plot in Brookline where the President's baby son had been laid to rest but it had eventually been decided that Arlington National Cemetery, would be more appropriate. One of the reasons was apparently the potential security nightmare if all the distinguished guests had to travel from Washington up to Boston for a burial in Brookline.

At eight o'clock on Saturday night Ted and I drove to the Chancery to collect our exhausted daughter. We met the diocesan Chancellor who was equally tired but told us that Liz had been a godsend and he could never have managed without her. A good part of her day had been spent in telephoning parish priests in connection with the requiem Masses as there were over 400 parishes in the Archdiocese. The Chancellor had warned her against 'protective' housekeepers who might refuse to 'disturb' the parish priest. If Liz encountered these formidable ladies she was instructed to tell them that she was speaking from the diocesan Chancery and that they were to get the parish priest NOW!

On Sunday 24 November, President Kennedy's body was taken to the Capitol, to lie in state at the seat of Congress. Over the next eighteen hours, two hundred and fifty thousand people filed past the casket. The following day, one million lined the route of the funeral procession from the Capitol to the White House and from there to St Matthew's Cathedral. That afternoon the 35th President of the United States was laid to rest in Arlington National Cemetery and his widow lit an eternal flame at his grave. Ted and I watched the ceremony on television and grieved for the Kennedy family. Little did we imagine that tragedy was to visit our own family within the decade.

Pamela, Anthony and Liz

The time had now come for Liz to leave the diocesan Chancery and prepare for her new life as nun. She wanted to spend a few months working in London before entering the novitiate and the Holy Child nuns invited her to live in their house in central London. Ted and I intended to visit her there and planned to take the opportunity to travel via Ireland. The trip got off to an ill starred beginning! We arrived at Dublin airport in the early morning to find that our plane was going to spend an extra two hours on the tarmac because Princess Grace of Monaco had also arrived and was receiving red carpet treatment. The Irish authorities were delaying disembarkation of all other travellers!

We were eventually decanted into the terminal building, only to discover that the Donovan luggage had travelled to Paris! We were fed tea and biscuits by kindly airport staff and assured that the missing suitcases were 'on their way'. In the meantime, Ted hired a car so that we could set off immediately the suitcases arrived. By the time they eventually reached us, night had fallen and we faced a long drive south westwards to our destination: the Eccles Hotel in Glengarrif, Co Cork. The road from Dublin to Glengarrif was long and winding and neither our journey nor our tempers were assisted by the number of sheep which had decided to go to sleep on the mountain road. Stupid animals, we thought! We were to discover that there was method in their madness. Sheep that spend too long in soggy grass are apparently subject to foot rot so the road was a sensible alternative.

We had only a box of chocolates to keep hunger at bay and Ted was afraid of falling asleep at the wheel. To keep ourselves awake, we prayed out loud, ate the chocolates, sang every hymn in our repertoire and yelled at the sheep! When we eventually staggered into the Eccles Hotel we were almost too tired to care that none of the bedroom doors appeared to have locks. The night receptionist was puzzled by our concern over keys: 'Who would be wanting to open anybody else's door?'

From Ireland, we had a trouble free journey to London where we discovered that Liz was having second thoughts about entering the Convent. She had been in contact with 'Himself' (Fr Gerald Orlando) who had written her a wonderful letter from Boston which she allowed me to see. Two days after our arrival Liz made a decision not to enter the convent but to return instead to the USA.

In June 1965, twenty-three year old Pamela graduated from St. Elizabeth's as a fully qualified nurse. Ted and I were very proud of her for succeeding in her ambition against considerable odds; not the least of which had been her total ignorance of any scientific subject when she elected to take up nursing. In honour of her graduation, Pamela had a studio portrait taken which shows her with firm jaw, determined mouth and her pretty hair looped beneath a perky little cap; the prized nursing badge well to the fore.

It was now time for our elder daughter to decide where she was going to practise her skills and she confided to Ted and me that she had for some time been thinking of entering a missionary nursing order. She was attracted towards the Medical Missionaries of Mary and had visited their Massachusetts convent in Winchester. She had also been offered a staff job at St Elizabeth's Hospital, which was a considerable feather in her cap. But she felt that the staff job would not provide her with the personal commitment she was seeking. As with Liz

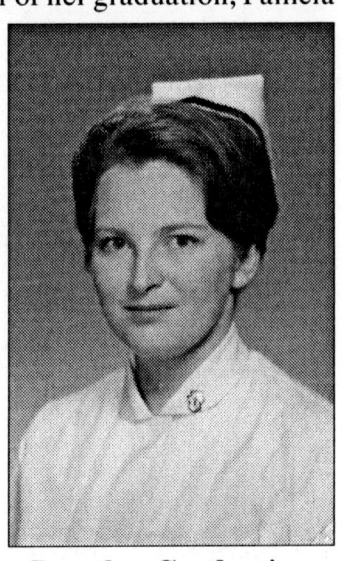

Pamela - Graduation

and Anthony, we felt honoured that God was choosing our children in this way but there was sadness at the inevitable parting.

The novice mistress at Winchester sent Pamela a list of requirements and we went shopping for the many and varied items, all of which had to be marked with her name. But what was that name to be? We were informed that Pamela would enter the novitiate as 'Sister Mary Donovan'. When she made her religious profession she would receive a different name but 'Sister Mary Donovan' would serve for the moment.

I sewed innumerable name tapes onto Pamela's clothes and belongings, remembering nostalgically the hundreds of tapes I had sewn for the children when they went away to boarding school. In my cupboard upstairs are still a couple of blankets marked 'Sister Mary Donovan' which bring back memories of those early days when I could at least console myself that novice Pamela would be close to us in Boston until she departed for the mission field.

On the appointed day, Ted and I delivered the future nun and her trunk to the convent in Winchester. We heard nothing and did not expect to do so. Nine days later the phone rang and it was Pamela's novice mistress: "Mrs Donovan, I am very upset. Pamela wants to leave. Please will you talk to her and try to persuade her to stay?" I gulped and thought fast: 'No, I won't try to persuade Pamela to stay. Please tell her that if she wants to leave, a warm welcome awaits her at home and my husband and I will be glad to collect her.' I replaced the receiver and wondered what to do next.

Ted and I could only wait and pray. The next thing we knew, a car was stopping outside our front door. The driver was a youngish nun and the passenger was Pamela! I hugged my daughter, welcoming her home and I tried to talk to the nun but she clearly did not wish to enter into any sort of conversation. 'Sister driver' decanted Pamela's belongings and her nursing books, got back into her car and drove off without saying goodbye to either of us.

Pamela seemed glad to be home. She did not want to talk about the convent and we did not press her. Later we learnt that matters had got off to a bad start on her first evening. The novice mistress had apparently addressed Pamela and her eight new companions, instructing them to forget about nursing and concentrate on becoming 'good nuns'. She told them that some of the group might never nurse again and reminded them that the novitiate was a time of testing; a place which they could be asked to leave because: 'the door swings both ways!' That was certainly an inauspicious beginning! Pamela later confided to Liz that when she told the novice mistress that she wanted to leave, she reminded her of what she had said on that first evening. "You told us that the door swings both ways, and 'I'm swinging out!'"

It had clearly been a very painful episode. Pamela decided to take a job at the nearby Veterans Hospital and moved into her own flat. Some time afterwards she left the Veterans and accepted a job at St Elizabeth's where she was welcomed with open arms and put to work in the maternity ward. She loved it. Ted and I found ourselves able to relate to Pamela ever more deeply as she became increasingly sensitive and compassionate. She moved house - this time closer to home. It was a lovely two-bedroom apartment which she shared with another nurse. The two girls were cat fanciers and acquired a beautiful Persian/angora kitten.

Ted and I continued to reflect on the mysterious way in which the Lord appeared to have called all three children into religious life with two of them eventually deciding against it. That left Anthony at Ampleforth. But Ted and I were becoming increasingly concerned about Anthony. The letters we were receiving indicated that he was neither happy nor settled and we felt powerless to help and support our son because we were so far away.

In our deep concern for Anthony, Ted and I clung ever more deeply to one another. We prayed as hard as we could and reminded ourselves that God was even more concerned about our children than their anxious parents. We longed to be able to share our concerns with like-minded people - strong Christians who would help and support us. Our dreams and hopes of Christian community were kindled afresh. We poured out our hearts to 'Himself' who did his best to comfort us - adding for good measure: 'You two will always be persecuted by 'good' people. Stick to your guns!' We felt that he was being something of a 'Job's comforter'. We had quite enough to contend with already and did not relish the thought of persecution on top!

Six months later, a letter from Anthony indicated that he was now suffering serious doubts about his vocation. He had moved to the Benedictine house of studies in Oxford, St Benet's Hall, from whence we received a phone call to tell us that he felt that his future did not lie with the Benedictines of Ampleforth. He would be leaving the community in the Spring of 1967 but intended to remain in Oxford to complete his degree and the board of education in York were providing the necessary grant. Sometime later he wrote to tell us about an undergraduate at St Anne's named Fiona McDonald and enclosed a photograph of a beautiful young girl. We liked the sound of Fiona and suspected that Anthony might be serious about her which proved to be the case. The two were married in July 1969 just after graduation.

Pamela in Vietnam

During the 1960's, American forces had entered south-east Asia to support the South Vietnamese in their struggle against perceived communist aggression. By 1967, the Vietnam War was at its height and television cameras were broadcasting horrific live coverage night after night. One evening Pamela dropped in to give us startling news. She was thinking seriously of volunteering to go out and assist the wounded and dying in Vietnam. She felt that she was needed because she had heard that the 400,000 American soldiers were entirely dependent upon the services of volunteer nurses to tend their wounded. To volunteer she would have to become an American citizen – a cost to Pamela because she was proud of being Irish.

For Ted and me, this was a bombshell. But we had always tried to support our children in their choices so we did not try to dissuade Pamela. Her first application to the Army Nursing Recruitment Centre was turned down by the recruiting officer on the grounds that she was thirty pounds overweight. Ted and I thought that would be the end of the matter but we had underestimated our daughter. Pamela lost thirty pounds in no time and returned to the Recruitment Centre, taking her mother with her! She saw the same recruiting officer who seemed kind and obviously remembered Pamela well from their previous meeting. This time her application was accepted and Pamela was drafted into the American Army Nurse Corps for a one year tour of duty as Second Lieutenant Pamela Donovan. She set off for Texas to begin her army medical training at Fort Sam Houston.

Pamela being sworn as US Citizen

In April 1968 she arrived back in Boston, radiantly happy as a fully fledged army nurse with her sights set on South Vietnam. On the day of her departure, Ted and I and Liz drove Pamela to Boston's Logan Airport. I was forcibly reminded of my final farewell to my mother at the same airport some ten years earlier. Pamela was radiant in her new military uniform with her name embossed on her badge. She kissed and hugged me goodbye and stood on tiptoe to kiss tall Ted. I can still see her happy smile as she walked out onto the tarmac and turned for one last wave. That picture will remain with me forever.

Pamela

Army nurses were normally sent out in pairs but the intended companion had fallen sick the previous day so Pamela was the only girl in a planeload of soldiers. Throughout the journey they apparently treated her royally and the pilot allowed her to join him on the flight deck. They all knew that the nurses were volunteers and wished to express their appreciation.

On her arrival, Pamela wrote immediately to tell us of her posting to the 85th Evacuation Hospital in Qui Nhon and continued to prove a faithful correspondent. She described parts of the country as 'like Ireland - but not when it comes to temperature!'. The heat was never less than ninety-five degrees and the limited air conditioning did not extend to Pamela's ward, nor to her living quarters. But there was never a word of complaint in her letters, despite the fact that she was working twelve hours shifts on six days out of seven. She frequently remarked on the bravery and the youth of the soldiers in her care. Pamela herself was only twenty six!

Before she left for Vietnam, Pamela had slipped away from the practice of her faith but now found herself nursing a number of soldiers who were Christians. Several had been blinded in action and wanted to listen to tapes with a Christian content. Pamela borrowed a number of tapes from our library and I received grateful letters from the parents of these young men.

In May she went to the beach and suffered extensive sunburn which might not sound too serious but proved to be a grave offence for a nurse who 'should have known better'. Pamela was in great pain and confined to bed where I suspect she received little sympathy from nursing staff who felt that she should have been on her feet nursing the wounded. During her recovery, Pamela made a tape for Ted and me in which she sounded happy and in good spirits. In a subsequent letter, she told us that she planned to go on to Japan and Australia at the conclusion of her one-year tour of duty. She had a friend in Australia who was also in touch with Ted and me and sounded enthusiastic at the prospect of being joined by Pamela. But our daughter also seemed to be thinking of applying to a number of nursing schools in the

USA with a view to taking an additional nursing degree. She seemed to be keeping her options open.

In one of her letters home, Pamela shared with us some news which filled us with foreboding. She had become aware of the existence of a 'heroin ring' in the hospital and had determined that it was her duty to report this. Ted and I cautioned Pamela to be very careful indeed. We knew little of the world of drugs but were deeply concerned that Pamela should not put herself into unnecessary danger. To this day I do not know whether or not she reported the existence of that ring and, if so, whether her report had anything to do with the tragedy that followed.

One day we received a telephone call out of the blue via two-way radio. Pamela spoke and then said 'Over'. We replied from the other side of the world, adding 'Over' in our turn. The conversation was somewhat stilted and frustrating but it was such a joy to hear her voice. I felt that Pamela was really and truly happy

On the home front, I was finding myself under ever increasing strain and was grieving over the separation from Anthony and from Pamela. I seemed to be exhausted all the time and very slow in doing anything. The doctor prescribed some pills but they did not suit me. At the beginning of June 1968, I finally suffered a mental breakdown which put me into hospital for several weeks. Ted was marvellously supportive throughout this whole painful period and we talked once more of our yearning for community with other Christians who wished to live according to Gospel values.

During this difficult time, Pamela really came into her own and proved herself the greatest support. She wrote to me every single day, as I know from the dates on her letters. The postal service proved less reliable and sometimes two or three letters would arrive on a single day, to be followed by several days of nothing at all. Her loving and constant concern helped me enormously and the knowledge that she cared so much was all-important.

The great American national holiday dawned happily on July 4th 1968. It was a steaming hot day which Ted, Liz and I spent lounging around in shorts. During the afternoon, the doorbell rang and a cable was handed in. This was rare indeed. What could it mean? We opened the envelope to find that the cable had been sent to us by the American Army and the news it contained was heart stopping:

"The Secretary of the Army has asked me to express his deep regret that your daughter Lieutenant Pamela Donovan was placed on the very seriously ill list in Vietnam on 3 July 68 as a result of an overdose of barbiturates. She was found unconscious in her billeting facility. In the judgment of the attending physician her condition is of such severity that there is cause for concern. Please be assured that facilities and doctors have been made available and that every measure is being taken to aid her. You will be kept informed of any significant changes in her condition.

She is hospitalised in Vietnam. Address mail to her at hospital mail section.'
  'Kenneth G Wickham, Major General.'

I felt numb with shock. Ted is always magnificent in a crisis and straightaway telephoned the Army Nursing Recruitment Headquarters in Boston where Pamela had enlisted. They could give him no information because none was available to them. We learnt only that the cable had been sent direct from Vietnam. Ted then decided that we should try the Red Cross. I telephoned the Boston branch and got through to a wonderful lady who was extremely sympathetic even though there was not much she could do in terms of getting additional information. She gave me some practical advice. 'Write a letter to Pamela every day starting right now.' That at least gave me something to do and it comforted me to think that my letters would be awaiting our daughter when she recovered.

The hours and days dragged endlessly as we waited in agonised concern. How could Pamela possibly have received 'an overdose of barbiturates'? I simply could not understand it. Another cable arrived from Vietnam, telling us that Pamela was still unconscious but was being flown to the capital, where she could receive 'more appropriate treatment'.

On July 9th I was sitting in our living room, when a limousine drew up. Out stepped a senior army officer. As soon as I saw him, I knew that he had come to bring the worst possible news. I invited the man in and before he could open his mouth I said:

'Pamela is dead, isn't she?' He nodded sorrowfully and my heart went out to this senior officer who had come on such a dreadful errand. I could only think to offer him a cup of tea which he refused. He offered to telephone Ted but I told him that I would 'manage'. He then made me sit down and handed me his card, telling me that he was in charge of 'the case' and would be available night or day to give us any help we might need.

He told me *all* that he knew which was that Pamela had died the previous day, July 8th and that the cause of her death was pneumonia. To my many questions, he had no answers. I was told that Pamela's body would be flown home in ten days time and would be transferred to whichever funeral home we designated. With reiterated expressions of sympathy and concern, the officer departed.

I had now to telephone Ted to break the terrible news. I could hear him weeping and when he arrived home we clung together in our grief. Ted knelt down and asked me to join him in prayer that we might accept the will of God, however agonising. After the first outburst of grief, there came numbness and a sort of disbelief. Yes, we knew that people lost children, but those people weren't us! We knew that Pamela was in a danger zone, but it was the soldiers who were supposed to get killed, not the nurses! Next we had to break the news to Liz who was grief stricken and to Anthony in Oxford.

Three days later, on July 12th, something so wonderful and extraordinary happened that I still can hardly believe it. The post brought us a letter from our dead daughter dated July 3rd, five days before her death and her words will remain forever engraved on our hearts.

> *Dearest Mummy and Daddy,*
>
> *I know over the years you have been unhappy, as I have been unfaithful to the Church and to going to Mass and the Sacraments. Well, I want you to know that last night I went to the Chaplain out here to Confession, and this morning I went to Mass and Holy Communion. I feel a new person......*
>
> *All my love, Pamela.*

In the midst of our grief, the knowledge of Pamela's return to her faith has remained an abiding source of joy and gratitude. Ted and I felt that we must express this at her funeral and we had heard that it was now possible to have a requiem Mass with flowers, joyful singing and white vestments, instead of the traditional black: a true Mass of the Resurrection. The parish priest was appalled at the idea of white vestments. We told him that if he would not accommodate our request we would contact Cardinal Cushing, and he capitulated.

We began to make arrangements with the funeral director who refused to accept a cent in payment, telling us that it was a privilege to be allowed to bury someone who had died for her country. We told him that we did not intend to hold a 'wake' because we wanted our visit to the funeral home to be entirely private. Anthony arrived from England and he and

Liz accompanied Ted and me to the funeral home as the only mourners. Pamela lay in an open casket lined with satin. Her beautiful face was peaceful and serene and her skin was its usual '˜peaches and cream' despite the recent sunburn. Her blonde hair was dressed back and she was wearing her military uniform with white gloves.

Ted and I were still very puzzled at the lack of information surrounding Pamela's death. None of the questions we asked received proper answers. We wrote to Pamela's Commanding Officer in Vietnam and to the Chaplain but received no response from either of them. The Senior Army Officer handling the case intimated that if we stopped asking questions Pamela would be given a full military funeral – the obvious implication being that a military funeral would be refused if we continued our enquiries. We were powerless to do anything and for Pamela's sake we decided not to question further.

We had wanted publicity kept to a minimum but learnt subsequently that Pamela was only the third nurse to be killed in Vietnam out of a total of eight. Her death made headlines in the newspapers and was reported on radio and television. Letters of condolence began to pour in, not only from relatives and friends but from men and women all over America. Ted and I placed these letters in a large suitcase 'to be read later'. I never acknowledged them and I have never been able to read them. It was just too much. Ted and I were just 'existing'; getting through each day as best we could. We obviously continued to wonder about the circumstances surrounding Pamela's death. There was no way in which her final letters to us could be seen as a prelude to self-destruction.

Many people told us that they were going to ask for a Mass to be offered for Pamela and a number of priest friends said they would be celebrating Mass for her. Ted and I decided that we should have memorial cards printed for these kind well-wishers. We calculated that about fifty Masses were going to be offered for Pamela so we had fifty cards printed, only to discover that we had seriously underestimated. Six hundred and thirty Masses were offered for the repose of the soul of Pamela Donovan and we had to put in hand a large reprint.

The day of the funeral dawned scorching hot. Ted and I drove up to the monastery church with Anthony and Liz. We felt as if we were in a dream. Ted said to me: 'I think we are going to miss having family here as there will not be many people'. We were puzzled to see so many vehicles in the car park. What could they all be doing there? When we walked into the large monastery church we saw to our astonishment that it was three quarters full. There must have been 500 people. 'Himself' was the principal celebrant and a number of our priest friends had told us they wanted to concelebrate with him. I counted nine priests at the altar. One of them I did not know at all.

A number of high ranking officers arrived for the Requiem and the coffin was carried into church on the shoulders of the military. It was covered in the Stars and Stripes and we had placed three red roses on the lid. At the conclusion of the Service, the military stood to attention as Ted and I walked down the steps of the parish church, and were helped into the large black car. The priest I did not know had followed us out of the church and I noticed that he was walking carefully. I heard him say to someone: 'Would you please put my hand into the hand of Mrs. Donovan?' The man was blind and it transpired that he was one of the priests who had received our tapes. I learnt that he lived hundreds of miles away in a different State but had made the long journey to express his support. He held my two hands and said only: 'Thank you'. I never learnt his name.

The funeral director led the procession to Mount Hope Cemetery where Pamela was to be buried with full military honours. We had been offered the choice between a burial at Washington's Arlington National cemetery or Mount Hope but decided on the latter. We wanted Pamela to be close to us. She rests beside soldiers who fell in battle during the Second World War.

Before the funeral there had been discussion as to who should receive the flag from the coffin and it had been agreed that it would be handed to me. The flag was carefully arranged in a tricorn shape and handed to the highest ranking officer who saluted and came across to place it in my hands. The bugle call 'Taps' was sounded followed by the Last Post. By the grace of God, I was able to contain my tears.

Aftermath

Immediately after the funeral Ted took me to New York for a few days - just to get away. We came back to Boston to try to take up the threads of our lives, nerving ourselves to face each day as it came It was only our faith in God and our love for one another that kept us going.

On our return, we found Pamela's death certificate awaiting us. It was dated 18 July and had been sent by The Office of the Adjutant General in Washington. It contained the stark words: 'Died 8 July 1968 in Vietnam from pneumonia secondary to an overdose of barbiturates'. Worse was to follow. In September a second death certificate reached us. This time an additional sentence had been added which turned me cold: 'Self destruction while mentally unsound'.

I knew that this could not be true. The girl who had found such joy in her work; the girl who had returned to the practice of her faith and was feeling 'a new person' could never have taken her own life. Ted and I showed the death certificates and Pamela's letters to medically qualified friends. They confirmed our conviction. The girl who had written so joyfully on July 3rd could never have taken her own life five days later.

Six months after Pamela's death, the telephone rang one morning and I picked it up to find that caller was a nurse friend of Pamela who had been out in Vietnam with her. When she had established that I was Pamela's mother she told me that she wanted to tell me 'the truth' about what had happened to our daughter. I waited with bated breath, but the young girl's voice faltered. She suddenly sounded very scared. 'No, I can't tell you. I am too afraid of what might happen to me!' With that the receiver was replaced. A few weeks later we received a similar phone call from another nurse friend of Pamela who wanted to tell us 'the truth' but was also afraid. We agonized and puzzled over these phone calls. What could they mean? What was 'the truth'? Why were Pamela's friends so frightened?

We were only too well aware that Pamela had known of the heroin addiction which was rife among American enlisted men in Vietnam during the 1960's, although this was only to come to the attention of the public in the spring of 1971. Had her death any connection with a 'heroin ring'? Had she made a report and was this related to her death? We were never to know. Ted drafted a letter of enquiry to a very senior officer in the Pentagon but in the end decided not to send it. Nothing was going to bring back our beloved daughter and we felt that we just could not take any more.

I continued to work at the tape library but went through each day like a zombie; just existing and getting through as best I could. Ted and I soon became aware that God was using our sorrow to help others. Pamela's death was providing us with the opportunity to stand alongside other bereaved parents and share their sorrow with an empathy and understanding that comes only from the reality of shared experience.

In 1969, the American Army Veterans Association asked whether we would allow a road to be named in memory of Pamela. They had chosen one leading up to the Passionist monastery church which we attended daily and where the tape library was based. For the formal opening of the road, Ted and I invited family and friends who had known Pamela to join us and a lunch was laid on. The experience passed in a haze but it was a consolation to meet so many people who had warm and loving memories of Pamela. We were deeply moved to meet people who had never met our daughter but had been deeply moved and impressed by her story and by the fact that a young girl who was not American born had wanted to go 'out there'.

In November 1993 the Women's Vietnam Memorial was dedicated in Washington DC on which the devoted service of these young women girls is publicly acknowledged and Pamela is remembered by name. Ted and I were unable to be present at the ceremony of dedication on Veterans Day, November 11th but were represented by Liz. Among the guests she met two nurses who had served with Pamela. Both had obviously been emotionally scarred by their experiences and one of them handed Liz a photograph of Pamela taken in Vietnam. She passed it on to me and I carry it always. The two women expressed their heartfelt condolences to Liz but clearly felt unable to enter into any of the details surrounding Pamela's death. On her return to Northants Liz undertook extensive research to contact anyone who had served with Pamela. She had a certain amount of success in tracing individuals but received conflicting accounts of Pamela's last days.

Pamela's memory lives on in the hearts and minds of friends and family who loved her dearly and will never cease to mourn her loss. She lives, too, in the hearts of unknown individuals whom we shall never meet but who honour the memory of our daughter.

One card which was left at the Vietnam Women's Memorial touched us especially deeply:

2nd Lieutenant Pamela Donovan: *Your kindness will never be forgotten* Don Sprecker

14

ENGLAND AGAIN
1969-1971

> And it shall come to pass that in later days that I
> will pour out My Spirit on all flesh…
> **Acts 2 17**

In 1969, we became aware that Liz really needed to get away from Boston and from sorrowful memories. Brian and Majsan suggested that she pay them a visit in England and we knew that the change would be beneficial. Liz was delighted at the prospect of getting to know her uncle and aunt and Brian and Majsan welcomed her as if she had been their own daughter. They could not have done more to make her feel at home.

At around the time of Liz's departure, Ted and I were invited to take part in a 'spiritual evening' at the Dominican House of Studies in Dover, Massachusetts. We were included because of our involvement in the Dominican Secular Institute and the group consisted of two priests, a number of former nuns and several ex seminarians. As the evening progressed we began to wonder what we had let ourselves in for.

We had begun with a time of fellowship during which we got to know one another. A Mass followed this, which was unlike any liturgy in which we had ever participated. The presiding priest was Father Stock whom we knew quite well and the Mass began with guitar music, which was followed by a lengthy period of silent reflection in which we were invited to meditate on our sins and shortcomings. Things began to get 'interesting' after the first reading when Ted and I discovered to our horror that people were expected to pray *out loud!* We had practised impromptu prayer, just the two of us together. The idea of sharing vocal prayer with a bunch of comparative strangers was toe curling! After the Gospel, the 'sermon' consisted of the congregation giving their personal thoughts and insights about the scripture readings. I was struck dumb and felt very scared and inadequate because I had always thought of myself as a very private person and all this 'sharing' was a bolt from the blue! Since I was seven years old I had prayed in a 'private language' which I had shared with nobody -not even Ted. All this 'sharing' seemed 'a very different cup of tea'.

At the time of Holy Communion we received the host but were also invited to receive from the chalice; very unusual at that time. More praying out loud again followed Communion and the Mass ended with guitar music

Ted and I discussed the evening and decided that we were not keen on 'that sort of thing'. Little did we know that we were witnessing the first stirrings of Holy Spirit inspired 'Renewal' in the Catholic Church. Still less did we realise that this Renewal was to be the means by which God was to answer our heartfelt prayers for community life with like-minded Christians. I was to discover that my 'private language' had a name: glossolalia, the gift of tongues. It had been a common phenomenon in New Testament times and two thousand years later was being re-experienced by Christians of many denominations throughout the world as Renewal spread. We realised afterwards that the Mass at the Dominican House of Studies had been the first intimation of the door that God was going to open in our lives. At that stage, we had no intimation of God's plan for our future and no intention of walking through any door whatsoever. We did not like 'that sort of thing'!

In England, Anthony had now become engaged to Fiona McDonald and we were anxious to meet our future daughter in law. The two had arranged their wedding for July 1969 and we flew to England full of expectation. We were overjoyed to meet the beautiful young girl who was so obviously going to make Anthony very happy. We felt that our son had indeed 'struck gold' in his bride and we have come to love Fiona very dearly. The wedding took place at The Old Palace, the Catholic Chaplaincy at Oxford and the celebrant was the Catholic chaplain, Father Michael Hollings. Father Hollings was to become very well known in the future as an outstanding priest of Westminster Archdiocese.

It was wonderful to see Liz in London and to meet up with Brian and Majsan after so long. They had become close to Anthony and Fiona who were going to start married life in Oxford where Anthony had a job in the Bodleian Library. They were not too far from Brian and Majsan in the village of Hurley between High Wycombe and Maidenhead. We returned to Boston but flew back to Europe the following year to meet our first grandchild, Stephen. Liz now had a little car and met us at Heathrow airport. Somehow she managed to fit us into it along with all the luggage and I was amazed at her courage in driving round the maelstrom of traffic at Marble Arch!

Back in Boston, the 'nest' seemed extremely empty. All our plans for a house full of young life with grandchildren running in and out had gone with the wind. We continued to work on the tape library and maintained our many commitments but there was a sense of emptiness. In April 1971 we celebrated our thirtieth wedding anniversary and realised that we each wanted the same anniversary present; a visit from Liz! We bought her a return ticket from London and asked if she could come for six weeks, in the hope that we might persuade her to come back for good!

When Liz arrived, the boot proved to be very much on the other foot. She spent most of her time persuading Ted and me to up sticks and return to England. At first we laughed at the idea, but Liz assured us that she did not intend to come back to Boston. She had put down roots in England and told us that Anthony and Fiona were going to stay there for good. Liz's idea began to make a lot of sense and Ted sounded out the president of his company about a transfer to the English office. The president was a good friend of ours. He agreed to the transfer but warned Ted that his salary would drop very substantially if he made such a move. We decided to risk it and bought a copy of the *Times* every week to check out the English housing market. We reckoned that a jolly good house could be had for eight thousand pounds; just as good as the house we had, and perhaps a little better.

Back to England

We flew to Ireland first and stayed in a ghastly hotel in Ballsbridge from whence we were glad to travel on to London. Ted knew that he would be working south of London, at Maidstone in Kent, so that was where we would be living. It was a part of the country we did not know at all and we discovered an attractive old town surrounded by beautiful countryside.

Alas, we also found that the price of houses had been going up by leaps and bounds since we had first looked at the property pages of the *Times*. We could get nothing for eight thousand pounds, and not much for twelve. We also discovered that some house sellers had a nasty habit of raising the price of a property when an offer had been accepted because they thought they could get a bit more. This, we learnt, was called 'gazumping' and it was rife! The nasty habit did not pertain north of the border between England and Scotland - as we were to learn to our advantage!

We tramped around wearily day after day and one afternoon came upon a beautiful house with a mature garden just outside Maidstone. It was for sale, had obviously been built by an architect and, astonishingly, it seemed to be within our price range. The owner was a Scotswoman, a Mrs May who was about forty and had originally put the house on the market eight months previously and then withdrawn it. She appeared to have put the house back on the market at the original price and without doing her homework about rocketing house prices.

We looked around house and garden, went home to think about it and hastened back to offer the asking price - with the nasty spectre of 'gazumping' at the back of our minds. Mrs May accepted our offer and then did something completely unexpected which made me thankful for her Scottish blood. She solemnly shook Ted's hand and then my hand, saying: 'You have my handshake on this. I am Scottish. You have my word that no one else shall have this house'.

Before we moved in Mrs May did something remarkably kind. She held a party for us so that we could meet all the other people in the road. She herself was moving into a cottage, but was unable to take possession of her new home for ten weeks which left Ted and me homeless - and unable to afford to spend ten weeks in a hotel. Someone told us about a Catholic retreat centre outside Maidstone called Allington Castle, which was owned by the Carmelite friars. The warden took pity on us and welcomed us in.

Allington had been the childhood home of the sixteenth century poet Thomas Wyatt who had carried out a number of foreign missions for Henry VIII. We were given to understand that we were staying in the King's bedchamber, known as 'Henry VIII's Room'. The main door to the room was large and presumably modern but there was a much older door which seemed inconveniently small and had apparently been so constructed to prevent enemies from rushing the King! Allington was a romantic place in which to stay apart from the big black spiders inhabiting the bathroom! We ate our meals with the other guests – fifteen or twenty of them during the week but rising to seventy or eighty at weekends when retreatants flooded in.

After ten years in Boston, our return to England was a considerable culture shock and we were grieving bitterly for our beloved Pamela. I was feeling shaky and insecure and had been prescribed tranquillisers and sleeping pills in Boston but wanted to wean myself away from these. A sympathetic young doctor in Maidstone helped me to do this and I found Dr McLaggan to be the kindest, most understanding and 'hopeful' physician I have ever encountered.

In many ways the ten weeks at Allington were a necessary 'watershed' between one life and the next. Among the Carmelite friars was the elderly Father Malachy Lynch who had been inspired to rebuild the thirteenth century Carmelite priory at nearby Aylesford which had been lost to the Catholic Church at the Reformation. Restoration work had only been completed in 1965 under the guidance of Father Malachy as the first prior. He had obtained the services of the architect Adrian Gilbert Scott, brother of Giles Gilbert Scott who had rebuilt the House of Commons after the war. To enhance Aylesford, Father Malachy had drafted in skilled Italian masons as well as local artists and sculptors. During our stay at Allington the Polish artist Adam Kossowski was working at Aylesford, completing the ceramic over the Blessed Sacrament altar in St Joseph's chapel. Most afternoons, Father Malachy and I would drive over to 'The Friars', as it was known, to say the rosary together and watch Adam at work

Mrs May was eventually able to move out of our house and we moved in at last. Thirty-five years previously the property had belonged to a horticultural specialist at the nearby East Malling Research Station who had laid out the garden. It seemed to contain every sort of vegetable and fruit, including a medlar, which was rare indeed, although medlars had been widely cultivated in England during the sixteenth century. The fruit of the medlar looked like rotten apples and should have been used in a variety of ways, but I was so taken up with the rest of the garden that I was seldom able to give this exotic fruit the culinary attention it deserved.

I now turned my attention to driving. My international driving licence gave me limited permission to drive in England but Ted and I both needed to pass the British driving test. Ted booked himself in straight away and passed first time – despite apparently driving straight over a zebra crossing on which there was a pedestrian. 'Whoops', said Ted, driving merrily on. The instructor must have turned a blind eye!

I took the test and failed; very shaming, after thirty years of driving all over Europe and North America. It was clear that I was going to need driving practice so I booked myself another test for six weeks hence and determined to spend every spare minute behind the wheel. 'Hill starts' were my particular bugbear, so I found a convenient steep hill in a residential street. Each morning after Ted had left for work I drove up to Allington Castle for very early Mass and then set aside half an hour for driving practice. At 7.00am on the dot I would drive slowly up 'my' hill, brake, stop, and look all around me with the exaggerated care required by driving examiners and restart the car; contriving not to roll backwards down the hill! I then turned around in the road and chugged down to a small side street where I stopped once more and practiced my 'looking around' technique.

One night Ted and I were sitting at home when the doorbell rang. On the step was a policeman with his helmet under his arm. 'Do you own car number WKT 607J?' he enquired. We did. Have you driven frequently in Larch Grove? We shook our heads, having never heard of Larch Grove. The policeman took out his notebook. 'It has been reported that car number WKT 607J has been seen each morning at 7.00am in Larch Grove. Residents allege that the driver regularly behaves in a suspicious manner! They suspect the driver of 'casing the joint' with a view to burglary! Ted and I looked at one another and burst out laughing. We explained my 'suspicious behaviour' but the policeman did not share our mirth. He stood up, completely deadpan and informed us that he would be explaining my actions to the residents of Larch Grove. I told Ted that I would probably have to find another road in which to practice driving. 'You jolly well won't' said Ted. 'If you find yourself another road, the residents there will complain all over again and we shall get another visit from a copper!'

When the time came for my second driving test, the examiner told me to make an 'emergency stop'™ when he tapped his hand on the dashboard. My 'emergency stop' was so sharp that the poor man nearly crashed through the windscreen and I thought he would fail me. He merely said: 'Relax, Mrs Donovan, You should be enjoying this!' When he told me I had passed I could have hugged the man.

I was missing my beloved Siamese left behind in Boston and decided that the time had come to buy another cat. I found a beautiful Siamese, which I named 'Yum-yum' and I longed to breed from her. Ted's reaction was: 'Over my dead body!' I managed to talk him round, on the understanding that he would be required to do absolutely nothing involving cat midwifery! The next step was to buy books on cat breeding, find a breeder who had a suitable sire and take the cat along at the right time. I had to pay a whopping fee for the privilege, but Yum-yum's increasing girth satisfied me that all had gone well.

One night we were getting ready to go out when Yum-yum started to purr very loudly. I knew that she was getting towards her due date and thought that I should stay with her. 'Nonsense' said Ted. When we returned the purring was still going on but nothing had 'happened'. I suggested that I took my knitting and a drink and sat with Yum-yum. Ted would not hear of it: 'That cat is quite capable of coping!'. At 5.00am I awoke and dashed into the 'labour ward'. Yum-yum had indeed coped, producing six tiny creatures that were all feeding busily and looked more like white mice than kittens. I would have liked to keep the lot but we compromised on one kitten to stay with me, and the other five to go to good homes.

I was so ignorant that I could not even discover the sex of the kittens. I phoned the breeder who suggested I bring them along. Easier said than done! I managed to get all six into a huge hatbox which I covered with rabbit netting. That, I thought would settle their hash! I set off on the seven-mile drive, but with six miles still to go I realised that one small demon had squeezed through the netting, followed by a second until all the wretched creatures were staggering about on the back seat. I stopped, replaced kittens and netting and tried again. This time they escaped within minutes and we were now entering a built-up area and I was unable to pull up. I stopped at the traffic lights with one kitten round my neck, two on my lap and a fourth walking up my leg. A lorry driver gazed down at me from the lofty eminence of his cab: 'Having problems, lady?'

When I eventually got them all into the breeder's house, she told me that I had five females and one male and showed me how to keep the wretches in place for the return journey. We decided to give the male to the cook at Allington Castle with whom we had become friendly. Her two small boys were fascinated by the kitten and could hardly believe that this tiny creature really belonged to them. They named him Pericles after the Greek statesman who was noted for his promotion of democracy. Allington Pericles had no time for democracy! He appointed himself '~King of the Castle', allowed no dogs on the premises and even tackled the swans.

One night Ted arrived home to tell me that the firm were closing the Maidstone branch and moving it to the Aldwych office in the heart of London. This was a blow - but a bigger one was in store. Shortly afterwards Liz arrived for the weekend wearing a large cross around her neck and telling us that she had been 'born again'. We could not think what she was talking about!

15

THE JESUS FELLOWSHIP
1971-1976

> "I have come to believe that it is not possible to live the [abundant] Christian life without being baptised in the Holy Spirit"
> **Merlin R Carothers** *Prison to Praise*

Liz had been working in London at a sophisticated secretarial bureau in Bond Street where she interviewed high flying multi-lingual secretaries of calibre, who had top business credentials and experience, the sort who could travel all over the world at the beck and call of senior business people, women who could deal with the ordering of a lavish dinner party and step in themselves if a guest failed to turn up. Twenty-four year old Liz had to suss out their backgrounds and any hidden assets.

One morning she had an appointment to interview a girl named Anneke who was half-English and half-Dutch. As part of the normal routine, Liz asked Anneke to name her principal interest in life.

'Jesus Christ' announced Anneke. Liz gulped and felt embarrassed. She placed Anneke in a company and thought no more about her until she wanted to place a second girl in the same company. She decided to find out how Anneke was getting along and suggested that they meet. Over lunch Anneke revealed that she belonged to a Bible study group which met regularly and included stockbrokers, barristers, and city men of all sorts but not many women. To cut a long story short, Liz was invited first to a dinner party and then to attend Anneke's weekly Bible study. Our daughter was keen to extend her social circle to include more men so she began to attend regularly. Liz told us that after the third meeting she had had a personal encounter with God. As a result of this precious experience she chose to make Jesus the Lord of her life.

Shortly afterwards Liz acquired a copy of *Prison to Praise* by the former American army chaplain Merlin Carothers. The book opened her eyes to a new aspect of Christianity; the concept of 'baptism in the Holy Spirit'.

Liz learnt that those who had received this gift apparently found themselves graced with a deeper awareness and understanding of the love of God and with the power to live and act in the name of Jesus. This was to prove to be the 'baited hook' which the Lord was dangling in front of our daughter. She decided that she wanted to receive 'baptism in the Holy Spirit' and brought the book along to the next Bible study meeting. There she enthused about this new form of 'baptism' which could be brought about through the laying on of hands. Liz asked whether members of the group would lay hands on her and pray that she might receive this gift. There was apparently a divergence of opinion among those present - some asserting that there was no such thing as 'baptism in the Holy Spirit' if one had already received normal Christian baptism, and others supporting Liz. She gave them time to argue it out, with the result that those who believed in 'baptism in the Spirit' gathered around Liz to pray that she might receive this gift. Liz had an experience of the supernatural which she later described to us as: 'a fountain bubbling up inside me while I laughed and cried at the same time'.

Some while afterwards Liz received the gift of speaking in tongues. This was the same gift that I had received at the age of seven but kept entirely to myself for fear of being considered mad. Liz of course knew nothing about my 'secret language'. I had not even mentioned it to Ted!

Liz had now 'found Jesus'. She continued to work at the secretarial bureau but visited Brian and Majsan at weekends where her arrival with a large cross around her neck, went down like a lead balloon! It was in similar guise that she arrived on our doorstep in Maidstone, announcing that she had been 'born again'. We were baffled by her description of 'baptism in the Holy Spirit' and found her somewhat self-righteous in her rediscovered Christianity.

I realised later on that Jesus does not call people alone, but links them up with brothers and sisters who can help them along the way. Liz now met a young girl called Janie St John who lived in Virginia Water and had undergone a similar experience of conversion. Liz and Janie decided to share a flat in West London with several other young Christian men and women. Ted and I found the whole thing rather odd but could do nothing except pray for them all and hope for the best.

When I met Liz's companions in the flat, I realised that they possessed enormous good will but seemed to be lacking any sense of direction in their Christian lives. In due course, Liz and several other girls moved on to live in a 'condemned' house in Wimbledon, having agreed that they would move on when the property was due for demolition. Liz and her friends cadged as much household equipment as possible from their doting parents and we were happy to think that at least the girls would have chairs, tables and cutlery in their temporary accommodation!

All this 'born again' Christianity was particularly hard on Brian and Majsan who were not churchgoers and had lavished endless love and affection on Liz. She would arrive on their doorstep brandishing a Bible and preaching Christianity to her uncle and aunt and their guests. To add to their difficulties, Brian was suddenly made redundant and he and Majsan decided to strike out anew. They took a course in restaurant management, sold their house in Hurley and moved to Devon where they bought a restaurant which they turned into a first class establishment. Majsan was a wonderful cook and the restaurant appeared in the Egon Ronay guide.

Wokingham

Ted had not been working for long in the Aldwych office when his firm dropped another bombshell. Central London premises were proving too expensive and they would be relocating yet again; this time to Brentford in Middlesex. For Ted, this meant four hours travelling each day with three changes of train. This was clearly impossible in terms of a regular routine and after two years in Maidstone we were going to have to up sticks once more.

We looked at various possibilities and eventually found a suitable house in Berkshire at Wokingham where we moved in November 1973. From Wokingham, the journey to Brentford took only fifty minutes by car and Ted joined up with two other men from his office that lived locally and took it in turns to drive.

I was sad to leave my lovely garden in Maidstone and the Wokingham 'garden' contained not a single flower bed; the sole occupant being a lonely pampas grass. Ted was only too well aware of my love for gardens and the Wokingham 'patch' certainly had potential. Ted arranged for a few flower beds to be dug and I planted bulbs in the hope of a little colour come the spring.

Wokingham was smaller than Maidstone and struck me as being exactly like something out of an Agatha Christie novel - minus the murders! I had always wanted to live in that sort of quiet homely town where the little shops all seemed to be privately owned - this was, of course, before the days of a supermarket around every corner. Clocks were mended by a retired general who had a collection of beautiful timepieces and one way or another we found ourselves surrounded by pleasant people. Our immediate neighbour was a retired Colonel who had spent most of his life in India and remained there in spirit. On the other side was a brigadier who had interesting stories of his war years in Burma and opposite there lived the widow of a judge.

The neighbours seemed to spend a good deal of their time holding drinks parties. No sooner had we moved in than the brigadier and his wife invited us to a little party on the pretext of introducing us to the locals. Unbeknownst to us, our immediate neighbours and a few others formed a sort of 'inner ring' into which you could not break unless you were considered 'acceptable'. The drinks party had been arranged to 'suss us out'. Fortunately one of the guests discovered that his daughter had been at school with Pamela and Liz which enabled us to 'pass muster'. We were 'in' before we knew that we could have been 'out'.

We also became involved in the local Catholic Church which we found somewhat lifeless but did not imagine that that would ever change. We just plodded along and I returned to my Boston habit of spending an hour in prayer after daily Mass.

Things began to look a little more interesting when another daily Mass attender, Elizabeth Walls, dropped a few hints about a group of people who were getting together to pray . She went into some detail and unfortunately it all began to sound suspiciously like the 'peculiar' evening Ted and I had attended at the Dominican House of Studies in Dover, Massachusetts. We certainly did not want to be involved in 'that sort of thing'! I made our excuses to Elizabeth but she was not one to give up. Ted and I were invited to come along to a prayer meeting at her house on New Year's Eve and Elizabeth was so warm and friendly that it seemed churlish to refuse.

The evening was friendly; gentle and very low key with people praying out loud if they wished and sometimes just sitting in silence. Eight other parishioners were present as well as the curate and there were none of the 'manifestations' which I later learnt to describe as 'charismatic'. The whole thing had an entirely different 'feel' to the Dover experience. We saw the New Year in and at the end of the evening were told that the group met every week in one house or another. We were invited to join them and Ted and I went along the following week. Soon we were regular attenders.

Leukemia

Unfortunately my health now began to play up again. I felt ghastly and my temperature was swooping up and down for no discoverable reason. I was also finding it hard to keep awake during the day and there was every sign that I was sinking into another depression. Ted thought that the problem was primarily exhaustion after yet another move and arranged a holiday in Cornwall. This, alas, was a flop.

Back home we made constant visits to the outpatient department of the local hospital. Whenever my temperature swooped up, Ted bundled me into the car and off we went to outpatients. They took all sorts of samples but were unable to give us any answers.

Eventually the consultant blood specialist arranged for me to spend a few days in hospital for tests. I was willing to try anything and trusted the consultant although I did not have much time for his registrar. This young man announced that they were considering the extraction of bone marrow samples from my neck and I understood him to tell me that the procedure was to be carried out without anaesthetic. The thought of an operation without anaesthetic threw me into a panic and when Ted arrived that evening I begged him to take me straight home.

The trouble was eventually diagnosed correctly as infection in a leaking heart valve; a legacy of my childhood diphtheria! I was taken into hospital for painful treatment but by that time I was feeling too ill to care whether I lived or died. I learned some time later that the Consultant had told Ted and Liz that I would not live to be an old women but that they had 'arrested the leukemia'! Eventually I was allowed home to convalesce, only to sink into deeper depression. Bad as the hospital stay had been, it was nothing to the wretchedness of that depression. For four months I was unable to get out to daily Mass and felt increasingly isolated because Ted had to be out of the house from seven in the morning until six at night. Medication failed to help and I wondered whether I was condemned to feeling dreadful for the rest of my life. Slowly I began to improve but it took me a long time to feel a hundred per cent once more.

The Jesus Fellowship

Liz had now left the Wimbledon house and had moved up to Northamptonshire where she joined other Christians in a village with the unlikely name of 'Bugbrooke'. The Baptist minister of Bugbrooke, Noel Stanton, had begun praying for 'revival' in the village in the 1950's and his prayer had been answered beyond all expectation. By 1973 Bugbrooke Baptist Chapel was the centre of an extraordinarily vibrant community inspired by the Holy Spirit and under the leadership of Noel. Two-thirds of the church membership lived in Christian community sharing all things in common and modelling themselves on the early Christian church of the Acts of the Apostles. They were to become known as the Jesus Fellowship or Jesus Army.

At this early stage Ted and I knew nothing about these people and were very much afraid that Liz was becoming involved in a 'cult'. She would turn up in Wokingham, not only with a cross around her neck but with her hair bound up in a headscarf and clad in a long dress which reminded me of 'Old Mother Hubbard'.

Liz

She assured me that all the women in the Jesus Fellowship wore similar clothes. Only later did I realise that Liz had come into genuine personal relationship with Jesus for the first time and was finding it a heady experience.

In the summer of 1976 Ted and I decided to go up to Bugbrooke for a weekend, just to see just what was 'going on'. We asked everyone we knew to pray for us during the weekend, and I learnt subsequently that Liz had been doing likewise! Throughout the two hour journey to Northamptonshire, we 'stormed heaven', asking the Holy Ghost to help us remain open to his will. We had not yet learnt to refer to 'The Holy Spirit'.

When we arrived at the main community house, Liz was at the door to meet us. She greeted us warmly and took us inside to introduce us to her companions. I was still praying frantically under my breath; alternating 'How do you do' with 'Lord let me be open'. I learnt afterwards that the Bugbrooke community had been just as curious about meeting Ted and me. We were among the first committed and practising Roman Catholics to cross their threshold and they wondered what sort of people we would be.

Liz told us that we had been assigned to stay with a couple living in a separate house, Lionel and Marion Orchard, who were a little younger than ourselves. The Orchards welcomed us graciously and Lionel showed us to our room, saying: 'Make this house your home. If there is anything that you want, please let us know.' Liz had told us that a meeting was to take place that night at the Baptist chapel and invited us to come along with the Orchards. Our hosts were obviously concerned for our well-being during this 'new experience'. Lionel told us to feel free to leave at any time: 'If you want to come out, just tell me and I will bring you back here.'

We arrived at the chapel early and Liz was there to greet us. She asked where we would like to sit and I said that we did not want to be near the front. Anthony had already visited Liz and attended a meeting where he had been placed near the front. He had told us that he felt 'psychologically assaulted'. Ted and I thought it would be safer to stay at the back!

More and more people crowded into the small chapel and we were amazed to see men embracing one another when they arrived and the women doing likewise. Ted and I sat like nervous ramrods as Liz brought people over to be introduced. I was again alternating between 'How do you do' and 'Lord, let me be open'. By the time the meeting was due to begin there must have been 450 people in the chapel. It was swelteringly hot and there was not a fan in sight.

Liz slipped into a place beside us just before the arrival of Noel Stanton, the minister. Noel was wearing ordinary clothes rather than clerical dress and we were extremely interested to see this man of whom Liz had spoken so warmly. Noel must have been in his early forties, and he led the congregation into a wonderful liberated time of worship followed by preaching the word. This was followed by singing and more worship.

At the end of one of the hymns something extraordinary happened. Those 450 people started to sing in the way that I had thought of as 'my secret' language since I was seven! Not only that, but I was able to join in with them, singing out 'my language' in public for the very first time. I glanced sideways at Ted and Liz. Both were looking at me, their faces filled with joy and tears running down Ted's cheeks.

Later on I heard Liz's side of the story. As I suspected, she had been very nervous about our visit and had warned the other women in the community about our probable reaction: 'Halfway through the service, Daddy will touch my arm, very politely, and say: "Liz, dear. It has been lovely to be with you, but this is not really our cup of tea!" Then they will both leave!' She was right about Ted touching her arm and Liz thought 'Here it comes!' Instead, Ted said to her: 'Look at Mummy. She is singing in tongues!'

The singing died away but the God of surprises had not finished with me for that night. For a long time I had been in bondage to my need for a drink every evening and became upset if I could not have it. I never drank during the day, but when Ted came home I would mix us each a gin and tonic and make mine much larger than Ted's. After the singing, I heard a voice call from the balcony: 'There is a visiting sister here who, although not an alcoholic, has to have a drink in the evening. The Lord says: "This night I am setting you free - I shall be your sweetness and delight!" I knew the message was for me! From that day onwards I have been able to have a drink if I feel like, but seldom more than once a week and I do not miss it on the other days.

That evening at Bugbrooke a door opened in my life. I walked through it and realised that all that had gone before had been a preparation for the moment when I experienced the full blossoming of the gift that I had received as a child. At last I understood that at the age of seven I had been baptised in the Holy Spirit and received the gift of tongues. I was not 'mad' and there were others in the world like me. For the first time, I had been able to share my gift in the company of 450 men and women who had also received it. Into the bargain, I had been freed from my attachment to alcohol!

16

THE LIVING SPIRIT
1976-1977

> You are the body of Christ and individually members of it
> **1 Cor 12.27**

Ted and I returned to the Orchard's house in a daze, and found lots of people spending the night on the floor in sleeping bags. On Sunday morning we drove off to a local church for Mass and returned in time to go back to the Bugbrooke chapel to hear Noel preaching again. He spoke for three hours on two verses from Ephesians 5 on the role of men and women in marriage. I agreed with every word he said, but found it difficult to accustom myself to the way in which he seemed sometimes to almost shout at the congregation. Over the years I have come to realise that Noel has had an anointing upon him and he had to shout in order to get through to some of his listeners who were rather passive and did not really 'hear' an ordinary voice. I consider Noel to be a very holy man; a true prophet of God in our day. At the end of his sermon we all said 'Amen' and sang a hymn about the truths of salvation.

That evening Ted and I sang all the way back to Wokingham and talked endlessly about the weekend. I had been particularly impressed by the extent to which the men 'walked tall'; as if they really appreciated that they were sons of God. We had both been impressed by the way in which everyone was welcome, regardless of their past life. People who were searching and willing to be open to Jesus had only to acknowledge their neediness. That was the only requirement.

Once we had settled back into respectable Wokingham, the whole experience began to seem rather remote. We wondered whether it would be appropriate to share 'Bugbrooke' with the weekly prayer group which had not yet manifested any of the charismatic gifts which had come crashing into our lives In the end, I decided to mention Bugbrooke initially to my friend Stella Kerr who was married to a local doctor. Stella was very devout and kindly and I made a date to see her although I was afraid that she might react coldly to my account of charismatic outpourings. I need not have worried. Stella obviously believed that our experience had been a gift from God and she proved extremely open to the idea of charismatic prayer.

Ted and I knew that we had entered a new phase in our lives, and were sure that God wanted us to pursue this. But how? We talked endlessly and concluded that if such gifts existed outside the Catholic Church, there must surely be something similar going on inside. Such an extraordinary outpouring of the Holy Spirit could not be confined to 450 people in the Midlands. We scouted around, and discovered that a Catholic 'charismatic' meeting was held regularly in London at the Westminster Cathedral Conference Centre.

We decided to drive down one Sunday and found ourselves immediately absorbed into an experience of fellowship which was radically different to anything we had experienced in all our years of Catholic parish life. When we arrived a time of 'free prayer' seemed to be in progress. One person was standing up and reading a passage from Scripture. He was followed by another who sang in tongues. A third person gave an 'interpretation' of the tongue; speaking in the first person like the woman at Bugbrooke who had assured me that the Lord had freed me from my attachment to alcohol. After this, the entire assembly sang in tongues and I was able to join in. Ted was to receive the gift of tongues on a subsequent visit to Bugbrooke.

The group broke for lunch and over sandwiches and tea Ted and I milled about and spoke to lots of friendly people - a far cry from the usual Catholic congregations who seemed to believe in 'keeping themselves to themselves'. After the lunch break we were addressed by an Anglican priest, Colin Urquhart, who was subsequently to launch into an international ministry, Kingdom Faith. It struck me as odd to find an Anglican addressing a Catholic gathering but Colin spoke extremely well and demonstrated great knowledge of Scripture. His words delighted my heart.

The next thing on the agenda was Mass with a number of priests concelebrating. This was like no other Mass Ted and I had ever attended. During the hymns, people raised their hands in praise – Ted and me included – and we sang in tongues. The short sermon was very much to the point and the sign of peace was more like a football scrum with 500 people milling around to give one another a 'hug of peace'. Despite my negative reactions to the Dover, Massachusetts experience, I was feeling calm and completely comfortable. I realised afterwards that I had been given a particular grace that Sunday. Some people are totally 'freaked out' by their first experience of charismatic worship. At the end of the Mass we all joined hands and sang: 'Bind us Together, Lord'.

Ted and I returned home full of joy and excitement and reported our Westminster experience to Liz at Bugbrooke, anticipating an equally enthusiastic response. She had, of course, realised how deeply Ted and I had been affected by our weekend with the Jesus Fellowship and we were surprised to find that she was not particularly inspired by our account of the Westminster Sunday. We realised afterwards that she had been hoping that we would leave the Catholic Church and follow her into the Jesus Fellowship. Ted and I were deeply grateful for the outpouring the Holy Spirit we had received at Bugbrooke but remained absolutely convinced that we belonged in the Catholic Church. There we have remained while retaining and deepening our links with the Jesus Fellowship.

In Wokingham we were again faced with the question of how much to 'tell' and whether or not to say anything at all to the prayer group. Numbers in the group had now increased to twenty six although there was a lot of coming and going and there seemed to be a general lack of commitment.

Elizabeth Walls remained a faithful member and it was through her that the decision about whether or not to mention the charismatic experience was taken out of our hands. Elizabeth had suffered from breast cancer some years previously and she now shared with the group the fact that she was experiencing constant pain in her leg and medical examinations had revealed the likelihood of bone cancer. We knew that the Westminster meeting included a ministry of healing and took this opportunity to share our charismatic experiences with the group. We invited them all to come to London with us one Sunday so that we could ask the healing team to pray over Elizabeth. On the appointed Sunday all twenty-six members of the group travelled to Westminster including our parish curate and Elizabeth's own doctor.

The Wokingham contingent was invited to come into a side room where Elizabeth sat on a chair and we formed a circle around her. We were led in prayer by an elderly Benedictine monk, Father Luke Ballweg, who laid his hands upon Elizabeth and prayed aloud that the Lord might free her completely from any sickness. During the time of prayer, Elizabeth told us that she had been aware of the most exquisite perfume but nobody else had noticed it. We returned home and Elizabeth kept a subsequent hospital appointment where X-rays revealed that the bone in her leg was completely healthy.

Life in the Spirit

Ted and I discovered that 'Westminster' was not the only charismatic meeting. Days of renewal, seminars and prayer groups were taking place all over the country and we rushed from one to another. One of our regular ports of call was the Church of St Mary of the Angels in West London where the parish priest was Father Michael Hollings who had officiated at the wedding of Anthony and Fiona at the Oxford chaplaincy. Father Michael was not personally involved in the renewal but extremely sympathetic, and very happy to allow us to use his facilities.

During a day of renewal in Reading, we met a jolly Benedictine monk from Douai Abbey, Nicholas Broadbridge, who was to become my 'co-discerner'. In former days I would have described such a relationship in terms of 'spiritual director' and 'penitent'. I found that the new concept of 'co-discernment' brought considerable benefit to both sides. Father Nicholas and I began to meet once a month for an hour to share the gifts we had received from the Lord as well as the mistakes we felt we had made. We found the relationship enriching.

Ted and I told Nicholas to go to Bugbrooke and spend a day with Liz who was still a sort of background mentor for us. At Bugbrooke, Father Nicholas was 'seized' by the Holy Spirit and it was almost as if he was drunk. He departed that evening, singing at the top of his voice and the Bugbrooke community were concerned about him. Liz telephoned Douai the following morning to make sure he had got home safely.

At the time of the day of renewal in Reading at which we met Nicholas he was still as green as the Donovans about all the new gifts being poured out. He rapidly became involved in the ministry of healing and was convinced that the root of many physical ailments lay in lack of forgiveness. Time and again I have found that conviction to be proved true. Ted and I were also drawn into the ministry of healing ourselves and Ted received a beautiful gift of discernment which has grown gently and quietly over the years. My own gift was different. I was enabled to see 'pictures' or 'words' in my mind while praying with someone. The picture or word seldom meant anything to me. I would nevertheless share it with my companion and it usually became clear that the picture or the 'word' contained a powerful message for that person. Sometimes it opened up a deep psychological wound which needed healing.

As the months passed, Ted and I made the acquaintance of many of the leaders of the movement in the Catholic Church. Several of them advised us to consider running a 'Life in the Spirit' course for the Wokingham prayer group which now held most of its meetings at our house. A Life in the Spirit course would normally run for several weeks and was designed to help participants to appreciate that the power of the Holy Spirit is available for every aspect of our lives and to prepare them for the possible reception of charismatic gifts such as 'baptism in the Holy Spirit' and the gift of tongues. Each session would last for about two and a half hours and Ted and I were well aware that we were 'babes in the wood' in terms of arranging and leading such an event. Our first idea was to draft in 'experts' to run the course for us so we asked advice about suitable 'experts' - only to be told by everybody that we should be running the course ourselves!

We were fortunate in our curate, Father Gabriel Cave, who had himself been baptized in the Holy Spirit and was supportive of our new ventures. He, too, made enquiries about 'experts' who could run a Life in the Spirit seminar and he too was told that 'do it yourself' was best. With the support of Father Gabriel we decided to trust in God and get hold of the Life in the Spirit manual in the hope that we would not go far wrong if we followed it word for word!

The Westminster group were also planning a Life in the Spirit seminar but theirs was apparently intended for 250 people with a session for seminar leaders scheduled for the week before our own preliminary meeting. Ted and I decided that it would be smart to drive down to London and get some ideas from the leaders' seminar. We arrived just before Mass and found most of the Westminster leaders assembled. The Mass was celebrated by Father Jim Overton whom we came to know very well indeed. Father Jim's Mass was an eye-opener from the word 'go' when Jim humbly shared aloud some of his own sins and members of the congregation also mentioned personal failures and shortcomings.

During the meeting afterwards, we realized that most of those present were going to lead one of the small groups of seven or eight people who would be meeting after each of the sessions for 250. These small groups would be discussing what had been said and raising any queries; they were a means of ensuring that everybody could join in and have their say. Ted and I were asked to become joint leaders of a small group. We were initially reluctant but the others were keen to have us and we realized that our attendance at the enormous Westminster seminar would at least keep us 'one step ahead' in terms of the Wokingham 'Life in the Spirit' group. Thus we were starting off in leadership without ever having the opportunity to be ordinary participants.

All 26 members of the Wokingham group attended the first Life in the Spirit seminar and Ted and I led it with our curate. We followed the manual faithfully and found our participation in the Westminster meetings extremely helpful. According to the manual, the fifth session was very significant because participants were now ready to pray over one another for the gift of release in the Holy Spirit and the gift of tongues. On our fifth evening together, we prayed as instructed and practically everybody received gifts from the Holy Spirit. The house practically rocked with the outpouring of the power of God. Some received gifts of prophecy and 'word of knowledge' through which the power and the will of God is made manifest. Others received the gift of tongues and gifts of discernment.

This was obviously a far cry from normal Sunday Mass in our parish church which nevertheless remains precious to Ted and me. Through the renewal we were experiencing a freedom in worship that we had never imagined possible and which brought us into a much closer walk with the Lord. We knew that God had liberated us in a wonderful way and we were also experiencing the extent to which the wisdom of God is revealed in the gathered body of believers.

We hungered to communicate these gifts to others and I came to realize that my own enthusiasm sometimes led me to 'share' in ways that were inappropriate and served merely to alienate those whom I wanted to approach. I pondered. How could I best describe 'Renewal' to a practicing Christian who had no experience of such a reality and how could I do it in such a way that I did not succeed in putting them off altogether! I had been praying about this just before I was due to attend a conference at Methodist Central Hall in Westminster, arranged by The Fountain Trust which had done so much to promote Renewal in Britain and further afield. More than two thousand people were expected to attend the conference and I was sure that somebody there could help me in my quest. I asked the Lord to lead me to that person.

During the conference, I talked to a great many people and a number asked me to pray with them. On the final day, I had still not met the person who could help me to 'communicate' and I was leaving after the coffee break. As I went down to the coffee room, I said to the Lord: 'I know You won't fail me; I will sit at an empty table, and I ask You to please send someone to sit at that table who will tell me how to describe this new movement in a nutshell!'

I picked up my coffee and sat down to wait. After a while, a little old lady ambled towards me. She looked an unlikely adviser and I sent up a prayer: 'Surely this cannot be the person you have in mind, Lord!' The old lady sat down, sipped her coffee and smiled across the table. I took a deep breath and plunged in: Where had she come from? Edinburgh, where she was a deaconess. Did they have Life in the Spirit seminars in Edinburgh? They did indeed - all the time! How would she describe this new life in the Lord and the experience of the Holy Spirit to someone who was 'new' to the Renewal and did not know anything about it?

No problem! My companion came out with exactly the answers I had been seeking. She reminded me that most people who come on a course such as the one we had been attending have some sort of relationship with God. They sincerely love and esteem the Lord, but their existing relationship can be compared with the friendship they might have with a very special and important guest. They invite him into their living room at particular times when the cushions are all plumped up, everything is clean and tidy with nice fresh flowers and they can sit and listen with reverence to whatever the Lord has to say - although they cannot always hear him very distinctly. The 'honoured guest' departs and the family get on with their lives.

The Scottish deaconess launched into an unforgettable description of the difference that comes about after 'release in the Spirit'. Sometime later, I shared her description with the congregation at a Service for

Women's World Day of Prayer. It was 'picked up' by Helena Wilkinson who had suffered acutely from anorexia nervosa and found the description helpful. She reproduced it in her autobiography: *Puppet on a String*, in which she refers to my talk:

'After release in the spirit...it's as if Our Lord says, "I know I am welcome here in this room, but I desire to be Lord of all your house." Panic usually seizes one! One thinks of the rest of the house and the disorder...in the different rooms. However, Jesus says, "Don't be afraid, take My hand and we shall go through your house together." He then says, "We shall start with the attic." This is usually a most disconcerting suggestion and maybe we remonstrate with Jesus, and say - politely, of course - "But Lord, there's so much rubbish and junk up there." "Yes, I know," says Jesus, "but take My hand and we'll go together. I quite agree there is junk, and we will discard this together, but also there are precious things up there that you don't know about, which I desire you to use for Me in My Kingdom."

`Jesus continues, "After the attic, may I go into your bedroom? This is the room where images are set in place, where masks are carefully put on. Maybe relationships aren't in My order in this room - do not fear, I am the answer to all problems." He says, "I will teach you to remove your mask and show you that I love and accept you unconditionally, just as you are, and also teach you to love and accept yourself unconditionally, because I do." He asks, "May we go into your kitchen, and may I sit in the corner and listen to all your conversations? May I hear the loving things you say about your family, to your family, and about your neighbours and friends? May I listen to you as you upbuild My body?"

'He then asks, "Do you have a basement?" We truly shudder. "Don't be afraid of the basement in your life - your hidden past, maybe guilt, resentment, fear, anxiety, even dark corners that have no name - don't be afraid. I am the Light of the World and I've taken you out of the darkness. Come; let Me heal all the wounds of your past, as I've promised to bind up all wounds. Will you invite Me to be Lord of every room in your life?"

Helena Wilkinson: *Puppet on a String* Hodder and Stoughton London 1984

Miriam

The Wokingham prayer group was blessed abundantly as a result of the Life in the Spirit seminar, and new members came to join us. Among them was a middle aged Irishwoman named Miriam who had been a senior nurse but was now very unwell and living in the local convent. We had the bright idea of suggesting that Miriam attend the healing service in Westminster. On the appointed day we drove her into the Cathedral Conference Centre with the intention of taking her into the usual side room where several people could pray with her.

By mistake -or so it seemed - we went into the 'wrong' room and Miriam, Ted and I ended up in a part of the building where the distinguished American evangelist, Jean Darnell was ministering to a small group. Jean looked somewhat surprised at our arrival and said: 'I did not expect so many. But that is no problem to Jesus! Jean entered into prayer and asked Jesus to send his Holy Spirit down upon us. There was an anointed silence and Jean then said quietly: 'There is someone here who has fallen off a bicycle and has difficulty in moving her leg. Would you please raise your hand? A hand immediately went up, and Jean said: 'Jesus has healed you!' The woman smiled, walked across the room unhesitatingly and said: 'Praise God'.

Jean spoke again: 'There is a person here with a cancerous growth on their cheek and the Lord wants to heal it'. The man beside me raised his hand immediately and although I had not noticed his cheek when we came into the room it was certainly blemish free now. He, too, praised God. Jean spoke a third time: There is someone here who is unable to raise their hands above their head. The Lord is healing you right now! A woman in the room raised both her hands and laughed joyfully. Jean spoke again: 'There is someone here who is in depression and is saying 'no' to the Lord'. She looked around but nobody spoke. Jean continued: 'The Lord asks you to take courage and step forward'. A nun rose to her feet and advanced towards Jean. 'Do you say 'yes' to the Lord?' The nun nodded.

I myself was to receive powerful ministry from Jean on a future occasion. That day I longed for her to say something which would 'touch' Miriam but it seemed that the Lord did not wish her to receive ministry that day. We returned to Wokingham somewhat downcast and wondered whether Miriam might be helped by The Jesus Fellowship where the Lord was working so powerfully. We contacted Liz and she consulted the community who generously agreed to welcome Miriam. She spent three weeks at Bugbrooke, after which the community contacted us. They told us that they were unable to be of help to Miriam as she, apparently, 'did not wish to be healed'.

The Wokingham prayer group continued to do their best, but Liz pointed out to us that the 'focus' of the group now appeared to be Miriam rather than Jesus! She told us that this must be making the devil very happy. I was stunned but, in retrospect I can see that Liz was right! We had got into the habit of praying with Miriam for hours and hours which pulled us down and left us feeling very drained and anything but Spirit filled.

We decided on one final attempt to help her and requested the assistance of Father Luke, the Benedictine monk who had prayed so powerfully for Elizabeth Walls. We drove Miriam up to Westminster and went once more into the side room. There Father Luke called on Miriam to repent and called on the Lord to deliver her from any power of evil which held her in thrall. The result was astonishing. Miriam's eyes changed from the hard agate to which we were accustomed and became beautifully soft and gentle. Her expression became docile and we gave thanks to God for releasing her and bringing her peace. We drove her back to Wokingham and left her at the convent, an altered woman - or so we thought.

The following morning, Miriam came to the parish Mass and afterwards told Father Cave and Ted and me that she had slept like a baby for the first time in years. She said that she could feel a tingling in her hands and wondered whether she herself had been gifted with a ministry of healing. Fortunately we had the sense to suggest that she just spent the day resting quietly. The following morning we again saw Miriam at Mass. Afterwards she suggested that the tingling might be a sign that she should return to Ireland and make peace with her nine brothers and sisters with whom she had quarrelled many years previously. We advised her to 'go slow'; to rest and to take her time. Miriam did no such thing. She telephoned one of her sisters who was a Reverend Mother and announced her plan to come straight across to Ireland where she clearly expected a family gathering to be arranged. Reverend Mother blew her top! She announced that Miriam wasn't considering anybody else's convenience and was doing her own thing - as usual! Miriam raged and Reverend Mother raged and both slammed down their receivers.

When we saw Miriam later in the day, her eyes had returned to 'hard agate' and we recalled the warning of Jesus about an evil spirit which is cast out of its original dwelling [Luke 11:24-26] If that spirit finds no rest elsewhere it may try to return to its original home. If it finds the house 'swept and put in order' it may decide to come back, bringing along seven other spirits who are even worse than itself. Was that happening to Miriam? We were never to know and the story does not have a happy ending because we lost touch, although we occasionally had news of her from other sources. The whole episode taught Ted and me the importance of delaying prayer for deliverance until other problems had been dealt with. In Miriam's case, we should have found out about the family rift and tried to encourage Miriam to mend her fences before taking her to Father Luke.

We also realized the great importance of community support for a person who has received the ministry of deliverance. On the days following her visit to Westminster, Miriam saw us at morning Mass but spent the rest of the day back in the convent when she really needed ongoing support from friends in the renewal.

Desolation

During our early days in the renewal, I suffered an attack of desolation which I now believe to have been demonic. At that stage I was too ignorant to understand what was going on but I knew that I had had a similar experience several years previously in Boston when we had been starting the Tape Library and I had suddenly told 'Himself' (Fr Gerald Orlando) that I was unable to record the meditation from *A Surgeon at the Foot of the Cross*. On that occasion 'Himself' had set the power of evil to flight with the powerful Passionist blessing. I was sure that prayer and ministry were needed once again to free me from desolation.

I was sitting in our church in the throes of this black experience and decided to ask the Lord how he saw me. Into my mind came an immediate picture of Hans Christian Anderson's 'Little Match Seller': poor, dirty, dishevelled, ragged and needy. My heart was moved with compassion and I knew that God was moved to far greater compassion at my poverty and littleness. The 'picture' changed and developed. The little girl – me - was sitting in a rowing boat pulling away at the oars to get the craft to shift. She was creating a lot of froth but getting nowhere. Then I saw that the boat was actually tethered to a sturdy peg on the shore. The little girl could row all she liked but she was never going to get that boat to move. The picture changed again, and now Jesus was walking across the water towards the little girl but she could not see him because she was facing the land, with her back to the open sea, rowing busily. Jesus very gently turned her around to face him, unloosed the tethering rope and set up a tiny sail. Then he breathed out -the breathing of the Holy Spirit - and the boat moved quietly and effortlessly away from the bank and towards the distant shore.

There was more to come. As the little girl sat in the boat a tiny child floated past, followed by a flock of ducks. She asked the Lord whether she should rescue the child and feed the ducks. The answer was: 'Yes'. This was followed by tremendous commotion and I 'saw' drowning people clinging to a raft and asking me to pull them into the boat. I was about to haul them on board when I remembered to turn to Jesus. 'No' he said: 'Just pray for them. I have other children in other boats'.

The Lord was teaching me an important lesson. Until then I had tried to help everybody, and never bothered to ask the Lord if He actually wanted me to come to the rescue or whether somebody else could do a better job for a particular individual! The new message was: 'Let go and let God!'

About a week after this experience I received a telephone call from someone who had helped Ted and me very much. She asked if we would take under our wing a young nurse who had just arrived in the area and did not know a soul. My immediate reaction was: 'Of course!' Suddenly the picture of the boat flashed into my mind with the memory of the words of Jesus: 'I have other children in other boats!' I asked if I could call back, and when I did so it was to suggest that a particular young woman might be a better support for this nurse. That seemed to have been the will of God because the two women were able to minister to one another in a way that would have been impossible for Ted and me.

It was at about this time that I received powerful ministry from Jean Darnell when she was sharing her ministry with leaders in the UK Renewal. There were powerful manifestations of the power of God until the last minute when Jean had to rush off to catch her plane. As she passed us, on the way to the door, she stopped suddenly and said: 'There is someone here who has trouble with their colon or lower bowel, and the Lord wants to heal them.' She looked at Ted, standing beside me, and he shook his head. I knew that the message was for me and told Jean that throughout my life I had been plagued with such problems. She put her hand on my stomach and said: 'The Lord wants to heal you!' I was healed immediately and the problems have never returned. Jean then looked at me intently and said: 'The Lord has some words for you and I don't know what they mean. You will have to ask him. They are: 'Write so that those on the run can read!' I immediately wrote the words down on a scrap of paper and then Jean was gone! What could the message mean? I puzzled and prayed about it. The answer did not come quickly and one cynic suggested that I might have a ministry to escaped convicts!

The answer to the cryptic message came totally unexpectedly while I was reading one of the letters of St Catherine of Siena in which she mentions the need to write for 'those who are running towards the Lord!' Her words, written in the fourteenth century, seemed to leap off the page. I had not only discovered my 'readers on the run', but I had been working for them for years without realizing it.

The work had started with the library for the blind when I had written to the busy people who believed themselves to be corresponding with 'Father Gerard Orlando'. I had felt totally unable to respond adequately to so many of the queries and time after time the necessary answer had been contained in whichever book I was currently reading onto tape. I had become a sort of conduit - passing on the 'living water' contained in one or another book. The message from Jean Darnell confirmed to me that the Lord wanted me to continue to write for 'those on the run!' I had to believe that he would continue to give me the words.

Marriage Ministry

Two very interesting people came into our lives in the early days of renewal, Richard and Joyce Connor who were in their seventies and very much alive in the Holy Spirit. Richard had spent his working life in the army so the family had moved from pillar to post. He was a member of the Church of England and had a real vision for the spiritual revival of England. Joyce was a Roman Catholic and the pair were regular participants in the Westminster Renewal group. I suspected that Richard suffered agonies of frustration with some members who were very taken up with their 'own' ministries and did not share his wonderful vision of renewal.

The Connors had a particular ministry to marriages and Joyce possessed a rare gift of discernment which helped countless married couples. At one point in their own marriage Richard and Joyce had become aware that their relationship had diminished to the point of non-existence - thanks in no small part to the constant disruption of army life. They were a courageous and prayerful pair and decided to take action in order to save their relationship. By the grace of God, the two were led to 'Marriage Encounter' which provides the time and space to enable couples to work on their own relationship with the help of experienced leaders. Marriage Encounter revitalised the Conner's marriage and left them with a burning desire to help other couples.

Richard and Joyce wanted to enable couples to achieve holier marriages as well as happier ones and Ted and I wondered whether it might be helpful to hold a Marriage Encounter weekend for the eight couples in the Wokingham prayer group. We wanted the Connors to animate the weekend which would take place in our house rather than at a residential conference centre which was the usual arrangement. We had enough room for the group sessions but needed to 'borrow' a room from a kindly neighbour for the sessions when the participants divide up by couples. This was going to be 'Marriage Encounter with a difference'!

The organizers of Marriage Encounter allowed the Connors to adapt the course for a non-residential setting which included prayer at the beginning, middle and end. We launched in with high hopes but no real idea of the possible result - and the results were extremely surprising. That weekend proved to be a real eye opener in terms of highlighting the extent to which the men had 'stepped back' and allowed their wives to take on intolerable burdens of leadership. Men and women alike were responsible for this and we were all suffering the consequences.

Ted and I were both concerned that our own marriage should rest on a sound biblical basis. We realised that if I was to step back and allow Ted to take the decisions, he would need to step forward and actually take them. I became aware of the extent to which I had manipulated Ted to do what I wanted and he realised that I had born burdens which were rightly his. Resentment and pain surfaced; not only in ourselves but in several other couples. One pair had a major row on the Saturday night and decided to quit. In accordance with the new teaching, the wife told her husband that it was his role to go and tell the leaders that they were leaving. In the end they managed to make their peace with one another and completed the weekend!

Six months later we held a 'reunion' when the eight couples returned and witnessed to the changes which had taken place in their marriages and the extent to which the Lord had worked a transformation in relationships.

17

COMMUNITY
1977-1978

'The responsibility of speaking the truth in love is very serious indeed'
Ralph Martin

It was many years since Ted had first said to me: 'I don't think we can live this Gospel message the way Our Lord wants it, without a community around us'. At one time I had thought he was off his head but had long since come to agree with him.

During one of the meetings in Father Michael Hollings' parish hall we met John Blatchley, director of the English National Opera and his French wife Catherine. We became firm friends and were very concerned about the number of people in the renewal who seemed to see it in terms of a spiritual 'pick-me-up' - a kind of 'quick-fix' which would not necessarily bear lasting fruit.

The Blatchleys had accompanied us to Bugbrooke on one occasion. Ted and I loved to visit the Jesus

Fellowship but were sure that we were called to remain in the Roman Catholic Church. This was a cause of puzzlement to the Fellowship with their perception of the Roman Catholic Church as 'dead'. They could not imagine why anyone would want to remain in a 'dead' church. We always received a very warm welcome at Bugbrooke and were offered every encouragement to 'jump ship' and join them. Zealous young men would challenge us along the lines of: 'How long are you two going to sit on the fence and compromise with the Lord? You could join us and give your lives to Jesus!' It was a sort of compliment because the Jesus Fellowship needed older members and they must have thought that we could be licked into shape!

Ted and I continued to attend charismatic conferences and sometimes helped to run them.

In June 1978 we decided to go to Dublin for an International Conference. It was anticipated that 20,000 members of the renewal would be gathering from the four corners of the world in the Royal Dublin Society International Convention and Exhibition Centre at Ballsbridge. I knew the place well because it was the site of the Dublin Horse Show to which Grandma Nettie had taken me year after year. Ted and I bought tickets for the conference which included accommodation but had no idea where we would be staying.

We found ourselves in a bed and breakfast out at Dun Laoghaire which was a good way from Ballsbridge. It was run by a poppet of a young mother who had three children who were as good as gold. She could not have been more helpful and told us to help ourselves to anything we could find – day or night – regardless of the fact that she had only signed up to give us breakfast! On the first morning we left her in plenty of time to get the bus and, lo and behold, a car drove up with two nuns from our Westminster group. They were thrilled to see us – but not half as thrilled as we were to see nuns in a car with two free spaces!

As we approached the conference location, I kept wondering where on earth we were going to park – I was only too well aware of the minimal parking space at Ballsbridge. Sister driver blithely drew up at the entrance of the Royal Dublin Society. A friendly Gardai in uniform approached: 'Can I help you Sister?' 'Yes, indeed', said Sister: 'I'm looking for a parking place!' 'You just bring your little car onto the pavement right here' said the policeman. 'This is *your* spot for the week!' Sister's spacious car sat outside the Royal Dublin Society in solitary splendour day after day! During that week we met important members of the conference who had had to walk miles from their parking place to the conference centre while we were just swanning in through the door.

June 1978 produced the worst Irish summer weather in history; bitterly cold with fearsome gales. One day the wind blew so savagely that the roof of the bandstand lifted right off. It was a miracle that the members of our music ministry from the United States did not all go down with pneumonia. I felt particularly sorry for the Americans who had arrived in Ireland from blazing summer heat. Some of them were accommodated in a so-called 'Holiday Camp' outside Dublin where they must have been freezing. Day after day they huddled in blankets around the arena but their spirit was wonderful.

Every day there was a choice of about twenty different workshops and one could move from one to another. Ted and I were particularly drawn to the workshop of the American Dominican friar Francis McNutt. Father McNutt had received a great gift of healing and his name was a household word in the Renewal.

We were all in our places – the room buzzing with expectancy – when a rumour began. The minister of healing was sick. Francis had in fact gone down with a bad bout of flu but was reluctant to disappoint those who had come to hear him. He staggered onto the stage looking ghastly and it was some time before he managed to say a word. When he began, he never mentioned the subject of healing. Instead he spoke of the power of prayer; the vital necessity for prayer and the importance of being faithful to prayer. He then moved onto the importance of parents praying with their children – an area in which I felt myself to have been short-changed by my own non-religious parents. I had always resented that fact and had had a few words with God on the subject!

That morning in Dublin in Father McNutt's workshop he asked how many people could remember their father praying with them every day – not the rosary or grace before meals, but spontaneous prayer. There seemed to be hundreds of people present and I imagined that a host of hands would go up. I was astonished to count only twenty. Father McNutt then asked the same question about mothers. How many people could remember their mother praying with them? The same minimal show of hands! This was truly an eye opener. I was far from being alone in my lack of praying parents. I had, however, been inundated with graces I had been too blind to see and too ungrateful to appreciate. That was the gift of the Dublin meeting as far as I was concerned. Father McNutt retired back to his sickbed having transformed my ungrateful heart.

At another of the workshops we listened to Ralph Martin of the American Ann Arbor Community. He stood on the platform in driving rain telling us about his community and the joy they experienced in serving God together. A man had to stand beside Ralph with an umbrella but it didn't do much to help - they were both drenched!

On the final day of the conference, Sunday Mass was due to be celebrated in the main arena at 11.00am and it was going to be televised. By Saturday afternoon the weather showed no sign of letting up and the organizers were seriously worried. Word went around that we should all pray especially hard for sunshine. Things happen when people pray!

Sunday dawned with blue skies and not a breath of wind. I hope I never forget that Mass. It took twenty minutes for 1200 priests, several bishops and three cardinals to process into the arena. We thought the line would never end. Ralph Martin's Word of God Community led the music and we sang and worshipped as part of a great outpouring of praise.

When it came to the distribution of Holy Communion, under both species, we saw why some of the priests were wearing red vestments while the others wore white. Those in red had been asked to place themselves at different 'stations' for the distribution of Holy Communion and they were each accompanied by a white robed priest. It was a long walk for some of the pairs and Ted whispered to me: 'It is like the 72 being sent out in twos'. Everything was orderly in the extreme; complete reverence and no rush or hurry. After the final hymn and blessing there was a spontaneous movement into the centre of the arena and people began to dance.

The Holy Land

In the summer of 1978 we heard of a two week tour to the Holy Land which was being arranged in October by friends in the renewal. This would be a 'once in a lifetime' opportunity and we added our names to the list. The pilgrimage was to be led by Father Mike Gwinnell and Sister Mary Peter whom we had known for some years. Within minutes of entering the arrivals hall at Tel Aviv Airport, Ted was deeply moved to hear a little girl calling out: 'Abba, Abba!' until her father turned around and she leapt into his arms. It was a 'wisdom picture' of our relationship with our Father God.

For the first week, we were accommodated in a crummy hotel in the centre of Jerusalem. We had to decide whether the pilgrimage was going to be a glorious experience or whether we were going to ruin it by complaining about everything. Fortunately we decided to make the best of what we had. That hotel was not all bad. From the window I saw my first camel. It was being used as ordinary transport and loped along with gaily coloured trappings and bells jingling. One morning I saw a sight in the street outside which took me right back to the Gospels. A group of friends was carrying a man with an ulcerated leg. They set him down by the Damascus Gate where he could unbandage his wounds and display his disfigurement to passers by in the hope of sympathetic donations. Suddenly I was back in the time of Jesus when he asked the man at the pool of Siloam: 'Do you want to be healed?'

We were blessed in having a leader who had made several visits to the Holy Land and knew the ropes. Father Mike was extremely knowledgeable and helped the Gospels to 'come alive'. We were very moved to walk the Via Dolorosa although we were told that the road was twenty feet higher than the route along which Jesus would have actually carried his cross. I think that there were only two places where I felt able to say with absolute certainty: 'Jesus stood here; on this spot'. One was the original flagstoned courtyard of Pontius Pilate's Antonia Fortress where the soldiers scourged and taunted Jesus and crowned Him with thorns. That courtyard now forms the basement of the Convent of Our Lady of Sion on the Via Dolorosa and the games played by Roman soldiers to while away the time were still marked out on the flagstones. The other place in which I felt Jesus had actually been present was Jacob's Well, north of Jerusalem where he had spoken to the Samaritan

Woman. Nobody moves a huge well like that! It must indeed have been the well where Jesus sat down and spoke to the woman.

In the little village of Cana we came upon, not a wedding but an engagement party. Nearly all the village seemed to be present and the happy couple walked through the town to the prepared feast including a magnificent multi-coloured cake.

Bethlehem I found awful because Christians seemed to disagree violently about the exact place in which Jesus had been born. At the Church of the Nativity we were shown gold 'star' marking the 'birthplace' and men collecting money were much in evidence! Fortunately Father Mike led us away to an entrance in the rock face which he described as 'the cave of the shepherds'. Here he celebrated Mass in peace and reverence and a wonderful stillness. It seemed to be just the sort of place that biblical shepherds might have used.

On my birthday we climbed Mount Tabor and Ted asked Mike to offer Mass for my intentions. It was wonderful to be up there in the place of the Transfiguration but it had been quite a climb. No wonder the disciples were often tired and had to be chivvied along!

Rather less wonderful was the indentation in the rock which George, our guide, presented as 'the footprint of Jesus'. The stories of George lost little in the telling! We took to describing them as 'The Gospel according to Saint George!' Our guide also had 'favourite' shops in which he encouraged us to purchase anything and everything - no doubt to the tune of hefty backhanders for George!

Israel is a country geared to the gullibility of pilgrims. Along the road from Jerusalem to Jericho we came upon 'The Inn of the Good Samaritan'. Several members of the party were very excited to see the 'real' inn to which the kind Samaritan had taken the wounded Jew - regardless of the fact that Jesus had created a story to make a point! We also came across three separate sites of the tomb in which the body of Jesus had been laid and there seemed to be a number of 'veils of St Veronica' with which she was supposed to have wiped the face of Christ.

In Nazareth we were mocked and derided as we approached the modern church. Jesus himself had failed to find faith in Nazareth so we were in good company! I found that church a vulgar hotchpotch of colours and styles – no doubt because so many nations had had input! At last I spotted a mosaic of the Good Shepherd - an image of Jesus which had never previously appealed to me because the 'Good Shepherd' is as often portrayed as weak and effeminate. The shepherd of Nazareth was different. He stood sturdily upright in his short tunic and had piercing eyes and a short black beard. Across his neck lay the lost sheep which was clearly very precious. That picture spoke to my heart.

In the second week we moved on to Tiberias - and another crummy hotel. But it was a joy to sit beside the Sea of Galilee. One day we took a boat ride across the Lake and a storm blew up - seemingly out of nowhere. Father Mike offered Mass where

Jesus might have proclaimed the Beatitudes and in the distance I could see a settlement on a small hill. I wondered whether Jesus had pointed to it when he told his listeners to be like 'a city set on a hill'.

During our week in Tiberias the Cardinals in Rome were in conclave to elect a successor to Pope John Paul I who had died after only 33 days in office. When we heard the announcement of a Polish Pope we presumed that it was the Polish primate, Cardinal Wyzinski of Warsaw. Off we went to toast the new Pope in champagne. Only later did we learn that John Paul II had been Cardinal Archbishop of Cracow.

Community

Our thirst for community was increasing. Among the priests who shared our longing was Father Jim Overton of Westminster who was half English and half Peruvian. Jim sensed that the Lord was calling him towards community and approached Cardinal Basil Hume who gave him leave of absence to visit a number of communities in the United States.

This was exciting. We knew that communities had sprung up in the USA as a direct result of the Renewal. Cardinal Suenens of Belgium who was a great supporter of the renewal had himself visited a number of the American communities and had invited several of them to his own archdiocese of Malines-Brussels including 'The Word of God' from Ann Arbor Michigan and 'People of Praise' from South Bend Indiana as well as 'Marriage Encounter' with which Ted and I were already in touch.

Jim Overton was eager to visit communities of renewal in the United States and he had quite a list. From us he needed practical details in terms of the best way to get from A to B. Should he fly or was it better to travel by Greyhound bus? We spent a day with Jim during which Ted and I doled out information and prayed with him. In the evening we made our farewells and Jim told us that he would keep in touch - which he did not. We heard not a word for nine months - at which point Jim erupted into our lives on a flying visit to Cardinal Hume. He told us that he could not tell us anything and disappeared once more!

Eighteen months afterwards Jim reappeared - now he was eager to share his news. He told us that one of the communities he had visited was in Gaithersburg, Maryland. It was called 'Mother of God' and had started in 1968 when two women began to pray together, Judith Tydings and Edith Difato. Judith had a Masters degree in history and was married to a man who was not at all interested in religion. Edith had not been to college but was an avid reader. Her husband was Catholic but not at all interested in the Renewal. Judith and Edith felt that the Lord was calling the two of them to start community and they did not like the idea one bit! They obeyed, nevertheless, and the community came to birth and flourished in its mission to glorify Jesus Christ and grow in the knowledge of God through prayer, fellowship, evangelization and service.

Jim decided to interview one of the founders and at the conclusion of their interview session she dropped a bombshell on him: '*This* is a sin in your life, and *this* and *this* and *this*. Your prayer life is completely passive!'. Jim told us that he had been furious with the lady. He stormed out of the room and returned to his hotel in a great rage. For three nights he was unable to sleep and eventually returned to the founder and humbly asked what he should do. She advised him to return to England and request permission from Cardinal Hume to spend three years in their community - the reason for Jim's flying visit to England. Cardinal Hume had given permission and Jim was now half way through his three year stint!

During this visit to England, Jim encouraged Ted and me and also John and Catherine Blatchley in our own yearnings for community. He suggested that we start by meeting weekly with like-minded members of the Westminster renewal group. The purpose being to share what the Lord had done in our lives during the previous week. The first meeting brought together thirty six people but gradually most of them dropped away and we were left with a faithful group of seven regular attenders at St Mark's, Kennington.

For eighteen months, we had met every Sunday afternoon for two hours which involved a lot of travelling - the Blatchleys coming from Kilburn in north London and Ted and me driving up from Wokingham. The meetings had no structure, no plan no programme - and no leader. Eventually six of us decided that we needed proper leadership and that the seventh member - John Blatchley - should become our leader. We did not mention this to John but during one meeting the six of us stood up, prayed over John and asked that he be blessed in the office of leader. He did not appear to mind being railroaded into leadership - and he was a very good leader! We were richly blessed in that group because we had all suffered in one way or another and we were all praying for community.

One Sunday John announced that he would not be with us for the next two Sundays because he was going to Brussels on business. This was news indeed. We knew that the American renewal community, 'The Word of God' was based in Brussels under the name 'Jerusalem Community'. We also knew that one of the founders, Ralph Martin, was visiting Brussels from the United States. John was commissioned to pay a visit to 'Jerusalem'! He returned at the end of his fortnight with good news and bad - the bad news was that it had taken him a week to find the community.

The good news was he had eventually attended a Sunday Mass at their meeting place. We sat John down and plied him with questions. Ralph Martin had apparently preached the Sunday sermon rather than the priest. We were rather taken aback by this: it was the first time we had heard of a priest listening to a layman preaching during Mass.

When John eventually came to a halt, Ted came out with: 'I think that we should pray about making a visit there ourselves'. More excitement! It was agreed that Ted and I should travel to Belgium and we wrote to the Brussels community to ask if we might visit. It took ages to receive a reply and was my first lesson in the time it can take to make arrangements with communities.

At last the longed for letter appeared. 'Jerusalem' would be happy to receive us and we would be staying with a family called Rowland. I phoned Madame Rowland to ask what they would like me to bring. The answer was: 'Something to eat!' I decided that a large ham might fit the bill as well as a huge Christmas cake - a twenty pounder!

Colette Rowland was a Frenchwoman; spiritual, compassionate and very determined. She was to have a profound influence upon me. Her husband Tony had been born in England. At the age of twenty-two he had emigrated to Canada where he met the beautiful Colette who was very much a career woman. Both were Catholic but Tony was very much more committed to his faith than Colette. They married and in due course Colette gave birth to eight children to whom she was devoted - but she remained indifferent to religion. The marriage began to drift and Colette eventually suffered a nervous breakdown. Shortly after her recovery Tony was swept into the charismatic renewal. Colette did not want to know! She told Tony that she was quite prepared to feed and welcome his charismatic friends to their house but she had no intention of getting involved in their prayer group.

The marriage was more or less at rock bottom with Colette very busy with the children and Tony working for the religious publishing house Ave Maria Press. The couple were leading separate lives albeit under the same roof. One day a woman friend came to visit Colette to tell her that she was coming to say good-bye because she was in deep despair and had decided to commit suicide. Colette was horrified and felt helpless to do anything to change her friend's mind. After the friend had departed Colette did something she had not done for years. She knelt down and said a prayer: 'O God, if you exist, *do* something to show it!' That night a weary Tony returned from his publishing job. He had decided that it was curtains as far as marriage and family life were concerned and he, too, had made a desperate plea to God. He came into the house and went to find Colette: 'I promise that I will never ask you anything like this again, but will you come to the Prayer Meeting with me tonight? Colette said: 'Yes'.

Colette told me that when they arrived at the meeting place, she felt cold as ice and very bolshie. Then something happened. In her mind's eye, she saw herself standing on a wide ledge. Below her was darkness and there seemed to be many people in that darkness. They were stretching up their hands towards her and she sensed a voice speaking 'You will be used to bring many people to Me. Some you will get to know, and some you will not know'. Colette knew that she was listening to the voice of an all powerful and all loving God. It changed her life. The whole family took part in a Life in the Spirit seminar. Rachel, the eldest, would have been about fifteen and over the years all the children came closer to God.

Ted and I did not of course learn the full story that first night but over the years we came much closer to Colette and Tony Rowland. One day I told her that I could see that I was lacking in humility. She responded that the only way to become humble was to serve. In Colette I met a woman who really put others before herself, was tireless in serving and very adaptable. . It was a real eye-opener to see the relationship between husband and wife in biblical order. I had heard and read about this – and began to feel that I might find it pretty hard going if we became involved in this community; always supposing that they would allow us in.

We were greatly interested and intrigued to learn from one of the Ann Arbor elders, Bruce Yocum, that a decision had been taken to try to create community in London. Among the many people we met was a young American with the unlikely name of Charles Christmas who was one of the possible pioneers of a London Community. Charles came from the 'Bible Belt' of the southern United States and was a convert to Catholicism. He was a lawyer, married with a little daughter and he had never set foot in England. Charles had a meeting with Ted and later with me to ask whether he and his family might be suitable for a community in London. We were thrilled at the prospect of a 'Jerusalem' Community beginning in London but their imminent arrival begged the question: 'Where?' London was so huge.

The week we spent in Brussels was very much a 'learning' experience. We had not known what to expect and I felt that Ted and I were under intense scrutiny. The general gathering of 'Jerusalem' included Mass at which Ted and I experienced the preaching of Ralph Martin while the priest sat quietly to one side. I began to see that these people really needed preachers who understood the vision of community and its teaching – and those preachers might very well be lay people. On that occasion, the priest celebrating Mass was himself a 'learner' while Ralph as one of the founders had years of experience behind him. During the week I met another priest who belonged to the community and was going off to join the 'mother house' in the USA at Ann Arbor. I asked why he was doing this and his answer seared my heart: 'I want to learn how to serve!'

18

CANCER
1979-1983

'You will be my witnesses not only in Jerusalem but throughout Judea and Samaria and indeed to the ends of the earth'
Acts 1:8:

Early in 1979 Charles Christmas and his wife Patti arrived in London with a mission from Brussels to found community. They looked at various houses and eventually settled on a West London property in Chiswick. The house was large and in addition to the Christmases and their baby daughter there were two young Americans from the People of Hope Covenant community in New Jersey coming to join them. Ted and I were eager to be as fully involved as possible.

In order to make the new community known, the Christmases decided to run a seven week Life in the Spirit seminar for people who were new to the Renewal. Those of us who were already in contact with them, including John and Catherine Blatchley, were asked not to attend the seminars for fear of 'swamping' the new enquirers and making them feel that we were the 'in' group while they were merely 'newcomers'. The 'old-timers' had to meet on their own.

In the final week of the Life in the Spirit seminar we were all invited to come together. When we arrived each 'oldtimer' was handed a slip of paper containing the cryptic words: 'Don't prophecy and don't speak in tongues!' -presumably intended to prevent us coming out with alarming charismatic manifestations. All the new enquirers seemed to be speaking in tongues anyway so I doubt if they would have been phased by our efforts.

We became known as: 'The West London Community': a non-residential community, all living in our own homes and running our own finances although each family agreed to donate a tenth part of their income to charitable and church purposes – which of course included community expenses. Every Sunday there was a meeting in London and members also came together for a weekly sharing group. As the community increased in number, the sharing groups multiplied in order to keep each one manageably small.

Ted and I were swept into this new way of life. Community is like family - you cannot choose your brothers and sisters, aunts and uncles. It is the same with community. We were a motley bunch and becoming motlier by the week with so many different characters and personalities joining in! Ted and I were fully convinced of our need for community – but the daily living out of that reality was a shock to the system! We found the sharing groups a strain – not least because they happened at the end of the working day. Ted finished work in Brentford at 5.30 and the meetings in London did not start until 7.30. I would pick him up in the car and we would go to Mass together, eat our sandwiches in the car, attend the meeting and drive home.

During our first summer, four married couples decided to try their hand at living under the same roof for a week. One of the community couples had a holiday home in Dorset available for rent – two small cottages knocked into one. The eight of us were more or less the same age but we soon discovered that one person's idea of holiday 'fun' was another person's boredom – or even misery! ! It was an education in the importance of laying down the ground rules before a holiday and getting a clear idea of likes and dislikes. One couple who lived in a flat wanted to spend the time sitting outside and reading. Another pair liked looking at stately homes and the third couple liked shopping and going to the theatre. We had some stormy sessions but in the end managed to settle our differences and have a good time.

The cooking of dinner was divided between the four families. I cooked with Annette of whom I was very fond. One evening we made a succulent mixed grill in the most enormous frying pan I had ever seen. I was intending to make gravy with the bits and pieces left over - only to discover to my horror that I had been using cocoa powder in place of gravy browning. Annette told me that I should throw it out but I decided to 'take a chance'. The cocoa did not contain sugar and I thought I might get away with it. Annette and I served up our 'gravy' without mentioning the content and everybody asked for more. The following day we told them the truth about 'Dorset gravy'!

At the end of the first week the other three families left and Ted and I stayed on – Anthony and Fiona came to join us and we had a wonderful week together.

From 1979 onwards Ted and I found ourselves taking part in all sorts of conferences and weekends where we came in contact with a great number of fascinating people. We saw the wonderful side of this renewal, and we saw as well the ugly side - the casualties; the nuns and priests and also the married couples who wanted to 'do their own thing'. Some ended up leaving their religious life or splitting up with their marriage partner. On the positive side, we witnessed great healings and the changing of lives. It was a time of coming to know the Lord better, knowing myself better and coming even closer to Ted.

One particularly memorable conference took place in an empty seminary during their holiday time. We arrived to discover that whoever had allocated the rooms had not only separated husbands and wives but a few couples including ourselves were actually accommodated in different buildings! Ted lugged his bed from the room he had been originally assigned so that we could be together. We made a point of encouraging other couples to do likewise.

Fortunately I was on the registration desk on the first day and made a point of advising 'separated brethren' to get back together. On the final day a lot of beds had to be lugged out of the 'double rooms' and back to their original places so that the seminarians would find everything in place when they returned.

As Ted and I were fairly experienced we were invited to start Prayer Groups in a number of places. It was exciting to witness God bringing people together people for praise and worship; men and women who were thirsting for the word of God and wanted to support one another in Christian fellowship.

It did not take me long to realise that I was in considerable danger of turning the renewal into an 'ego' trip. Renewal was tailor-made for this in the sense that anyone with a particular gift from the Lord would have no difficulty in pushing themselves forward and using their gift as a means of getting other people to look up to them. There was so much in me that wanted to be 'centre stage'; so much that wanted to shine before others. I knew that I was walking a tightrope but with the help of Ted and wise elders in the community I think was enabled to avoid the dangers on either side. But I was well aware of them and of the fact that my strong personality was a mixed blessing.

A great number of very wounded and needy people were attracted to the movement. I know with all my heart that we are *all* the walking wounded; we are all in need of healing; but it requires great discernment to differentiate between those who genuinely want to change and those who like a lot of attention but have no real intention of altering their lives. Our unfortunate experience with Miriam in Wokingham was a considerable help in this area.

I was often reminded of the story of Jesus and the man at the healing pool of Bethsaida [John 5;7]. I had always found the man's response strange when Jesus asked him whether he wished to be made well. "Sir," said the man: "I have no-one to put me into the pool." Perhaps the man did not want to be healed because he would no longer be assured of a livelihood from the kind people who brought him offerings. Within the renewal I found many people who behaved like this man. They wanted the support and attention which assured them of a place centre-stage - but they did not really want to be healed. It was as if 'sickness' – mental or physical - gave them a sense of importance and gave meaning to their lives and there were kind people who would meet all their needs.

With our entry into the charismatic renewal, we were introduced to a whole new world of books. I would almost rather read than eat and in the Renewal I was exposed to authors from every Christian tradition. One of the most remarkable books was Jackie Pullinger's *Chasing the Dragon* in which this young girl describes her extraordinary experiences in Hong Kong. Jackie had been 'zapped' by the Lord at the time of her confirmation and decided that she wanted to be a missionary. Like Gladys Aylward 'The Small Woman', Jackie could find nobody to accept her services. One night at a prayer meeting in West Croydon she received a message which she was sure came from God: 'Go. Trust me and I will lead you. I will instruct you and teach you in the way which you shall go; I will guide you...' With a few pounds in her pocket, Jackie set off on the cheapest ship she could find. At Hong Kong she sensed that this was the place that God had chosen for her. She disembarked – not without difficulty – and found herself in the horror of the 'Walled City'; a den of lawlessness which had become a haven for gold smuggling, drug smuggling, illegal gambling dens and every sort of vice. There she discovered young girls of twelve or thirteen who had been sold into sexual slavery. Their hands were scarred with the needle marks from heroin injections – the only thing that made their lives remotely bearable.

God worked powerfully through Jackie Pullinger to bring help and humanity to this terrible place and her achievements have now been acknowledged. Ted and I met Jackie at a seminar in London and found her fascinating. She was completely natural and had no hesitation about witnessing to Jesus. We were impressed.

Cancer

In 1982 I went down with shingles. I had been aware of a few spots around my waist and when I received the diagnosis I decided that shingles could not be too bad after all. The doctor, however, left me in little doubt about the potential effects of shingles on a sixty one year old! Then the pain started. I had never imagined such agony and I was prescribed painkillers to be taken every four hours. Ted and I decided that I was well enough to travel to the community weekend which had been planned and I spent the entire weekend watching the hands of the clock creep round to the moment when I could take my next dose.

The following week Ted was booked into hospital for a prostate operation and I wanted to be well enough to drive him to the nursing home and to visit him every day. The doctor changed my pills and I managed it!

Ted's operation went very well and was followed by six weeks convalescence during which we did our best to relax at home. It was great to have him back safely but I still had the shingles and began to be wary of becoming reliant on painkillers. I decided to reduce the dose because I knew that suffering could be used to good effect. I decided to offer mine to God for the many people who needed prayers and support.

Ted returned to work in December and three days later another blow fell. He arrived home with the news that he was being made redundant in January. Ted told me later that the news had not come as a very great shock and I believe that he was able to be of great help to some of his colleagues who were also being made redundant. Word apparently went around that Ted was the person to go to if one was in need of support. During that time something lovely happened. Anthony and Fiona offered us financial assistance, should we need it. We did not need to take up their kind offer which was as unexpected as it was generous.

When Ted left the firm for the last time we took a three day break in Christchurch as a sort of 'adjustment'. Life was going to be completely different and we had to make new plans. Ted and I were going to be seeing much more of one another and I thought of the old saying about husbands at home in the daytime: 'For better, for worse, but not for lunch!"

On Holy Saturday night I noticed a small swelling in my breast. I thought nothing of it but mentioned the matter to Ted. He was adamant that we should get a doctor to take a look on Easter Monday. Dr John Kerr duly examined me and made an immediate referral to the Royal Berkshire Hospital.

The examination at the Royal Berkshire was detailed and very thorough. The surgeon told me that he would not know the result for several days and I would then be asked to return. The word 'cancer' was never mentioned, but I made a point of telling the surgeon that I was a Christian and wanted to know the truth and the whole truth. I had known too many women who had been 'fobbed off' with references to 'a tiny lump' or 'a small growth'!

A week later we were asked to return. We were told that I definitely had cancer but the extent was unknown. I was going to need an operation which might involve total or partial removal of the breast. It is hard now to describe my reaction to the news. The very word 'cancer' is sinister and can produce a sense of unreality: 'This can't be happening to me'. Needless to say, Ted was magnificent and totally supportive. With hindsight, we should have asked for a second opinion but Ted and I were 'dumb bunnies' when it came to dealing with doctors - we just accepted whatever we were told.

The operation was scheduled for two weeks hence – I was thankful not to have to wait longer and knew in my heart that I was being tested. Did I really believe everything that I had told others about 'trusting God'? Words are easy when you don't have to act on them yourself! However I felt that in some mysterious way I was 'hearing' from God the words: 'Let Me enfold you in My arms, and show you how much I love you'.

I had to break the news to Liz and that was hard. I tried to soften the blow by telling her that I knew God was in the midst of this and was only permitting it for some greater good. Liz was scared. She told me later that she went into shock as she tried to take in the news. Fortunately she was able to tell herself that if God had given me the grace to accept the situation he would certainly not withhold that grace from her.

Ted phoned Anthony who came over to Wokingham. He wanted to take us out to a large lunch but I could not manage it and we settled for Ploughman's at a local pub. I sensed his concern and was so grateful for his prompt arrival.

In the fortnight between diagnosis and operation life took on a new perspective. We had tickets for a play and I found myself thinking: 'Will this be the last play I shall ever see?" Ted took me down to West Wittering to look at the sea which I love so much. Was this the last time I would watch the waves? – not that we could see any waves because the tide was out and we were treated to an expanse of mud-flat!

I was torn between grief at the idea of leaving my beloved Ted and a sort of excitement at the thought that

I might be going to heaven to meet Jesus. There was no physical pain – apart from the wretched shingles. I was aware only of the slight swelling in my breast. I thought of my mother's operation in the United States when the cancer was discovered to be so advanced that nothing could be done. She had been given three months to live but survived for nearly a year.

I felt that I had to come to terms with the possibility of dying under the anaesthetic. It was impossible to know the extent of the cancer until I was on the operating table but I had known for years that my heart would present problems to an anaesthetist.

We broke the news to the members of the community who were deeply concerned and assured us of the support of their prayers. I knew that prayers were being offered for me in all parts of the world because we had lived in such a lot of places and remained in contact with many friends overseas. I thought back to Ted's assertion, early in our marriage, that I was a 'spiritual snob' because I 'collected' people who had the ear of the Lord. I now 'called in' their services on my own behalf and they responded magnificently.

Operation

The operation was due to be carried out at Battle Hospital in Reading and I was asked to arrive 48 hours in advance. Ted drove me there and as I walked through the front entrance I seemed to hear an inner voice telling me: "You are walking on holy ground and I am just one step ahead of you." I was shown into a light and airy ward – eight beds and five patients – I was the sixth.

That evening some of the sisters from the community drove down from London to pray with me. The following day I had various medical visitors, including a student who had been sent with instructions to diagnose my heart condition and its probable cause – not the first time I had been used as a 'test case' for trainee doctors. It quickly became apparent that this young man was a Christian and we talked animatedly for twenty minutes and then prayed together. I reminded him that he had done nothing about examining my heart at which he laughed and proceeded to do so. To help him on his way I told him about my childhood diphtheria and the leaking heart valve!

I made friends with two of the cleaning women who were Christians and I was given the courage to share my faith with other patients in the ward, some of whom were believers. Two of the women were much less well than the others and I felt able to ask if we could all pray for them and lift them before the throne of God. Later in the day, one of the visitors came over to speak to me and when he heard that my operation was scheduled for the following day he remarked on my apparent calm. I told him that I was a Christian to whom he responded: 'I wish I had your faith'. I seemed to be given the heart of an evangelist and asked him if he wanted faith. The answer was: 'Yes!' I prayed aloud for the man and I know that the Lord touched him.

I was convinced that I was on my way to heaven and had a strange sense of being 'withdrawn' from the world and even from my beloved Ted as well as from Anthony and Liz. Ted came in that night and as we said goodbye I felt buoyed up with the knowledge that God would care for him if I was 'going home'.

The operation was scheduled for 11.00 the following morning and I was given a sleeping pill to take me through the night. At 10.00am I was given a pre-med but did not feel particularly drowsy and was wide awake when they lifted me onto the trolley. As I was about to be wheeled out of the ward a beautiful bouquet was delivered from friends and their note read 'With love and prayers...' I thought to myself that the words described perfectly the feelings with which I was going to Jesus – love and prayers. This, I 'knew' was my final departure!

A lovely nurse walked beside the trolley holding my hand until I was wheeled into the operating area. A number of doctors gathered around, including the anaesthetist who wanted to have a few words and explain that he would be giving me the injection which would 'put me under'. I told him that I was a Christian and believed I might be going to meet my Father in heaven. I would appreciate a few seconds warning before the 'knockout' injection. They fussed around and the anaesthetist then said: 'I am going to give you the injection in five seconds –does that give you enough time?". "Yes", I said: and added, loudly and clearly: 'Father, Into Your Hands, I commend my spirit."

Several hours later I returned to consciousness, back in my own bed in the ward with a kindly nurse mopping my brow. There was no physical pain – but a stab of disappointment that I was in Battle Hospital and had not gone to Jesus in heaven. Sensation returned slowly and I became aware of strapping and bandages around my chest. My left breast had been removed. Ted arrived shortly afterwards with tears running down his face.

Then the pain began with an acute sensation of burning on my left side. I had been warned that the shingles would cause severe nerve pain at the site of the operation but had paid little heed because I had been so sure that I would not be alive to feel anything at all! I was aware of a doctor trying to decide whether or not to give me a blood transfusion and then, mercifully, I was given an injection and knew no more.

When I came round, Ted was there again and this time Liz was with him. She was weeping but these were tears of joy at the fact that I had survived after all – though we still had no idea of the extent of the cancer; only that the breast had been removed and I was on a drip. There was a message from Anthony to say that he would be coming to the hospital the following day. He arrived with Fiona – my daughter-in-law was bearing a beautiful little china bird which she called 'a bluebird for hope!' I was deeply touched.

April 19th was our wedding anniversary and I confided the news to Matron when she visited the ward first thing in the morning. She passed it on to the Scottish registrar when she came on her rounds. I usually found that registrar tight lipped and unfriendly but she responded kindly to the news of my wedding anniversary: 'You should not be in here – you ought to be back home having a bottle of champagne and celebrating with your husband." If only!

Ted, me Fiona, Anthony and our three grandchildren: Stephen, Alan and Jonathan

The next step was measurement for the prosthesis and five days after the operation I was given a prescription for pain killers and told that I could leave hospital. The stitches were still in place and I staggered to the phone, longing to share the news with Ted, but nervous at the thought of leaving hospital so soon after major surgery. The following day Liz and Ted came to pick me up and a nurse helped me to dress. It was a long and exhausting walk from the ward to the main entrance and I should have made the journey in a wheelchair. There are no words to describe the agony of that drive home, with me lying sideways in the back of the car. Ted and Liz had brought pillows, but I realised vividly the importance of travelling by ambulance so that the patient can be completely flat!

During the journey, Ted said suddenly: "Let's celebrate - What would you like?" I think that if I had asked him for the moon on a cream cracker he would have tried to get it for me. All I could think of for 'celebration' was a fresh cream finger bun with icing on top and butter in the middle so Ted stopped at a bakery. At long last we arrived home and they helped me out of the car and up to the front door. Ted and Liz were obviously overjoyed to have me home but the pain was too great for me even to take my coat off, let alone climb upstairs to bed. We sat in the kitchen where I managed to eat half the iced bun!

I had been told to return five days later for removal of the stitches and news at last. Had the cancer been completely removed and what sort of treatment would I need? It was a long five days. Two of the stitches gave me great pain and the painkillers helped only to a limited extent. Our friendly local doctor advised me to call the district nurse and ask her to remove the offending stitches.. Alas, she was unable to do so because my surgeon would apparently have come down on her like a ton of bricks for interfering with his handiwork! Sleep was well nigh impossible but Ted was indefatigable in his efforts to distract me from the pain and I know that he stormed heaven on my behalf. We spent much of the time praying together and that certainly helped.

The fifth day came round eventually and Ted drove me back to hospital where my stitches were removed by a delightful nurse from the island of St Kitts. She was gentle and kind but I wished that she had not started by telling me that there were thirteen stitches to be removed - adding, for good measure, 'thirteen is unlucky!' I then waited to see the surgeon but who should call me in but the Scottish registrar who I did not like: "You can leave now" she said: "There is no further treatment!" Her 'bedside manner' left something to be desired but I was able to establish that the operation had been a success and that the cancer had been completely removed as far as anyone could tell.

Ted took me to stay with a nurse friend and I found myself extremely short of energy and able to do little more than lie on my bed. Our friend felt that I should be making more of an effort but I was completely incapable. Unbeknownst to any of us, I was in the very early stages of leukaemia and this, coupled with my leaking heart valve and general post-operative condition was probably responsible for general malaise.

Meanwhile, our community was wonderfully supportive and the leader of our sharing group kindly arranged for meetings to take place at our home so that I would not have to travel to London too frequently. While I had been in hospital, Ted had clearly been doing some thinking. One day he gently raised the possibility of a move from Wokingham to London. My answer was prompt and to the point: 'No way!" I was horrified by the very idea of leaving our lovely home for a new start in London - not to mention all the work involved in selling one house and moving into another. Despite the kindness of our sharing group in coming to Wokingham we still seemed to be driving to London a couple of times a week – but I much preferred that to the prospect of actually living there!

One morning at Mass Ted was the designated reader. He proclaimed the words of Jesus from Acts 1:8: 'You will be my witnesses not only in Jerusalem but throughout Judea and Samaria and indeed to the ends of the earth'. I had heard the words many times before but on this occasion it was as if a shaft of light had 'pierced' my heart – no pain but just a sense that the words were addressed to me personally. Here was a call from the Lord to invest my energies not only in my local parish and in regular visits to Chiswick but in actually making the move I had previously found so unthinkable. At least I wasn't being asked to travel to 'Judea and Samaria'! The prospect of a move to London now brought great peace. I said nothing to Ted until I had prayed about the matter and then surprised him with my decision: 'I believe the Lord is calling us to London – I am ready!'

19

THE LAST LAP
1983-2000

Our first step was a visit to Tony Rowland as leader of the community. Tony's response was a real confirmation from the Lord that we were on the right track. "I was just going to give you a call because the leaders of the community have decided that it would be right for you to move to London!" Tony did not want us to come to Chiswick but to the Acton area just next door. We started visiting house agents and put our house in Wokingham on the market.

We found a house in Julian Avenue which suited us but was going to need quite a lot of work including complete redecoration. We would be unable to move in for several months but had to be out of our Wokingham house by early September. We spent the interim living in a flat we were lent in Mayfair and moved to Julian Avenue on 8th November.

I missed Wokingham far less than I feared and was so pleased to be close to the centre of community activities in West London. Our new house had four bedrooms and a triangular rear garden which was paved but had flower beds along both sides and a beautiful passion flower in the front garden. We settled in, picked up the threads of Community life and felt that at long last we were really living in a Christian community.

In December 1983 Ted began to work part-time for a computer company run by another community member and later he took on part- time work in the community office. Ted was 64 and I was 62. 'Officially' we were at an age when we could think of ourselves as `retired' but we seemed to be getting busier all the time.

Fortunately we managed a few trips away and some theatre visits but much of our time was spent in supporting other community members and in deepening our understanding and involvement in various aspects of the work of the community.

We became increasingly involved in the ministry of deliverance and were in absolutely no doubt about the tangible presence of evil in the world and its power to disrupt the lives of communities and individuals. On one particularly dramatic occasion we were asked to pray for a very disturbed man, who I will call John, and was being evangelised by members of the community. He was European but spoke good English. The community elders asked Ted and me to minister to John and he was open to this. We met with him in one of the reception rooms at the back of the brothers' house.

John sat facing us and we began by calling on the power of the Holy Spirit to be with us and to strengthen us. We invited John to share some aspects of his life and he described experiences of anger, bitterness, resentment and unforgiveness which had their roots in his disturbed childhood. We asked the Holy Spirit to enter into John and free him from the bitter memories which were poisoning his life. We felt that we were making some progress as we moved from one area of distress to another.

After about an hour, John suddenly rose from his seat and threw himself onto the ground, where he remained on all fours. He began to growl and make similar animal noises. Such behaviour was completely out of character and Ted and I were sufficiently experienced to realise that we might be in the presence of demonic possession. We continued to pray and minister to John but his rage only increased. The animal noises continued and he began to pull and tear at the carpet and upholstery. We were now convinced that we were in the presence of an evil spirit inhabiting this unfortunate man. We called on the power of the name of Jesus to deliver John from the demon but there was little change. We realised that we needed the support of the prayers of others. Ted went next door and asked the four brothers there to pray together until we had dislodged this demon. Ted returned and we continued to pray and to minister. The support of the brothers' prayer enabled John to be released. The animal noises ceased and John became quiet again. He rose to his feet and returned to his chair. It was a great joy to witness the power of

God restoring this troubled man to his senses. John was able to forgive those who had wronged him, to repent and to seek forgiveness for himself. The evil spirit had lost its power to control his life.

In 1985 we came into close touch with David Pytches of St Andrew's Chorleywood on the outskirts of London. David had spent a number of years as a bishop in Chile and when he returned to parish ministry in the UK he was concerned to bring about the `spontaneous expansion' of the church in his own country as he had experienced it in Chile. David and his wife Mary had developed a deepening friendship with John Wimber founder of the US based Vineyard Fellowship. With John's support the Pytches had launched a powerful ministry to church leaders.

Ted and I took part in a training course at Chorleywood on the healing ministry and found it immensely valuable and later shared in courses run by David Pytches' wife Mary. The following year there was an opportunity to take part in a course in Brighton led by John Wimber and entitled Teach us to Pray. This was followed by another Brighton conference in October 1987 which John Wimber entitled 'Worship'. That same year, we had a wonderful fortnight with the People of Hope Community in New Jersey during which I was strongly encouraged by my friend Joanne Quense to write a book. Joanne provided the motivation; telling me that the book would be for my grandchildren! How the project has grown!

In April 1988 there was another John Wimber conference on `Spiritual Warfare' and in 1989 came Billy Graham's great Mission to the UK in which we participated as helpers. In that same year the name of the West London community was changed to The Antioch Community.

For several years we thus divided our time between living and working with the West London community and visiting other communities in the UK and overseas to give and receive ministry. We witnessed some dramatic examples of the healing power of Jesus and one in particular has always remained with me. While we were visiting a community in the United States, a young lady I will call Ann came to us for prayer. Ann had been married for ten years and she and her husband Rory had four children. Their relationship had started off well but had now diminished to the point where divorce seemed inevitable. While praying with Ann we dealt with a number of hurts from her childhood: areas in which repentance and forgiveness were required. Ann had no difficulty here but we sensed that there were hidden areas in her life where healing was still required. With the help of the Holy Spirit and his gift of knowledge and wisdom it came to light that Ann had had an affair before her marriage which resulted in pregnancy and abortion. She had never been able to come to terms with the guilt of abortion and had been unable to share any of this with Rory. At last she was able to speak out her repentance to Jesus and to bring to an end the cycle of guilt and misery in which she had existed. I suggested that Ann give a name to her unborn baby. She chose the name 'Matt' and asked Jesus to allow her to see her child. Through the power of the Holy Spirit Ann was enabled to 'see' a picture of a radiant young man holding the hand of Jesus. She left us feeling very much happier but still unable to consider telling Rory the full story.

Some days afterwards Ted and I were surprised to receive a phone call from Rory himself, asking to come and see us for ministry because he had seen a great change in his wife since her visit. Ted told him that we would like to pray about his request. We did so and decided that Ted should ask Rory to come and see us and bring Ann with him.

When they arrived we could sense the strain between them. We seated Ann opposite Rory and asked her to pray silently for our ministry to her husband but not to say or do anything else. We began by inviting Rory to tell us about his upbringing and his early life. This revealed areas which needed repentance and forgiveness and Rory had no difficulty about that. With the help of the Holy Spirit, I sensed that Rory was still boiling with an anger which had nothing to do with his childhood and early upbringing. I told him that I sensed his anger and asked if he could explain. Rory began to talk about experiences as a soldier in Vietnam which he had never shared with anybody. He had gone out as a young soldier and one day had been asked to drive a truck in which three of his mates were passengers. They drove for a little way and then the vehicle hit a mine which exploded. Rory's three mates were killed and he was the sole survivor. His boiling anger was directed at the military authorities who had sent young soldiers into such a place of danger. Rory had buried that anger and never even shared it with his wife. He was as deeply wounded as Ann had been.

As he finished his story Ann rose from her chair, came across to her husband. She took him into her arms, hugging him tightly and shared with him the story of her previous relationship and the abortion. They wept together and it was wonderful to see the love between Ann and Rory reborn and deepening in that precious moment. There was no longer any question of separation and divorce.

In 1993 a valuable visit took us to Vienna and in 1995 it was a great blessing to have the opportunity to visit the Washtenaw Community. In 1991 the original Word of God Community in Ann Arbor had split into two groups: one changed its name to 'the Washtenaw Community' later to 'The Word of Life'. It was from the original Word of God Community that the Jerusalem community had sprung and thus our own West London Community so it was a joy to visit them in their new incarnation as Washtenaw.

While at Washtenaw in 1995 1 was taken ill and found myself gasping for breath before each session. We were greatly blessed in the kindness and care of the community but I ended up in hospital and eventually came home to London having left my gall bladder in America after my first experience of a new technique called 'keyhole surgery'!

Back in the UK, we continued to minister and on one occasion were asked to visit a lady who was blind in one eye as a result of cancer. During our time together it became apparent that she had suffered throughout her life from the resentment and anger resulting from a serious incident during childhood. We prayed with her that she might be released from her inner suffering. The prayer was answered spectacularly and the woman was not only enabled to forgive but she was cured of the blindness in her left eye. We praised and thanked God and returned home to Acton.

Two days later I suffered severe pain in my left eye and almost overnight lost the sight in it. Was there any connection between this loss and our experience with the lady over whom we had prayed? We were never to know. I was referred to Moorfields Eye Hospital where I learnt that the cancer had returned. I attended Moorfields regularly for radiotherapy which was painful but well worth it because the cancer seemed to be halted. Ted and I were able to continue in ministry. This was not, however, my final experience of treatment for cancer; the next one would be far more wretched.

New Zealand

In 1998, we received an invitation out of the blue from the Lamb of God Community in New Zealand. Neither of us had visited the southern hemisphere before although we had met members of the Lamb of God Community when they visited London. We also had members of our own families in New Zealand. We prayed long and hard about undertaking such a long journey and it was almost as if we could hear the Lord saying: `I want you in a different part of my vineyard now - Go!'

My precarious health always obliged us to travel in faith that nothing drastic would go wrong while we were out of the country. When leaving on any journey we were invariably aware that the Holy Spirit had `taken over'. There was such an awareness of the hand of God outstretched over Ted and me and upon those whose lives we were allowed to touch. We were always given the energy we needed and I never fell seriously ill overseas with the exception of the one occasion in Ann Arbor where I lost my gall bladder!

The object of our visit to New Zealand was to make ourselves available for prayer ministry to anyone in the Lamb of God community who requested this. The two main community centres were in Christchurch in the south island and Auckland in the north. We were to spend five weeks in New Zealand, two weeks at each centre and a week off in the middle. This suited us well, especially as the Christchurch community were kind enough to lend us a car for our week's holiday so that we could tour the northern part of the south island. We spent the first two weeks in Christchurch and, on the recommendation of the community, we started our holiday week with a visit to the Lewis Pass with its spectacular views.. We then descended to the coast and stopped off in two places where members of the community put us up. We then drove east across the island and at midday found ourselves entering the town of Kaikoura.

The first thing we spotted in Kaikoura was a large notice advertising sailing trips around the bay to see schools of whales and dolphins - departure in one hour! We both had a soft spot for dolphins so we joined the sailing in order to see them. There were twelve of us in the motor launch and it was wonderful to see these beautiful affectionate creatures. Some of the passengers dived into the water to join the dolphins but Ted and I decided that swimming with dolphins was not for us! We returned happily and spent the night in the home of a wonderful friendly couple who made us completely at home. During that week we saw so many beautiful sights and enjoyed the friendliness of the people we met.

At the end of the week we returned the car to our kind friends and flew up to Auckland for the second leg of our trip. Here, as in Christchurch, it was a great privilege to be allowed to pray with and minister to those who requested this service - members of the community and many others. We were in no doubt that many people were set free from bondages of differing sorts through the power of the Holy Spirit. As always, the content of ministry was completely confidential and it was perhaps beneficial that Ted and I came from the other side of the world and would be leaving in a few days - people who had shared deeply with us might have felt uncomfortable if they had had to meet us socially. Fortunately, they could be sure that they were very unlikely to see us again!

We thanked God for allowing us to be used as channels of his grace and power and we constantly kept in mind the words of Luke 5:31: `Those who are healthy have no need of a physician, but those who are sick'. We are all wounded and God, in his love and mercy, allowed Ted and me to minister as `wounded healers'. Throughout our ministry we operated under the `cover' of an elder of our own community to whom we reported back. This was Mike Shaughnessy who had taken over from Tony Rowland and Charles Christmas as leader in London.

During our visit to New Zealand we took part in the community meetings on Sundays. These usually consisted of worship and praise at the start followed by a teaching on some aspect of community life in the light of biblical teaching. Afterwards community members would share news of the ways in which the Lord had been working in their lives and the meeting would end with more singing. During one of the meetings in Auckland the session ended with a beautiful song which Ted and I liked very much: 'Because he lives, I can face tomorrow'. We asked if it would he possible to have either a tape of the song or some sheet music and were told a day or two later that neither was available. We were disappointed but thought no more about it. As the time of our departure drew near we received a lovely surprise. A member of the community's music ministry had got together with one of the leaders of the community to make a special tape of the song for us to take back to England.

Moving to Northampton

Over Christmas 1998, I went down with a severe attack of bronchitis followed by pneumonia and poor Ted acquired a nasty dose of salmonella. We were in a desperate state and for almost a week we just lay in bed, too ill and miserable to do anything. I think that we both hoped that we might die. Dear Liz came down from Northampton to look after us and 'commuted' regularly between Northampton and Acton. When she was unable to be with us herself she arranged for a member of the Jesus Fellowship who was a nurse to come and look after us as needed.

As we made a slow recovery, Liz came up with a radical suggestion. How would we feel about leaving our London home and moving up to Northamptonshire to be close to the Jesus Fellowship so that Liz could keep an eye on us?

We had spent nearly sixteen years in Acton - the longest time we had spent anywhere in the whole of our married life - Acton felt like home. On the other hand, Ted was now nearly eighty and I was 77. Was it really sensible to think that we could go on being independent for ever? We thought and prayed about Liz's suggestion and the result was that in July 1999 we moved up to Northamptonshire to stay in one of the Jesus Fellowship community houses, Cornhill Manor. We spent several months with the Fellowship while Liz went to great trouble to find a suitable house for us. She came up with a lovely three bedroom bungalow with beautiful garden in the village of Pattishall not far from Cornhill which had a small shop although we needed to go further afield for most of our shopping.

No sooner had we moved into the bungalow than my health took a severe turn for the worse. I have nothing but praise for our local doctor who made himself available far beyond the call of duty and the doctors and nurses at the hospital in Northampton were magnificent. I came to know them very well indeed and was in and out of that hospital so frequently that the car was almost able to find its own way there!

A second valve in my fragile heart had started to play up which resulted in breathing difficulties and there were times when I could get around only with the help of a wheelchair. The cancer had also returned with a vengeance and I found myself afflicted with chemotherapy which left me feeling like `death warmed up'. I told Ted that I had felt like putting my head in a gas oven.

Water retention was another very trying condition and the medication produced painful mouth ulcers as a side effect. They almost destroyed my desire for food and on one occasion Ted was told by the doctor that I had not more than two months to live. 1 was feeling so wretched that I hardly cared except for the grief of leaving my beloved Ted. I have never been more grateful for the enduring bond of love between me and my dearest husband. I would never have survived without it and I know that he suffered with me. There is nothing worse than having to watch the suffering of a loved one and knowing that one is powerless to relieve it.

But it has not all been gloom and doom. One of the most joyous and important 'happenings' was the increasingly close relationship which developed with our dear son. He arrived one evening to cook us a meal and it was wonderful to be able to embrace him and express our love for him and our admiration for the way in which he and Fiona have brought up their three wonderful sons, Stephen, Alan and Jonathan, who are a great credit to parental devotion. In retrospect Ted and I regret that we sent our own children away to boarding schools and wish that we had had those precious years with them growing up at home in the house with us.

Another cause of great joy is the loving kindness and care we continue to receive from the Jesus Fellowship. I cannot express the admiration and gratitude that Ted and I feel for Liz and her `extended family'. They provide a team of people who continually nurse us, care for us and meet our every need. At the drop of a hat they are on the front doorstep or at my hospital bedside!

A third cause of joy is the fact that although I fall frequently I never suffer a broken bone! What does the future hold now? There is increasing pain and breathlessness and every likelihood that I shall receive the home call before my dearest Ted. I do not know when the Lord will come to take me but I live each day in joy and thanksgiving for all that he has blessed us with and in glorious expectation of the heavenly homeland!

EPILOGUE
2000-2001

"[Becoming 'Real'] doesn't happen all at once…. It takes a long time. That's why it doesn't happen often to people who break easily, or have sharp edges, or who have to be carefully kept. Generally, by the time you are Real, most of your hair has been loved off, and your eyes drop out and you get loose in the joints and very shabby. But these things don't matter at all, because once you are Real you can't be ugly, except to people who don't understand."

***The Velveteen Rabbit,* Margery Williams**

As Joyce's health declined she became ever more 'real' in the sense of Margery Williams words quoted above. With two leaking valves in her heart, recurring cancer, leukaemia and the loss of the sight in one eye she remained my beloved 'Donny' - as I had always called her. She was always stalwart, courageous warm hearted and a valiant warrior. As her health declined, she became ever more vibrant, tender and understanding. I was so proud of her.

The events Joyce recounts in this book are only part of the story. The full account of her life and work would take volumes! As the reader will appreciate, she was a magnificent storyteller and a wonderful and faithful letter writer who remained in touch with friends in all corners of the world.

I felt that God had been preparing me throughout my life for the moment of Joyce's death. It was my job to act as 'Joseph' who protected Mary and it was to be my privilege to care for her to the best of my ability until God chose to call her 'home'. It would be the understatement of the century to say that I was going to miss her dreadfully. After nearly sixty years together I would be losing half of myself! At the same time I could not but be aware that God would be doing the best possible thing for my beloved Joyce in taking her to Himself. That was what she wanted. Her relationship with Jesus had always been deep but it became far deeper in the final months of her life. Her health was diminishing rapidly and we suffered together – she in her agony and I in my inability to do anything but 'be' with her and experience my powerlessness to relieve her pain. She confided to me that it helped to know that we were 'in this together!' I thank God every day for His gift of Joyce to me and the wonderful years He gave us. We trusted one another other fully in every way and we were blessed with three beautiful children and three wonderful grandchildren.

In early 1999 Donny went to London for a cancer check at the Royal Marsden Hospital. The news was not good and her professor arranged two cycles of chemotherapy which really knocked the stuffing out of her. In October I was told that she had not more than two months to live. But, like her mother before her, Joyce defied the doctors. She was longing to go to the Lord but she fought her illness every inch of the way.

By the end of the year 2000 she was regularly 'at death's door'. Anthony had been travelling up regularly from Salisbury and before Christmas he and Fiona came to stay for a few days because the doctor assured us that the end was very close. It brought Joyce great joy to be held in the strong arms of her son as they said their last goodbyes. Anthony and Fiona made their departure – but once again Joyce defied the doctors!

In January 2001 carers were coming to the house twice a day and Liz was with us almost constantly cooking and cleaning and running the house. We were both overwhelmed by her love and by the devotion of the Jesus Fellowship and their constant loving presence. Spring came and Joyce was still with us. Our doctor decided that she needed 24 hour care and arranged for Joyce to be admitted to the local hospital for a few weeks from whence she was transferred to a nursing home where I was allowed to remain day and night at her side. Although, in the end our doctor came and chased me out and told me that I should be sleeping in my own bed! Joyce supported him! Liz and I prayed regularly with Joyce and we knew that her body was breaking down.

We spent Easter Sunday together. Joyce had been eating very little. On Easter Monday morning the nurse had helped her out of bed and settled her comfortably in an armchair. Joyce said to the nurse: 'I'm hungry'. The nurse went away to prepare breakfast and, in those few minutes, Joyce was called home! Unfortunately I arrived a few minutes afterwards so was not there when she died. It was April 16th 2001 and Joyce was 79 years old. Three days later we were to have celebrated our sixtieth wedding anniversary! Joyce had asked one of the nurses to buy an anniversary card for her to give to me. The words she wrote touched me to the core of my being and my tears did not want to stop.

The funeral Mass -in white robes - took place in the church of St Thomas More in Towcester on April 24th. At Joyce's wish, she was buried in our village cemetery at Pattishall which belongs to Holy Cross Church. Her funeral was a real celebration of our life together and of Joyce's entry into a new life in Jesus. As we finished praying around the grave someone began the chorus "We will enter His gates with thanksgiving in our hearts..." That was exactly the way I felt! Joyce had truly entered His gates with thanksgiving. She had fought long and valiantly – and she'd won!

Joyce is in glory after a full and blessed life of 79 years – not bad going for someone who had suffered a heart condition from the age of eight and had been told she would not live to be an old woman! My daughter Liz now lives in the Jesus Fellowship House in Oxford and I live in a flat close by. Anthony and Fiona are still in Salisbury. I have told the Lord that I am ready to go to Him anytime but it seems that He wants me to get this book into the shops and maybe even work on another volume - there is no shortage of material! Meanwhile I long for the day when I will see my beloved Joyce again in heaven – I can't wait!

Ted Donovan,   Easter Sunday, April 16th 2006

Index

85th Evacuation Hospital, Qui Nhon,
    S. Vietnam 279

A Surgeon at the Foot of the Cross,
    Pierre Barabet 181, 248, 250, 253
Allington Castle (Carmelite Retreat Centre)
    Maidstone, Kent 298-9,301,303
American Army Nurse Corp 278
Ampleforth College,
    Yorks. 73, 88, 93, 197, 245, 277
Antioch Community, The (The West London
    Community) London .... xvii, 362, 383
Attlee, Prime Minister Clement 22
Avstreih, Pat ix

Bayley-Butler, Professor James, University College,
    Dublin (Buggy) 137
Ballweg, Fr Luke, OSB 323, 331
Betjeman, John (poet laureate) 99
Blake, Fr Simon, OP 222

Blatchley, John & Catherine 343, 354, 362
Broadbridge, Fr Nicholas, OSB,
    Douai Abbey.. 324-5
Byrne, Abbot Herbert, OSB 74

Cantwell, Kay (aunt) 37
Cardinal Basil Hume OSB 352-4, 370
Cardinal Cushing, Boston, Mass... 242, 244, 263, 285,
Cardinal Suenens, Brussels 352
Cave, Fr Gabriel, Wokingham 326, 333
Chamberlain, Prime Minister Neville 75, 83
Charlton, Selina ix
Chasing the Dragon by Jackie Pullinger 366, 367
Christmas, Charles & Patti 358, 361, 389
Clark, Steve, Ann Arbor, MI xviii
Collins, Fr Pat, cm, Dublin, Ireland xv
Connor, Richard & Joyce 338-40
Convent of the Holy Child Jesus, Mayfield,
    Sussex 217, 238, 241
Convent of the Sacred Heart, Mount Anville,
    Dundrum, Dublin 203, 206
Courtnedge, Cicely 59

Darnell, Jean, American Evangelist 331-2, 337-8
de Bertodano, Teresa (editor) ix
deHueck Doherty, Catherine, Madonna House
    Apostolate, Canada 178
Depression (1920-1930) 51
Donovan, Alan (grandson) .... v, 375, 391
Donovan, Anthony (son) .... v 375
Donovan, Arthur (Ted's brother) 78
Donovan, Cecil, Dom Bruno
    (Ted's brother) 78, 88, 93, 186, 243

Donovan, Dorothy (Ted's sister).......... 76, 79-80, 117
Donovan, Edward (great uncle, Ted's father) 66
Donovan, Edward A (Ted) 38, 64,183
Donovan, Elizabeth, Liz (daughter)................. vi, 313
Donovan, Fiona nee MacDonald
    (daughter in law) 217, 295,296,374, 365, 391,395
Donovan, Freda (Ted's sister).... 67, 76, 79, 80,117,126
Donovan, Jonathan (grandson) .... vi, 375, 391
Donovan, Mollie (great aunt, Ted's mother).... 66, 76
Donovan, Pamela 2nd Lieutnenat
    (daughter)......................... 129, 154, 155, 273, 278
Donovan, Stephen (grandson)........... vi, 296, 375, 391

Evergloss Polish Ltd 48,88, 89, 99, 186

From Prison to Praise by
    Merlin Carothers 305, 306

Gallagher, Brian, Irish Ambassador to the
    Netherlands 215
Graham, Billy, Evangelist 382
Gwinnell, Fr Mike 348-350

Hale, Sonny 59
Halpin, Gavin 38
Hitler, Adolfe 58, 75, 83
Hollings, Fr Michael 295, 324, 343

Jeffers, Julie, Liverpool 90, 91, 118
Jerusalem Community, Brussels 355
Jesus Fellowship, Jesus Army, Bugbrooke
    Chapel, Northants ..... Chap 15, 319-22, 333, 343-4
    390, 392, 396

Jonsonn, Majsan Langford (sister in law,
    Brian's wife).. photo
Joyce, William (Lord Haw-haw)............................92

Keating, Alyce Langford (mother).................... photo
Keating, Annette (Grandma Nettie).................. photo
Keating, Sean, President Royal Hibernian
    Academy, Dublin 159
Kennedy, President John F...................... 266-269, 271
King Edward VIII 59
King George V and Queen Mary 1935 59
King George VI..60

Lamb of God Community, New Zealand......386, 387
Langford, Brian Frederick (brother) .... photo
Langford, Ernie (uncle)............................25, 26, 120
Langford, Fred (father) .... photo
Langford, Granny & Grandpa........................... 59, 98
Langford, Mabel (aunt)..?
Langford, Stanley (uncle) 26
Langford, William (uncle) 25, 114
Little Match Seller by Hans Christian
    Anderson.. 335

Marmion, Abbot Columba, OSB 157, 174
Marriage Encounter 339, 340, 352
Martin, Ralph, Ann Arbor, MI 342, 347, 355, 358
Matthews, Jessie 59
McNutt, Fr Francis..346-48, 359
Milltown Golf Club, Dublin 23, 68, 82
Mother of God Community, Gaithersburg, ML... 353
Museum of Fine Arts, Boston, Mass................... 240

National Gallery of Ireland, Dublin 158
Nisbet, Tom (Irish Painter), Dublin 158

O'Donovan, Fred (Film & Theatre Director)
    Dublin 23
Orchard, Lionel & Marion 314, 318
Orlando, Fr Gerard A, CP Rector of St. Gabriel's
    ('Himself'), Boston.................... Chap 12, 287-289
Our Lady of Sorrows Library, Boston,
    Mass .... Chap 12,
Overton, Fr Jim 326, 352, 353
Owen, Tracy ix

People of Hope Community, NJ 382
People of Praise Community, South Bend, IN 352
Prince Philip... 219
Princess Grace of Monaco 271
Puppet on a String Helena Wilkinson................ 330
Pytches, Bishop David & Mary .... xiii, 372

Queen Elizabeth II 209, 210
Queen Juliana of the Netherlands 209

Rowland, Tony & Colette 356, 379, 389
Royal Hibernian Academy, Dublin 158

Scott, Olivia ix
Shaughnessy, Mike, Servants of the Word........... 389
Sheridan, Monsignor, Belmont,
    Boston, Mass USA.......................... 193, 198, 200
St. Andrew's Church, Chorleywood, Herts. UK....xiii
St. Cecilia's Guild for the Blind, UK.................... 261

St. Elizabeth's Hospital, Brighton,
    Boston, Mass... 241, 273
St. Gabriel's Passionist Monastery,
    Boston, Mass.. 231
Stanton, Noel, Senior Pastor,
    Jesus Fellowship 313, 315, 319

The Crazy Gang 115
The Small Woman by Gladys Aylward 366
The Velveteen Rabbit by Margery Williams 393
M & Mme Thivy, Indian Ambassador
    to the Netherlands 214-216
Trinder, Tommy.. 115
Trinity College, Dublin 23, 74

Uncle Tom's Cabin by Harriet Beecher Stowe....... 27
Urquhart, Colin Kingdom Faith Ministries......... 321

Valentine, Fr Ferdinand, OP.................... 45, 157, 261
Vietnam 277, 279, 280, 283, 286, 290, 291

Walls, Elizabeth, Wokingham 310, 311, 323, 333,
Washtenaw Community, Ann Arbor 385
Waters, Elsie and Doris... 115
Westminster Cathedral Renewal 321, 324, 326
Wilberforce, William 26
Wimber, John, founder Vineyard Fellowship 382
Women's Vietnam Memorial,
    Washington, DC... 291. 292
Women's World Day of Prayer 329, 330
Word of God Community,
    Ann Arbor, MI.......................... 352, 355, 358, 385
Word of Life Community, Ann Arbor, MI 385

Yocum, Bruce (Servants of the Word,
    Ann Arbor, MI) .... xii, 358

Printed in the United Kingdom
by Lightning Source UK Ltd.
117261UKS00001BA/1-36